SKY SPIES

Above: The sigint antennae protruding from this Lockheed Orion clearly define it as one of the US Navy's ten EP-3E 'Aries', which equip VQ-1 at NAS Agana, Guam, and VQ-2 at NAS Rota, Spain. Equipment includes AN/APS-115 ASW radar, AN/ALQ-70 ESM, AN/ALQ-110 elint and AN/ALR-60 comint, plus IFF and radar countermeasures. (Lockheed)

SKY SPIES

THREE DECADES OF
AIRBORNE RECONNAISSANCE

Anthony M. Thornborough

ARMS AND
ARMOUR

Arms & Armour Press
A Cassell Imprint
Villiers House, 41–47 Strand, London WC2N 5JE

Distributed in the USA by Sterling Publishing Co Inc, 387 Park
Avenue South, New York, NY 10016–8810

Distributed in Australia by Capricorn Link (Australia) Pty Ltd, P.O.
Box 665, Lane Cove, New South Wales 2066

British Library Cataloguing-in-Publication data:
A catalogue record for this book is available from the British Library

ISBN 1 85409 147 6

Edited and designed by Roger Chesneau/DAG Publications Ltd
Monochrome reproduction by M&E Reproductions, North
Fambridge, Essex
Typesetting by Ronset Typesetters Ltd, Darwen, Lancashire
Printed and bound in Great Britain

CONTENTS

INTRODUCTION

EIGHTY-FIVE years ago, the role of observation gave military aviation its vital kick-start. Height and a respectable payload capability launched the fixed-wing flying machine into war. That the aeroplane rapidly evolved into a fighter to deny others reconnaissance, later became the means for depositing bombs, even paratroopers, with an element of surprise, and was eventually exploited as a means of transporting vast cargoes speedily across the globe, merely followed as an extension of the basic concept of using aircraft as a 'platform' for cameras.

Today's wide-ranging air-crew roles also sprang from the same embryonic beginnings. In the pioneering days there existed only pilots and their observers. (Up until 1943, by which time the Royal Air Force had truly came of age, RAF navigators, in deference to their traditional role, continued to wear the distinctive 'winged O' insignia—known to all as the 'flying a***hole'—until replaced by the now well-known winged 'N'!) As 'observation' equipment advanced from hand-held cameras, binoculars and a map-plus-grease-pencil to embrace state-of-the-art gyro-stabilized optical systems, finely tuned signals-receiving apparatus and active mapping devices, so whole new professions allied to the world of 'recce' were created in the wake of this technology—electronic warfare officer, radar observer, signals analyst, communications interpreter and a host of other specialists (some requiring much less training than navigators and others needing additional courses and hands-on experience). Today, these professionals range from pilots and their do-it-all back-seaters who continue to hone their skills on a full-time, almost daily basis to language experts drawn from academia and the diplomatic service who are specially seconded to one-off assignments. For over thirty years, such professionals have flown solo or in pairs on penetration missions while cocooned in aircraft whose performance has customarily driven the leading edge forward; or as co-ordinated teams comprising up to twenty-five officers and enlisted or contractor personnel, sitting behind sensor-linked airborne consoles stuffed into the giant sentinels—converted cargo or passenger machines, which orbit at some distance from hostile airspace—to provide a 'God's-eye view' of events.

Indeed, the human 'need to know' has continued to be a catalyst for the post-war development of much weird and wonderful 'sky spy' equipment. In today's fast-paced, information-greedy world, the 'snoopers' come equipped with a mind-boggling array of sensors tailored to fit specific missions. Amongst the more conventional types are high-resolution autofocus cameras capable of 'shooting' patches, swathes or entire vistas in conjunction with a variety of film types. They are supplemented by electro-optic and infra-red 'eyes', plus mysterious passive and intrusive devices which are capable of perusing other branches of the electromagnetic spectrum in the radio-frequency end, from which other 'invisible' data—such as communications chatter and radar signals—can be gleaned. Add to this the facility of 'near real-time' reconnaissance, whereby these devices, through a chain of microwave relay and deciphering networks, are able to convey their tell-tale data within a few minutes to virtually any authorized agency willing and able to support them, then reconnaissance has become a formidable tool which can be employed with equal efficacy during times of peace and war, at the diplomatic table and on the battlefront.

An unadulterated picture still tells a thousand words, and at no time recently was this made more apparent than during the conflict in the Persian Gulf, where theatre recce forces were in short supply and high demand. The lessons learnt were clear: reconnaissance products which were speedily collected, transmitted, processed and disseminated in 'near real-time' before Saddam Hussein and his entourage had the opportunity to shift their hapless forces elsewhere—a feature which gave rise to the term 'perishable intelligence'—proved invaluable. 'Platforms' performing these duties which outstripped all expectations, and whose development has been accelerated in the aftermath of 'Desert Storm', include the remarkable E-8 Joint-STARS and the E-3 AWACS, which latter will shortly be reconfigured to perform passive intelligence-gathering duties to add to its already impressive all-seeing radar capabilities. Other newcomers comprised the hitherto poorly tapped resources offered by relatively inexpensive, and expendable, UAVs (Unmanned Air Vehicles),

Above: The author samples the accommodation of an F-4G Phantom 'Wild Weasel' under the guidance of Gulf veteran pilot Capt Bruce Beynshek. (Courtesy Peter E. Davies)

which can ply their obedient track in hostile airspace without fear of putting airmen in jeopardy. After having been left to stagnate for a decade, the UAVs have had their value once again recognized.

Many old lessons had to be re-learned during the lightning six-week Gulf War. Despite all the state-of-the-art intelligence-gathering hardware (or possibly because of it), there existed a dire shortage of aircraft capable of performing traditional high-resolution photography for pre- and post-strike planning (otherwise known as BDA or battle damage assessment). None of the latter-day 'near real-time' technology has diminished the need for the commander— be he an admiral, a general or a head of state—to acquire top-quality photographs based on celluloid, which can be processed and enlarged to show remarkable detail only *after* the recce aircraft has returned to base to disgorge its cumbersome film magazines. Reconnaissance jets packing old-fashioned conventional cameras are no less vital than they ever were. Even General 'Stormin' Norman' Schwarzkopf acknowledged that 'Desert Storm' represented one of the few occasions in which pilots were tasked to fly combat missions without 'fresh'

photos of their targets (some of which, 36 hours old, were well and truly past their 'sell-by date'). 'It was a void all of us felt,' he later acknowledged, brought about by the fast-paced nature of the conflict.

This glaring shortfall in tac-recon products in the Coalition's otherwise near-optimum repertoire became especially clear during the prosecution of the preparatory air war, when the need for accurate BDA was causing some anxiety at the planning level, just when the enemy introduced the unexpected in the form of 'Scud' terror-tactics, which diverted the attention of the hard-pressed recce-strike forces. The nature of 'near-real time' digitalized reconnaissance, which sacrificed acuity for the sake of speed, brought with it a loss of image quality, resulting in too many sorties which tasked bombers against hastily chosen targets (the Al-Amiriyah bunker among them, where 400 civilians perished), together with the expenditure of vast resources on locate-and-destroy assignments against the elusive Iraqi rocket forces (very few of which were successfully knocked out, as they could not be adequately differentiated from the droves of decoy articulated lorries driven out to the desert). The need for a speedy interpretation of recce products also resulted in a certain loss of attention to detail which on one occasion caused enemy forces to slip through unnoticed into Kuwait, and some unfortunate 'Blue-on-Blue' casualties when the fog of war was thicker than anticipated, possibly owing to the *expectancy* of a continuous flow of useful information from the otherwise well-oiled Command, Control and Communications chain. Finally, the dependence upon satellites in order to glean an overview of enemy movements deep within the heavily defended sanctuaries of Iraq was a technological leap forward which produced a commensurate loss of localized authority, in which theatre commanders were obliged to rely on material processed and disseminated by specialists in Washington, thousands of miles distant. A joint intelligence centre was established in the Pentagon which pooled some 500 staff from the DIA (Defense Intelligence Agency), National Security Agency and branches of the US military, who took time to draw useful conclusions from their varying extrapolations. All of these shortcomings were made all the more poignant by the absence of the United States' star performer, the SR-71A, which was grounded only eight months prior to the Iraqi incursion into Kuwait. The greatest irony of all is that O&M (Operations and Maintenance) funds for the Blackbird had finally been withdrawn as a hand-slapping exercise because of the incoherent state of the US military's reconnaissance programmes, which allegedly were 'in complete disarray'! There is little doubt that the rapid and untimely retirement of the glamorous SR-71A cost a great deal in lost intelligence. The much-lauded U-2R was unable to match the Blackbird's ability to survey up to a quarter of a million square miles of territory in one sortie (enough to capture the entire theatre of operation on high-resolution camera and radar film) and, besides, it was needed for equally urgent signals-gathering tasks. Ultimately, this in turn placed an excessive burden on the CIA/DIA KH-9 and -11 'Big Bird' satellite community, which soon became bogged down in a tremendous backlog of unprocessed data, some of which 'perished' before it could be put to proper use. Moreover, satellites were unable to provide continuous through-the-weather coverage of enemy movements deep in Iraq. (In the ten years prior to the conflict, the SR-71 force had obtained vital reconnaissance imagery pertaining to Middle Eastern interests on no fewer than eighty occasions when satellites broke down or were unable to poke through the atmosphere.) Meanwhile, modest numbers of US Air National Guard RF-4C 'Photo-Phantoms', US Navy F-14 TARPS Tomcat fighters, British GR.1A Tornados, French Mirage F1CRs and Saudi Arabian RF-5E Tigereyes, a veritable circus of tac-recon types (and a mere shadow of the enormous fleets of dedicated machines available only a decade beforehand), were press-ganged into what were tantamount to *strategic* reconnaissance duties. That the commanders were able to make relatively good

use of the diverse intelligence is testimony to a highly co-ordinated, motivated force of military staff able to make use of the disparate sources at its disposal. However, that is not to say that the 'high-tech gear' was nothing short of invaluable, rather that the abandonment of traditional resources for technology's sake needs rethinking. The two elements—old and new—should be combined. Each has its merits and drawbacks.

Whatever conclusions can be drawn from the war in the Gulf, it is clear that the 'big-league' nations will continue to maintain fleets of specialized sentinels with which they can support their more clandestine, earthbound shenanigans. Moreover, several interesting—and much-welcomed—trends are discernible, for example the revitalization of an 'open skies' policy over Europe, first proposed by President Eisenhower in July 1955 but rejected outright by Premier Khrushchev (and now starting to become evident in the commercial airline industry, with military operations to follow—on established tracks, using a vetted sensor suite), and the clear desire, in the post-'Cold War' climate, to mix the best of East and West as opposed to chasing partisan pursuits which fuelled the paranoia and xenophobia that brought the world to the brink of nuclear war at the zenith of the Cuban Missile Crisis. The Russian design bureaux Mikoyan-Gurevich and Sukhoi are actively exploring the possibilities of incorporating Western sensor technology as 'strap-ons' to expand the capabilities of their prestigious fighters (which are already incorporating compatible Western cockpit technology), while at the frontier of signals intelligence and radar observation the United States and Europe are adding yet more oddities to the already bizarre cornucopia of 'sky spies' in an effort to put an end to international drugs trafficking.

The only unresolved question that remains is what is to become of *tactical* reconnaissance given the expense of maintaining the 'platform' aircraft at the top of the performance chart? Will generic systems like the new ATARS (Advanced Tactical Reconnaissance System), designed to be fitted to older fighters and UAVs, finally sound the death knell of the chisel-nosed, high-speed reconnaissance jet? It is a fast-disappearing breed.

This book examines the 'leading edge' of recce technology and discusses the 'platforms' and their sensors which have been moulded by three decades of reconnaissance duties, including those which helped to push back the boundaries during the 1960s and which, because of the lack of worthy successors, continue to ply their trade years beyond their originally projected retirement dates; the make-shift 'recce-strike' machines which are gradually ousting them; and the great Californian 'Blackworld'

Above: The Lockheed Advanced Development Company's high-flying 'dynamic duo', the SR-71A and U-2R, joined up for this rare formation shot, taken over the Mojave Desert at the end of separate test flights from Palmdale in 1981. (Lockheed/Robert C. Ferguson)

giants like the SR-71A (which, although no longer operational in a military capacity, form an essential part of the story). The mission profiles describing the Lockheed 'Black Velvet' hardware were drafted by the author and his associate Peter E. Davies several years ago, but have been substantially rewritten to incorporate updates and corrections, with special attention devoted to the sensor fits, using information which has only just recently entered the public domain. UAVs are also given consideration, with the emphasis on Teledyne Ryan Aeronautical's accomplishments. (The multifarious miniature UAV platforms used by the world's armies, many of which fall into the 'radio-controlled aircraft' category, merit a book in their own right.) Finally, mention has been made of East European reconnaissance aircraft, technologically impressive in areas which all too sadly are running aground for want of adequate funding in the aftermath of the collapse of the Soviet Union.

Compiling this book has proved to be both an enlightening and an exasperating experience owing to the secretive nature of the world of spy planes, and

so the author is especially indebted to all those who provided information, diagrams and photographs. Without the generous assistance of the following people, the book would barely have got off the ground: TSgt James R. Clark; Peter E. Davies; John Ford; Ga'bor Szekeres; Christian Gerard; Ian Hunter; Tim Laming; Lois Lovisolo; Douglas McCurrach; Frank B. Mormillo; David Oliver, editor of *Air Forces Monthly*; Jim Rotramel; Eric Schulzinger; Bettie E. Sprigg; Lt-Col Jim Uken; Frank Visser; and Keith Watson of *Flying Colours*. Many thanks go also to the following organizations for their instrumental help: GEC Ferranti; the GEC Marconi Research Centre; Grumman Aerospace; the Loral Corporation; the Lockheed Advanced Development Company; Martin Marietta; the Office of the Assistant Secretary for Defense in Washington; Headquarters RAF Strike Command; and Teledyne Ryan Aeronautical. Finally, special thanks are due to Rod Dymott, Director of A&AP, and his senior editor Peter Burton who, even at the 'one o'clock' stage in the proceedings, acquiesced in the need for additional research in certain areas. Thanks also to David Gibbons and his design team, who turned a morass of diagrams, photographs and support text into a coherent end product in record time.

Anthony M. Thornborough
Bristol, England, October 1992

1. DRAGON LADY

IT WAS 1 August 1955, out on the 'Ranch' at Groom Lake, Nevada. Lockheed Test Pilot Tony Vier was strapped in the cockpit of a strange, silver-coloured, glider-like jet perched on tandem twin wheels and fitted with wing outriggers or 'pogos' to keep it from toppling on to its wings, preparing the machine—known solely as '001'—for its first taxi run.

11:26	LeVier	Starting engine.
11:30		Rolling.
	Car chase	37mph. Pogos still on ground.
	LeVier	Carrying a little rudder to roll straight.
11:35		Brakes not too hot!
		End of run.
11:39		Start of fast run . . .

With those words echoing in the radio observer's headset, '001' made an unscheduled departure from *terra firma*. As the test pilot subsequently reported, 'The aircraft appeared to accelerate rapidly and at 70 knots the throttle was placed in idle . . . it was at this point that I became aware of being airborne, which left me with utter amazement!' The pilot had to fight to keep the metallic beast from soaring aloft, owing to its light structure and 10.6:1 high-aspect-ratio wing. Although the delicate machine's first hop culminated in a bouncy landing and two blown tyres, three days later it was let off its leash and, at 85 per cent engine rpm, it rose majestically up into the atypically cloudy desert skies to mark the launch of

Below: The 'Dragon Lady' first left the ground—albeit to an altitude of just 35ft—on 1 August 1955. Aircraft 66701 remains intact today, residing at the SAC Museum at Offutt AFB, Nebraska. (Lockheed)

Above: 'Silver Ladies' in their element. The U-2 gained public attention when Francis Gary Powers was shot down near Sverdlovsk on May Day 1960. Carrying cameras and particle samplers, he had as his target the Soviet bomb factory at Mayak on the River Techa. The Americans became aware of the plant following an accident there in December 1957 and believed it to be a nuclear test site! One of the waste storage bins exploded with a 1-kiloton force, releasing 20 million Curies of radio-activity. The town is arguably the most radio-active inhabited place on Earth, and it remained secret until 1990. (Lockheed)

the world's most illustrious (and infamous) spy-plane—the Lockheed U-2.[1]

Designed and built amidst the utmost secrecy for the CIA by the cost-cutting, technological trail-blazers at the 'Skunk Works', headed by the inimit-able Clarence 'Kelly' Johnson, the spuriously titled 'Utility Two' was to result in an eventual total of 103 machines in four separate batches between 1955 and 1989, during which time it grew in size and dispro-portionately greater in capability. These aircraft comprised 54 of the original Project 'Aquatone' 80ft-span versions, with the balance made up of the 40 per cent enlarged, more sophisticated U-2R series. The story of the original U-2A, its numerous deriva-tives and the photo intelligence (photint), signals

intelligence (sigint) and air sampling missions it flew over the Soviet Union and Communist China, initial-ly with Agency pilots operating 'weather reconnais-sance' sorties and later in the hands of daring USAF and courageous Taiwanese airmen, has been told many times. In the public eye, this began with the belated admission by the Eisenhower Administration that an American spyplane had been shot down over Russia on May Day 1960. Francis Gary Powers was assigned to garner intelligence on the rocket facilities at Mayak and Plesetsk, and all went well until a salvo of fourteen SA-2 'Guideline' surface-to-air missiles exploded around his U-2B (56-6693). The aircraft subsequently entered a flat inverted spin, from which Powers threw himself free, and thus began the jokes about the CIA standing for 'Caught In the Act'! 'Utility Twos' made headline news again two years later during the Cuban Missile Crisis. A U-2 piloted by Maj Richard S. Heyser flew over the island on 14 October 1962 and obtained the first photographic evidence of the Soviet military build-up there. Further photint was gathered during daily sorties in the ensuing two tense weeks under the express orders of President John F. Kennedy, adding to the Lockheed jet's

Above: The driving force behind Lockheed's famous 'Skunk Works' was designer Clarence 'Kelly' Johnson. The CIA's U-2B behind, N803X (a Palmdale registration), is equipped with an infrared signature-suppressing 'sugar scoop' extension to its tail-pipe. (Lockheed)

growing notoriety on both sides of the 'Iron Curtain'.[2] Oddly enough, none of the popular press reflected on the fact that the aircraft flew unescorted—and completely unarmed except for modest self-defence electronics. Throughout the protracted Vietnam War the USAF expanded the type's sigint-gathering role, while flying 'Lucky Dragon', 'Trojan Horse' and 'Giant Dragon' missions from Operating Location 20 (OL-20) at Bien Hoa, South Vietnam, during which time the Pratt & Whitney J57 engines were replaced by that company's more powerful J75 model and the sinister overall 'Velvet Black', ironball, radar-attenuating paint scheme was introduced,

adding to the machine's wonder and unjustified infamy. The little model's career finally ended on 26 April 1989 when Doyle Krumrey flew U-2C 56-6682 (former NASA N709NA) into Robins AFB, Georgia, for permanent display. It was retired with 8,860 hours on the clock.[3]

The fabrication of a dozen U-2Rs followed during 1967 and 1968—the beginnings of the current armada of the 103ft-span giants. These were not mere scaled-up attrition replacements, but brand new designs stressed for the J75 engine. The development of the U-2R by 'Kelly' Johnson, Ben Rich, Fred Cavanaugh and others sprang from a 1965 proposal for a U-2L, and the first example (N803X/68-10329) made its maiden flight on 28 August 1967 from Edwards North Base, California, with Lockheed veteran William M. Parks at the controls. North Base became home for the CIA's sextet, two of which were

---

[1]The flight of 4 August was unofficial. A record 2in of rainfall which fell during the test flight did not dampen spirits, and the design and test team spent the evening celebrating the sortie with beer-drinking and arm-wrestling contests! The first official flight took place on 8 August, with CIA clients in attendance.

[2]Taiwan operated both U-2s and RF-101As over mainland China and suffered several losses before these 'programs' were terminated. By 1983, this disparate collection of obsolescent hardware had been replaced by Lockheed RF-104G Starfighters equipped with stand-off Itek KA-102A 66in LOROPS, more than sufficient to meet their needs without the embarrassing repercussions associated with previous 'Dragon Lady' and Voodoo losses. The Taiwanese appear happy to retain their Starfighters. Three days after the President's 22 October 1962 announcement of an arms quarantine against shipments destined for the island, Maj Rudolph Anderson Jr was killed when his machine was hit by shrapnel from a SAM missile. The whole subject of sigint is aired in detail in Chapter 5 under the sub-heading 'Sentinels'.

[3]The USAF received its first U-2As in June 1957 at Laughlin AFB, Texas. These were attached to the 4080th Strategic Reconnaissance Wing, parent unit for all the OLs, including the Bien Hoa operation in Vietnam. Squadrons comprised the 4025th equipped with AQM-34 'Lightning Bugs' (described below, under the sub-heading 'Combat Angel') and the 4028th with the U-2s; in June 1966 the force was re-labelled the 100th Strategic Reconnaissance Wing and the squadrons the 350th SRS and 349th SRS, respectively, and later moved to OL-RU at U-Tapao, Thailand, while the parent Wing and its training mission shifted to Davis-Monthan AFB, Arizona. Headquarters moved again in July 1976 to Beale AFB, California, as the 9th SRW. U-2C 56-6682 was specially repainted in its all-black decor by this time. Previously it had belonged to NASA as N709NA and on 17 and 18 April had successfully clinched two time-to-climb records for Class C-1F and C-1G aircraft. In even earlier service, the machine had earlier been one of the heaviest modifications, flying as a U-2H with AAR receiver and an arresting hook. The last two Air Force jets from the original series—the pair of U-2CT 'Two Headed Goat' trainers—were retired from service during late 1987.

Above: Five U-2Cs were painted in two-tone blue-grey camouflage for European field trials of the ALSS (Advanced Location Strike System) in 1975; the customary 'Black Velvet' scheme introduced nine years previously was considered to be too sinister for British and German sensibilities. (Lockheed)

U-2 PRODUCTION ('SMALL-WING')

Article no	Serial batches	Numbers
341	'001'	1 (prototype)
342-389	56-6675 to -6722	48
390?		
391-395	56-6951 to -6955	5

INTACT SURVIVING 'SMALL-WING' AIRFRAMES

Model	Serial no	Location
U-2C	56-6680	National Air & Space Museum, Washington DC
U-2C	56-6681/N708NA	NASA Ames Research Center, California
U-2C	56-6682/N709NA	Robins AFB Museum, Georgia
U-2C	56-6701	SAC Museum, Offutt AFB, Nebraska
U-2C	56-6707	Laughlin AFB, Texas
U-2C	56-6714	Beale AFB Museum, California
U-2C	56-6716	Davis-Monthan AFB, Arizona
U-2D	56-6721	March AFB, California
U-2A	56-6722	USAF Museum, Wright-Patterson AFB, Ohio
U-2CT	56-6953	Edwards AFB, California

All these aircraft have been inactive for at least five years, apart from former U-2CT 56-6692 which was used for some time as a battle-damage repair trainer at RAF Alconbury. All remaining aircraft were written off in accidents or shot down, or scrapped.

dispatched to Taiwan for the surreptitious Chinese overflights (which endured until 1974, when the survivors were passed over to the Air Force), while the USAF's six were absorbed into the 100th Strategic Reconnaissance Wing (SRW) at Davis-Monthan AFB, Arizona, primarily to keep an eye on Cuba from OL-19 at McCoy AFB, Florida, and on North Vietnam and Laos from OL-20. On 11 July 1970, the South-East Asian 'Olympic Torch' missions shifted to U-Tapao in Thailand and for four straight years demonstrated a 98 per cent dispatch rate, reaping photint and sigint in support of the Strategic Air Command's B-52D/G bombers. The unit received SAC's Paul T. Cullen Memorial Trophy for best reconnaissance Wing in the 15th Air Force before returning to its headquarters in the Arizona desert.

The pressing need for additional surveillance platforms generated by a wealth of 'netted' sensor systems in development in the post-Vietnam years overtaxed the dwindling force—which was by then down to eight aircraft. To fill the gap, the USAF had intended to procure long-endurance, high-altitude Unmanned Air Vehicles and sponsored two 'Compass Cope' contenders, the Ryan YQM-94 and the Boeing YQM-98, to fulfil the task. However, continued mistrust in UAVs led to the cancellation of Boeing's winning submission in July 1977. Only one solution would suit the generals—more U-2Rs. It all became official on 16 November 1979 when Lockheed were awarded a start-up $10.2 million contract to take tooling out of storage at Norton AFB, California, and set it up at its Palmdale facility (Site 7, part of the huge Air Force Plant 42) with Pratt & Whitney in on the act. The latter company would refurbish spare

J75 turbojets removed from recently retired F-105 'Thuds' and F-106 'Darts' and modify them to the non-afterburning, wide-fan, high-altitude task. A 37-aircraft production run ensued, including a pair of virtually identical 'Earth Resource Two' machines for the National Aeronautics and Space Administration. NASA would eventually receive three ER-2s, and their initial glossy white and blue machine (N706NA/80-1063) marked the launch of the new series when Art Peterson roared off the Palmdale runway on 11 May 1981. The Air Force followed suit on 1 August with Ken Weir in charge of 80-1066, his ship bearing its standard military overall 'Velvet Black' decor devoid of unit regalia and the curious new title TR-1A. The late 'Kelly' Johnson's account is that Joint Chiefs of Staff Chairman Gen David C. Jones insisted on the new designation: 'We have to get the U-2 name off that plane. We'll call it the TR-1, Tactical Reconnaissance One.' The stigma attached to the 'Utility Two' was considered to be potentially inflammatory to the Europeans, who would play hosts to a big slice of the force. In fact, when production ended with the delivery of 80-1099 on 3 October 1989, the expansion in numbers had passed by virtually unnoticed, and, somewhat ironically, only well-informed observers seemed to be beguiled by the new title. Meanwhile, U-2Rs and TR-1As went about their business much as the type had for three decades!

UP AND AWAY

Today's mighty establishment of thirty-nine remaining military aircraft is flown and maintained by the 9th Wing, headquartered at Beale AFB, twelve miles from Marysville, California, under the banner 'Semper Paratus'—'Always Ready'. Now part of Brig-Gen Lawrence A. Mitchell's 2nd Air Force (head-quartered at Beale, and overseer of all the Service's global reconnaissance and C3 assets), the aircraft are split among four squadrons: the 5th RTS *Dragon Tamers*, responsible for training new air crews and for conducting the Standardization & Evaluation (Stan/Eval, a type of 'quality control') of operational pilots; the 99th RS, a mission-ready unit whose cartographic bison insignia reflects its worldwide reconnaissance commitment; the 95th, forward deployed to RAF Alconbury in Cambridgeshire, England, in support of NATO and Middle Eastern interests, whose crews wear the distinctive kicking donkey patch, from which is derived their unofficial nickname, the 'Ass Kickers'; and the 6th RS, which grew out of the famous 'Black Cat' detachment at Osan AB, South Korea, and continues to patrol the sensitive borders of the republic and its neighbours.[4] Mission objectives, passed along normal Air Tasking Order channels, originate anywhere from the JCS down to 'hard-hatted' theatre commanders and typically comprise scrutinizing the assigned target area with cameras or a mapping radar while simultaneously recording sigint. Until very recently, the 'Dragon Lady' community continued to draw distinctions between the 'strategic' U-2R and the 'tactical' TR-1A and ostensibly went about its business as two distinct operations, despite the fact that both teams were SAC-run and heavily engaged in sigint using almost identical equipment: 6th and 99th SRS

Below: The famous 'Skunk Works' logo of the Lockheed Advanced Development Projects office adorns the tail of this 'little-wing' U-2, one of only ten survivors. Aircraft 66722 can now be seen at the USAF Museum at Wright-Patterson AFB, Ohio. (Via Peter E. Davies)

---

[4]The entire U-2 establishment was consolidated under the 9th Wing at Beale on 28 June 1991, when Alconbury's parent Wing, the 17th RW *Toujours au Danger*, was formally disbanded. Two months later, on 1 September, the force was realigned under the 2nd Air Force. The 5th RTS was originally formed in August 1981 as the 4029th Strategic Reconnaissance Training Squadron, responsible for training U-2R/TR-1 (and, between 1983 and 1989, SR-71A) crews. It was redesignated the 5th SRTS on 1 July 1986 and dropped the 'Strategic' prefix in June 1992 when Air Combat Command merged former Tactical and Strategic Air Command reconnaissance and strike aircraft. The future of the 95th RS is under review. Three of Alconbury's machines (80-1070, -1074 and -1077) returned to the US between 19 and 21 October 1992, leaving only two (80-1079 and -1080) in place.

U-2 PRODUCTION ('BIG-WING')

Serial no	Model	Notes
68-10329/N-803X	U-2R	Served as Lockheed test-bed
68-10330	U-2R	Written-off 7 Dec 1977 RAF Akrotiri, Cyprus
68-10331	U-2R	C-Span III modified
68-10332	U-2R	Written off 15 Jan 1992
68-10333	U-2R	
68-10334	U-2R	Written off 15 Aug 1975
68-10335	U-2R	Written off
68-10336	U-2R	Original Lockheed ASARS-2 test-bed
68-10337	U-2R	
68-10338	U-2R	
68-10339	U-2R	USN EP-X test-bed; later ASARS-1 test-bed
68-10340	U-2R	
80-1063/N706NA	ER-2	NASA-Ames
80-1064	TR-1B	Twin-seat trainer
80-1065	TR-1B	Twin-seat trainer
80-1066	TR-1A	First TR-1 to fly; later reassigned as U-2R
80-1067	TR-1A	Lockheed-Palmdale test-bed
80-1068	TR-1A	Reassigned as U-2R
80-1069/N708NA	TR-1A	On loan to NASA-Ames
80-1070	TR-1A	Reassigned as U-2R; C-Span III modified
80-1071	U-2R	C-Span III modified
80-1072	TR-1A	Written off
80-1073	TR-1A	
80-1074	TR-1A	Initial PLSS test-bed
80-1075	TR-1A	Written off
80-1076	U-2R	
80-1077	TR-1A	
80-1078	TR-1A	
80-1079	TR-1A	
80-1080	TR-1A	PLSS test-bed
80-1081	TR-1A	
80-1082	TR-1A	
80-1083	TR-1A	
80-1084	TR-1A	
80-1085	TR-1A	
80-1086	TR-1A	
80-1087	TR-1A	
80-1088	TR-1A	
80-1089	U-2R	
80-1090	TR-1A	Lockheed-Palmdale test-bed
80-1091	U-2R(T)	Twin-seat trainer
80-1092	TR-1A	
80-1093	TR-1A	
80-1094	TR-1A	
80-1095	U-2R	
80-1096	U-2R	
80-1097/N709NA	ER-2	NASA-Ames
80-1098	U-2R	
80-1099	TR-1A	

All surviving TR-1As were redesignated U-2R and both TR-1B trainers U-2RT, respectively, by December 1991. An additional five FY68 U-2R 'tails' (including '10342' and '10345') were sighted during the 1970s but are all believed to be spurious. Thirty-six U-2Rs, three U-2RTs and three ER-2s remain operational, though ACC plans to reduce the force to two dozen U-2R/RTs over the next two years.

machines concentrated on photint, while the 95th RS honed its efforts in radar-mapping. However, the demarcation line gradually became so blurred that in December 1991 it was abandoned altogether. At that juncture, the military force was streamlined into U-2Rs and U-2RT trainers, though it will take several years' worth of subtle modifications during depot tear-downs at Palmdale to achieve a truly homogeneous 'baseline' configuration. Moreover, the sensor fit is adjusted as required, so it is a moot point whether or not the aircraft will ever catch up with the changes in the paperwork! In theory at least, the 99th RS is now just as likely to monitor enemy troop concentrations just behind the battlefront as the 95th RS is to tune in to CIS (Commonwealth of Independent States) missile telemetry or 'sniff' French or Chinese nuclear tests with radioactive particulate samplers.

Flying the 'big wing' is a challenging experience for the best of pilots (who must have logged a minimum of 1,500 hours' flying time before they are even considered for training—and most have amassed double that), though apparently less so than in the early days of the U-2 programme. The newer, stronger design, the trio of purpose-built twin-seat trainers which wean novices on to the type in stages and an 'institutional knowledge' that spans thirty-six years of experience are all contributing factors—and then there are the simple human comforts to consider. The current David Clark Company S1010B full-pressure rubber suit has much more 'give' in it than the cyberman-like MC-2/3 outfits which inspired the creative *Dr Who* spin-off, the cockpit is commensurately roomier and the Lockheed zero-zero ejection seat is superbly reliable. However, exhaustive preparations need to be made prior to each physically and mentally taxing mission. This begins a day in advance, with two pilots going through the drill. One will make the flight, the other is the standby. This arrangement is necessary for two reasons: one is medical, the other is that flying the U-2R is actually a two-man job in the pre-launch and landing phases of the mission. Long-duration, high-altitude missions also require a fit pilot, and the 'primary' receives a thorough medical from the PSD (Physiological Support Division) immediately before each high-altitude sortie. Temperature, blood pressure, pulse and weight are recorded and checked before the 'Dragon rider' is passed fit to fly.

Descending from altitude with blocked Eustachian tubes, for example, could cause anything ranging from a severe headache to black-out. The back-up man, known as the 'mobile' for reasons which will become clearer as the hypothetical sortie unfolds, is always ready to step in should any of the medical parameters miss the mark. Psychological preparation

Above: Lockheed test pilot Bill Park flew Agency U-2R N812X gently off and on to the deck of the USS *America* during secret trials held between 21 and 23 November 1969. All U-2Rs have folding wing tips so that they may ride up and down on a carrier's lifts (elevators), but the arrester hook and wing-tip skids were specially added for the test job. (Lockheed)

Right: A crisp driftsight view of Seattle-Tacoma (SEATAC) Airport in Washington, photographed by NASA contract pilot Ronald W. Williams from a height of 65,000ft and at an indicated air speed of 120kts. (NASA)

Below right: At the helm of NASA U-2C N709NA, Ron Williams observes Mount St Helens through his driftsight, shortly after the mountain 'blew its top'. Note the digital co-ordinates displayed on the INS panel on the right. (Lockheed)

is important too, and the 'mobile' needs to know as far in advance as possible if he will be obliged to face a session in the rubber suit in lieu of a colleague suffering from the sniffles. Mission-planning precedes this, based on the air tasking handed down from higher authority, which is carefully drawn out on a Mission Support System (MSS) computer and then fed into the U-2R while it remains dormant, using a data load transfer module which will hold a series of carefully set out co-ordinates, one for each leg of the mission. Sensor equipment similarly is fine-tuned and checked ready by the jet's Crew Chief, assisted by a pool of technical specialists, backed by contractor Technical Representatives, who possess exemplary knowledge of the sensors and avionics. More detailed briefing, including copious notes on weather, projected enemy defences and diversionary airfields, follows two hours prior to take-off. All settled, the pilot strolls along to be processed by the PSD, to begin the lengthy suiting-up. The cotton undergarment, nylon mesh and insulated rubber layers (with built-in 'pee tube') is topped with the

Above: The first TR-1A production aircraft destined for the USAF was rolled out at Lockheed-Palmdale on 15 July 1981 and was flown by Ken Weir on 1 August; the first TR-1B followed on 23 February 1983. Both types have dropped the 'tactical' nomenclature and are now known simply as the U-2R and U-2RT respectively. (Lockheed)

flame-resistant gold outer cover featuring integral booties and pressure-tight glove and helmet rings and usually adds several inches to the pilot's girth. Over it go the parachute harness, self-inflating life preservers and flying boots. Once the gloves are clipped in place and the helmet screwed on to its circular capstan neck band, the mission has effectively commenced, for it remains in place, with the clear inner visor sealed, for anything up to fourteen hours. Surprisingly, most U-2R jockeys have few objections to this world of space-suited privation. They are well aware of the hazards resulting from high-altitude cockpit depressurization, such as the 'bends', and the outfit is mandatory for all flights above 45,000ft (FL450). In the last decade of training at Beale, only one individual was washed out on account of suit claustrophobia. That occurred during the temporary suspension of the interview process when candidates are expected to sit in the suit for a free one-hour trial period. Once in the cockpit, with the air conditioning ventilating the busy pilot, the only real reminder of the suit is the extra weight of the helmet. Before embarking on his slow 'moon walk' from PSD van to the cockpit, he spends at least an hour reclined in a armchair, breathing pure oxygen. This lengthy process purges the body of nitrogen as a further hedge against gas embolisms bubbling in the bloodstream in the event of depressurization (the symptoms of which are variously unpleasant, ranging from patches of hot, itchy but inaccessible skin to severe pains in the joints with, in the worst cases, cyanosis, partial paralysis or even coma resulting). A steady flow of oxygen is maintained via a hand-held portable pack right up to the time when the pilot straps himself into the ejection seat, assisted by the Crew Chief and 'mobile', and is connected to the jet's life-preserving umbilicals. It is also standard procedure to keep the cockpit cool prior to take-off, by means of the 'Howdah' built into the access gantry. This is seldom a problem at Alconbury, but temperatures can often exceed 100°F at Beale. Pilots often lose 6–7lb per flight as it is!

The pilot steps into a mission-ready machine, its engines already spooled into action by a 'huffer' ground starter and its instrument panel alive. The 'mobile' would have taken care of just about everything, including the initial alignment of the INS (inertial navigation set) or AINS (astro-inertial navigation system), depending on aircraft configuration, many of the built-in test functions of the avionics, the pre-flight 'walkaround' to check that the portions look healthy, and even the laborious paperwork. With everything ticking over, the crewmen exchange 'thumbs-up' and the sideways-folding canopy hood is clamped shut. This final layer seals the cockpit and will only be opened again after the aircraft has

Above: Prior to the advent of the U-2RT, this duo of U-2CT trainers—nicknamed 'Two-Headed Goats'—handled all initial pilot familiarization and conversion training. Aircraft 66953 (its tail is visible on the left) was first flown at Palmdale on 13 February 1973 and was joined three years later by 66692 (here dominating the camera frame). The distinctive sunshade-cum-access gantry is nicknamed the 'Howdah'. Both 'Goats' were retired by 1987. (Via Peter E. Davies)

ground to a halt at the conclusion of its long mission—or possibly earlier if shot off by bullet-shaped canopy breakers initiated by an ejection. With the Pratt & Whitney J75-P-13B whining away, the 'mobile' dashes to his 5-litre Ford automatic car, ready to supervise the stately progress of the 'Dragon Lady' to the runway via a UHF radio link. Turn radius on the ground is usually 'a tad under 300 feet', increased if cross-winds are pushing the tall fin or if the manually operated cables which control the steerable, solid tail wheels are slightly slack. While this ponderous process takes place a second 'chase' vehicle completes a final FOD (foreign object damage) examination of the runway, ensuring that it is free of debris that might be sucked up by the finely tuned powerplant or thrown on to the protruding sensor arrays.

On the runway centreline, with cockpit checks complete, pins pulled from the undercarriage (including the 'pogos', which will drop free), wind and pressure checked with the tower and the rumbling beast cleared for take-off, all is ready to roll. It is here that it becomes apparent that the 'Dragon Lady' is anything but a quiet, docile sailplane. The full-

blooded bellow of the J75's 17,000lb s.t. punch creates a unique noise and smell that reminds one of the engine's origins as the powerhorse of the 'Thud' and 'Dart', and even though the U-2R adaptation lacks an afterburner there still is plenty of kick on take-off. Even a heavily laden aircraft has to be carefully trimmed to avoid over-rotation. Take-off runs, depending on weight, range from as little as 500ft to three times that for an operational launch. Climb-out is always impressive, even at around 112kts: the aircraft appears to rise vertically on a smoke plume. According to Bob Uebelacker, the old C-model, a 'little wing' with a J75, 'could stand on its tail!' Initial climb-out is performed at 25–30° pitch, with the machine rising like a feather on a thermal. This drops off to 5–10° pitch in the thinner, upper air. Power is kept at 90–95 per cent until it reaches FL500, when the aircraft enters a 'Mach schedule' to keep the airframe within its structural limits. Normally this would involve a Mach 0.72 cruise at altitude, with a much wider stall margin to play around in than the 6–7kt 'coffin corner' that beset the original U-2 series and gave the machine its curious nickname. The crews reckon it is something like 15kts now, with the top speed 'red-lined' at Mach 0.8. In any event, the aircraft is flown in a 'constant cruise climb' so that, as fuel burns off and weight is reduced, the machine gains height. Ceiling is contentious as the relevant graphs in the pilot's manual remain classified, but operational configurations—bearing the burden of heavy-duty sensors—limit it to

Above: 95th RS U-2R 01086 lays in wait at RAF Alconbury, Cambridgeshire, between missions. The aircraft carries the full 'Senior Spear'/'Senior Ruby' sigint fit but has a 'slick' nose. The latter features a small panel for the installation of an F35 survey camera. (Author)

about 70,000ft. Autopilot is used for the greater part of the cruise and this manages most control functions, including trim. One unique feature of the 'big-wing' series is the all-moving tail: the whole assembly, including vertical tail and horizontal stabilizers, moves about an arc of 5° as one unit for trim purposes. Pitch trim is adjusted using a switch on the side of the control yoke, and is possible at all altitudes and air speeds, the idea being to reduce loads on the most fragile part of the U-2's anatomy—its tail. This is assisted by the gust flap system, used to dampen turbulence. Double spoilers on the wing provide roll authority. Bank angles of 20° on autopilot and 45° on command (15° greater than was possible on the old 'little-wing' models) are the usual practice, but are not limits.

Those who have examined the U-2's cockpit often express surprise at the big, two-handed control yoke, seemingly poached from a B-52. However, an emphasis on weight-saving throughout the structure and flight systems ruled out the use of power-assisted controls, and the high aspect ratio aircraft demands powerful aileron inputs to hold the wings steady, particularly in strong winds at lower altitudes, yet minimal pitch inputs. Physical strains of this type are an unwelcome addition to the already heavy pilot workload on long-range flights (for example the laborious ferry excursions from the United States to England, which cover 5,600 miles in just under thirteen hours using a ground speed of 430kts). The suit is not pressurized in flight, though would inflate instantly if its automatic sensors detected a loss of cabin pressure. It has been calculated that a pilot would be conscious for no more than three seconds

in the event of sudden decompression, allowing no time to secure a visor or suit opening. In slightly longer than this he would suffer the hideous symptoms encountered above 'Armstrong's Line'. Here, all bodily fluids would literally boil. The suit is therefore kept secure at all times. Having reached his orbit zone, the jet-jockey then settles into what is normally a lengthy surveillance span. This customarily means staying well back from the FEBA (Forward Edge of the Battle Area) as an insurance against being hacked down by SAMs such as the SA-12 (NATO code-name 'Gladiator') or being scarred irreparably by the sharp claws of a marauding MiG. However, overflights can

Below: Wing stability for ground operations is provided by these sprung 'pogo' outriggers, which drop free on take-off. Simplicity was the key to the U-2's success, and a lightweight structure ruled out the use of a heavy conventional undercarriage. (Peter E. Davies)

be and still are practised, and measures to improve the aircraft's defensive ('Def') systems are under way, including a new Cincinnati Electronics cryogenic missile approach warning receiver (to replace the old 'System 20') and more effective active counter-measures (for example, *active* decoy dispensers which emulate those of the U-2R). However, the black lady is anything but a sitting duck. It can pull relatively hard, 2.5*g* manaoeuvres at altitude, out-turning most fighters and creating homing problems for the most tenacious missile in the thin upper air. Nevertheless, it would not take much shrapnel damage to force her down. Mostly, the biggest threat is pilot complacency arising out of boredom, as the machine goes about collecting its data by remote control. Pilots just switch buttons on and off, as briefed. 'We've finally got most of our buttons, switches and dials glove-sized rather than pinkie-finger sized so that we can manipulate them,' observed Maj Steve Randle. 'Elaborate moves are ruled out by the bulky glove.' As a rule, this is done in complete radio silence on a 'door-to-door' basis, a standard procedure for all of Lockheed's 'black' birds, past and present, which prefer to maintain their anonymity while on the wing. The high workload is dictated by physical factors as much as anything else: 'You can get real tired if you have to exert yourself.' High-altitude glare is another source of fatigue if not checked. The intensity of the sun at FL700 *et environs* is much more ferocious than most people imagine. Sunshades are built into the canopy hood, yet pilots often devise additional protection using mapboards and other checklist paraphernalia: 'I build a sort of house of cards in there. Let's face it, there's not much other traffic at altitude so I don't have to look out and see what's coming!' Solar radiation, especially during peak sunspot activity, is another hazard crews have learned to cope with by keeping the tinted visors lowered. The engine is kept going throughout the proceedings. Contrary to mythology, U-2 pilots have never voluntarily glided anywhere except in a dire emergency. Steve Randle's succinct comment was, 'If the engine's out, my heart's palpitating!' Remaining virtually immobile in the cockpit for long periods at altitude with little to do except swivel the driftsight is undoubtedly a salutary experience. A food warmer is provided to heat up rations resembling toothpaste tubes which can be inserted through a seal in the helmet and squeezed. These contain various delights such as beef and gravy or peach sauce, though few pilots profess to being regulars at the 'Dragon Lady diner' and force the food and fluids down to maintain minimum energy levels. Cold water, to mitigate dehydration, is much more popular. With or without a tube of food to suck on, with the sensor equipment

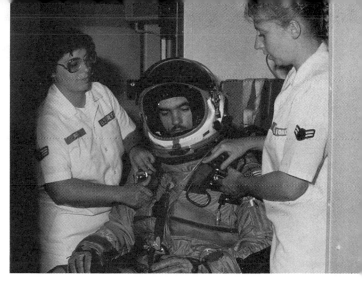

Above: 'Suiting up' takes the best part of half an hour and is followed by just under an hour's worth of 'pre-breathing' pure oxygen, overseen by the PSD (Physiological Support Division) staff. (USAF)

Below: Dressed up in the life-saving David Clark Co S1010B suit and plumbed into the standard air conditioning pack, a 'Dragon Driver' poses for Lockheed photographer Eric Schulzinger. (Lockheed)

warmed up and the pilot monitoring his position by means of the driftsight, maps and LN33 INS or AINS digital read-out to ensure that the beast is on course for the reconnaissance pass—composed of one or more 'destinations' in a point-to-point flight plan, a fly-by in parallel coverage or a monotonous, continuous racetrack orbit—then 'spying' may commence.

LOOK, LISTEN AND LEARN

Protruding as 'farms' of antennae are the sigint receivers. The U-2R's listening equipment originally comprised two closely allied sets of communications-intelligence (comint) receivers, 'Senior Book', manifested as an array of ventral VHF and UHF direction-finding antennae, and 'Senior Spear', packaged into two large slipper tanks fitted at quarter-span. Both packages were linked to onboard recorders and dorsal VHF relay aerials, alongside the up-link/down-link AN/UPQ-3 microwave which permitted the dispatch of sigint and the reception of instructions at line-of-sight ranges of up to 400 miles from the ground station. At altitude, the systems could pick up chatter and telemetry at ranges of up to 350 miles, thus providing a potential real-time 'reach' of 750

miles. The Defense Intelligence Agency's appetite for sigint was voracious, and routine missions from the home-drome Beale, its four primary detachment bases and numerous OLs kept the force extremely busy throughout the final decade of the 'Cold War', often filling in for other NRO (National Reconnaissance Office) resources which were unable to fulfil their brief. For example, the loss of remote listening outposts in the highlands north of Mashhad and Teheran following the collapse of the Shah of Iran's regime was keenly felt, and Diego Garcia in the Indian Ocean was activated as a new OL, permitting the 99th SRS to assist with the monitoring of Soviet rocketry as a precursor to the ratification of SALT 2.

Above: U-2R 01068 trolls over RAF Alconbury, complete with ASARS-2 but lacking sigint equipment. The all-up package was known as the TRS (or Tactical Reconnaissance System) and conveyed radar images and sigint to a ground-based TREDS receiving station located near Hahn AFB, Germany. (Peter R. Foster via Peter E. Davies)

Below: 'Ass Kickers' U-2R 01077 ambles along the runway at Alconbury in October 1985 with the all-up ASARS-2 and sigint fit. The first such mission was flown by Lt-Col John Sanders on 9 July that year. Note the dipping, laden wings. (Peter R. Foster via Peter E. Davies)

Meanwhile, Det 2 (the 'Black Cat' detachment) at Osan AB, South Korea, kept an eye on the ROK's ever-belligerent neighbour North Korea and on the fragile DMZ; Det 3 continued to trawl for intelligence over the Sinai, Persian Gulf and North Africa, from its Mediterrannean enclave at RAF Akrotiri, Cyprus; Det 4 kept an ear on central Europe and the crisis in Poland, flying out of RAF Mildenhall in Suffolk; and Det 5, stationed at Patrick AFB in Florida, wheeled in never-ending offshore loops near Cuba, plotted activities in troubled El Salvador and Nicaragua and provided essential support for the later contingency operations conducted in Grenada ('Storm Fury') and Panama ('Just Cause').[5]

Numerous new passive comint and electronic intelligence (elint) devices steadily increased the sigint repertoire in support of these tasks. Following close on the heels of 'Senior Book' and the consolidation of the strategic recce force at Beale AFB in July 1976, E-Systems' 'Senior Ruby' was added. This is an elint receiver which was packaged alongside an updated 'Senior Spear' Phase IV comint sensor array in two extended slipper tanks known as 'superpods', which split the full-span trailing edge flaps in two. The combined sigint fit bears the acronym RTASS (Remote Tactical Airborne Sigint System) and is connected to a Sperry data-link sprouting from under the tail to relay the tell-tale sigint back to a ground-receiving TGIF (Transportable Ground Intercept Facility). RTASS achieved IOC during 1978, when the 99th SRS deployed its first 'superpodded' U-2R (68-10339) to RAF Mildenhall in England for 'Creek Spectre' sigint missions over central Europe. These missions expanded the following year when another U-2R (68-10338, nicknamed 'Snoopy') doubled the force in an arrangement which, with aircraft and crews rotating in and out on a temporary duty (TDY) basis, would endure until 22 February 1983, ten days after RAF Alconbury had been deemed suitably 'bedded down' and the 95th RS had received the first pair (80-1068 and -1070) out of an eventual dozen TR-1As—shortly to be reduced to an expanded 'Det' of four aircraft, one for each of the purpose-built wide hardened shelters. Further elint sensors are in the works. PLSS/SLATS (the Precision Location Strike System/Signal Location Targeting System) was aborted in 1988 after gestating steadily for over fifteen years; however, a more self-contained package code-named 'Senior Smart' is about to enter flight test and promises to do much much more.[6]

If the evolution of multiplex 'farms' of bent and twisted ground-brushing antennae have transformed

---

[5]Operations 'Storm Fury' and 'Just Cause' are described in further detail in Chapter 4.

[6]See Chapter 5.

Above: NASA U-2C N709NA soars into the sky on its J75 engine. On 17 and 18 April 1989 the machine rocketed to the stratosphere to clinch several Class 1F/G time-to-climb records previously held by a Gates Learjet 28. The pilots concerned were Jerry Hoyt and Ron Williams. (Lockheed)

Above: A U-2R climb-out at an initial 25–30° pitch amidst the bellowing and thunder of the 17,000lb static thrust produced by the P&WA J75-P-13B turbojet is an impressive sight. (John Dunnell via Peter E. Davies)

Below: This multiplex of bent and crooked protrusions is associated with the 'Senior Book' sigint fit, comprising UHF/VHF direction-finding antennae. The dorsal relay antennae were later replaced by internal data-link equipment. (Peter E. Davies)

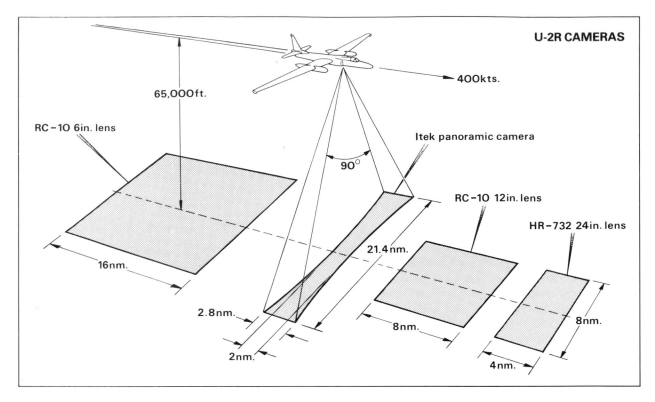

65,000ft.

400kts.

RC–10 6in. lens

Itek panoramic camera

90°

RC–10 12in. lens

HR–732 24in. lens

21.4nm.

16nm.

2.8nm.

8nm.

8nm.

2nm.

8nm.

4nm.

the originally slick 'Dragon Lady' into a demonic flying machine, then the nasal infection of warts that have sprouted on the force's steadily elongating snouts over the past decade have surely earned it a place in a witch's coven. Its crews eschew the notion that they are warlocks riding a 'Black Velvet' broomstick, aware that behind all those lumps and bumps is housed one of the U-2R's gem sensors—the Hughes

ASARS-2 (Advanced Synthetic Aperture Radar System), capable of radar-mapping tracts of ground twenty miles wide at stand-off ranges of eighty miles or more, deep behind the FEBA, to identify rear-echelon forces in all weather conditions. It remains the only *active* device amidst the plethora of available sensors. Photo-like imagery is made possible by the use of *synthetic* as opposed to *real* aperture radar.

U-2 CAMERAS

Camera designation	Image format (in)	Optical angular coverage	Focal length (in)	Notes
Type A-3	9×18	41°21'	24	Three HR732 24in lenses for multi-emulsion coverage
Type A-4			6/12+36	RC-10 plus Fairchild HR73B
Type B/HR733B Fairchild	18×18	28°	36	Imagery captured on two 9in wide film frames; first high-acuity camera
RC-10 Wild-Heerburg	9×9	73°12' / 41°	6 / 12	Dual camera for multiple emulsion of multiple scale coverage of the target area
Multi-Spectral Camera IIS	9×9	47°	3.95	Four separate lenses for multi-spectral coverage of a target area
Type H Hycon	4.5×4.5	3°54°	66	LOROP with adjustable look-angle, pointed using driftsight; introduced in April 1965
KA-80A Itek	4.5×50	120°	24	OBC high-resolution panoramic camera; angled mirror sits in front of lens and rotates to provide panoramic coverage
KA-102A Itek	4.5×4.5	3°54'	66	Daytime stand-off LOROP

These are some of the key USAF and NASA camera sensors which have since been supplemented by E-O systems. 'Multiple emulsions' refers to different films—monochrome, colour (usually positive Ektachrome) or infra-red—which reveal different features. Multiple lenses also permit increased area coverage, or different scales by the use of lenses of varying focal length.

Above: Old and new drift above the clouds over San Francisco Bay. NASA obtained two ER-2s for various peaceful assignments which range from land management survey and ozone sampling to pre-launch trials of satellite-based sensors. A third 'ER-2', USAF U-2R 80-1069/N708NA, has been added to the fleet and will in all likelihood remain there. The old U-2Cs are now museum exhibits. (Lockheed)

The technique is aired elsewhere, but the net effect is to compress the along-track 'spot size' of the resultant imagery, for significantly improved resolution. ASARS-2 furnishes exceptional detail, with only minimum 'radar shadows', by means of a trainable set of planar radar dishes which can speedily re-scan certain strips to reveal features otherwise hidden in the lee of the 'look angle'—such as forces concealed behind a hill. A 'spotlight' mode also permits repeated scanning, for greater acuity.[7] The first European mission was flown on 9 July 1985 with 95th commander Lt-Col John Sanders at the yoke, and testing climaxed the following September during NATO 'Reforger' manoeuvres, when the 'Ass Kickers' provided continuous coverage of the central front for 48 hours, paving the way for series production. By 1988 Hughes had fine-tuned the radar system further, and was bold enough to assert that ASARS 'produces long-range images superior to those delivered by photo techniques'.

However, trusty old photography has never been abandoned. This sound policy was brought to the fore following the loss of the space shuttle *Challenger* on 28 January 1986. Apart from the tragic loss of life, the spaceship exploded with a valuable spy satellite aboard, while the resultant long-term grounding order—including that of the orbiter's intended cargo of KH-11 space spies, equipped with optical, infra-red and radar sensors—created programme delays that caused gaping holes to appear in the United States'

strategic reconnaissance-gathering capability. This salutary lesson did not go unheeded. Instead, 'photint' progressed to new heights, and included 66in focal length LOROP cameras such as the 'Q-Bay'-mounted Hycon Type H (distinguished by a large glass oriel for vertical or oblique work) and nose-mounted 'Senior Open' fit (identified by a large porthole), which permit photographs to be snatched adjacent to the flight path traced by the 'Dragon' by means of a projection mirror contained in the servo-rotating extremity of the nose. By 1990 the U-2R community had been furnished with 'near real-time' camera sensors too. These do not use celluloid at all, the film plane having been replaced with a Charged Coupled Device (CCD) array which converts the raw pictures into digital signals which can be conveyed to ground stations and then decoded back into good quality images—all within five minutes, for presentation in 'soft copy' format on screen and as prints.

[7] SAR radar is aired in Chapter 3 in the context of the Goodyear/Loral UPD systems fitted to 'Photo-Phantoms'. The ASARS-1 which originated from the same supplier was tested on U-2R 68-10339 under Project 'Senior Lance'. This was contained in the 'Q-Bay', with the antenna sprouting below in a rubberized radome.

Most such electro-optical (E-O) sensors are believed to be variable FOV (field of view) zooms effectively operating in the 12–66in focal length range, capable of taking both wide-angle 'pushbrooms' in swaths up to 140° wide and of producing close-up scans with an approximate 10° FOV. Flexibility and speed are just two of many advantages offered by E-O sensors: the imagery can be manipulated by interpreters to highlight different features by simply adjusting contrast or employing more sophisticated computer image enhancement techniques (some of which, on the debit side, may be used to prejudice the truth); the airborne sensors can be redirected to re-scan areas of special interest within a short time of their dicovery, a process assisted by the variable FOV 'zoom'; while the use of 'dry film' techniques means that interpretation is an unmessy, electronic process, which eases logistics and placates environmentalists to boot (there are no hazardous waste products which would otherwise result from photo-processing chemicals and gallons of contaminated water). The use to which such E-O sensors can be put is exemplified the quality of the U-2R imagery gleaned by 1704th Wing 'Dragons' flying out of Taif in Saudi Arabia during the Gulf War in support of the Coalition HQ at Riyadh, some of which is reproduced in the accompanying illustrations. Code-named 'Senior Glass', the technology is continually maturing.

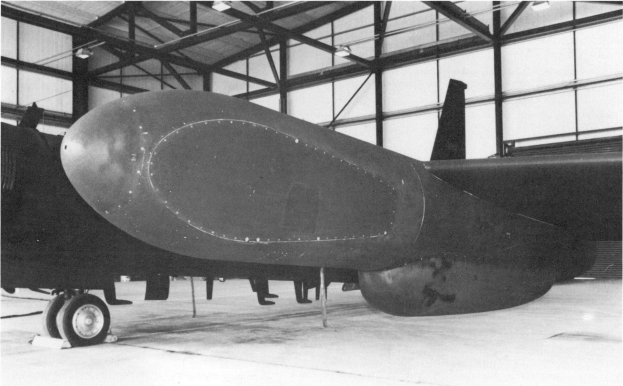

Above left: Aircraft 01099 was the last U-2R to be delivered, handed over to the USAF on 3 October 1989. The artwork is typical of the decorative treatment applied to the aircraft in recent years, much of which appears to be temporary, applied using artists' grease pencils. (Author)

Left: During the late 1970s the U-2R began to feature mission-tailored 'super pods' housing 'Senior Spear' comint (aft) and 'Senior Ruby' elint (forward) and sigint receivers. The system is currently updated to 'Phase IV' standard. (Author)

Above: The San Francisco Golden Gate bridge provides a favourite photographic opportunity. (Lockheed)

As seems to be the case throughout the history of the U-2 programme, 'development' and 'operational' sensor suites are difficult to distinguish owing to the never-ending influx of new technology. As 'Dragon Tamer' Steve Randle points out, 'There are so many combinations, almost endless; it seems that the aircraft are sprouting new antennas or other devices every time I turn around. As far as *combinations* of mission equipment are concerned, it's incredible!' However, it is not all cloak-and-dagger. Just before the 349th SRS set up shop at Beale under the 99th SRS, two surveillance flights over earthquake-stricken Guatemala were made at the request of the US Agency for International Development. These helped to ascertain just what kind of aid was required, and furnished photos for added political

clout. On 22 October 1976 Maj David Hahn located Bruce Collins, the sole survivor of a yachting accident in the Pacific. After three weeks of fruitless searches the U-2R was called in and Hahn's colour camera registered the yellow dot that proved to be Collins' liferaft, 780 miles west of San Francisco. In 1985 U-2s joined in the search for MV *Amazing Grace*. Many other sorties have been requested and granted in support of search and rescue, flood control and hurricane-damage assessment, while NASA's tireless trio continue to take false and real images in support of land management and 'resource control' and to test satellite sensors before they are committed on a long journey into Earth orbit.

'Senior Book', 'Senior Ruby' and 'Senior Spear' introduced sigint sensor management by remote control, and to this day U-2 pilots have very little to do with the sensor functions *per se*. Instead, these have traditionally been pre-programmed, packaged and processed by ESC personnel from such units as Alconbury's 6952nd Electronic Security Squadron and by joint-Service teams operating in remote fixed ground processing stations who can 'tweak' the sensors from afar. The 95th RS were the first to conduct field trials with U-2R 'near real-time' receiving stations, beginning with the semi-mobile Ford Aerospace TREDS (Tactical Reconnaissance Exploit-

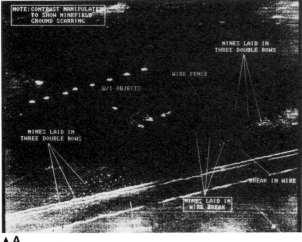

▲A

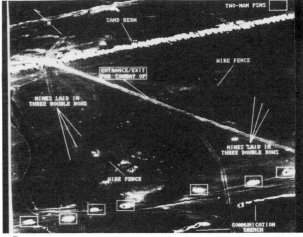

▲B

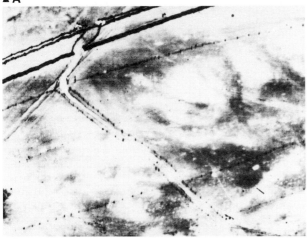

▲C

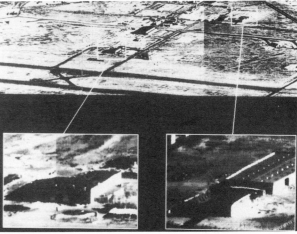

▲D

▲E

▲F

Above: These six U-2R images show the kind of information that can be gleaned from its photint and radar sensors. Photo A shows a multi-layered Iraqi defensive network, including (by means of contrast adjustment) the exact whereabouts of the individual mines! Photo B shows similar obstacles, including an earthen berm. Photo C reveals a gap in a wire obstacle. This could have been used by the enemy to move among his various defensive positions as well as to funnel invading Coalition forces into 'kill zones'. The data proved vital to Gen Schwarzkopf's staff. Photo D shows how the U-2R was used for BDA after the commencement of 'Desert Storm' and how the imagery can be magnified, in this instance to highlight the satisfactory destruction of Iraqi storage hangars. Photo E shows 'before and after' images of a naval depot that received the attention of Coalition strike aircraft. Photo F depicts the alarming scene of the destruction the Iraqis wrought on Kuwait's oil industry. (US DoD)

ation Demonstration System), which was deployed to 'Metro Tango', the code-name for a missile maintenance facility located near Hahn AFB in Germany, in late 1987, in support of the all-up TR-1A sigint/ASARS-2 fit (known as the TRS, or Tactical Reconnaissance System). Its automated operational successor TRIGS (TR-1 Ground Station) was on the point of being installed underground at Gossberg Hill near Weuscheim prior to the collapse of the Soviet Union, but little has been said about it since except that ways are being devised to make the package air transportable, for deployment near any potential trouble spot. It reputedly will form part of Air Combat Command's CARS (Contingency Airborne Reconnaissance System). As pioneered at 'Metro Tango', TREDS fuses data from the U-2R's miscellaneous sensors, filters out the rubbish and transmits a final series of synthesized reports down the hot lines to commanders. The system works so fast that U-2 sensors can be directed to re-examine areas of special interest before the 'Dragon Lady' has had time to drift much further along its pre briefed flightplan. 'Look' angles and 'zooming' of the E-O fit or ASARS-2 may be adjusted by remote control or manipulated after it has been received. Total sensor integration is the ultimate objective, to create an 'all-up' tactical recce system: in this manner, E-O or radar may be directed to spots where sigint indicates a high level of enemy activity, and the combined data can be 'fused' to provide a much fuller picture—on the *spot*, literally. The 40ft trailer housing TREDS was deployed to the Gulf region in support of Operation 'Desert Storm', along with a dozen 'Dragon Ladies', 28 pilots (on a sixty-day TDY rotational basis) and 220 other personnel drawn from Alconbury and Beale. Flying from Taif, the crews averaged 7–8 sorties each of 9 hours' duration on a daily basis, providing round-the-clock coverage with ASARS-2 and E-O sensors, using TREDS for mission-planning and mission-monitoring as well as image-processing. None of Lt-Col Stephen M. Peterson's force received a single shrapnel hole, despite operations deep into Kuwait and Iraq with a dated package of 'Def' systems.

Fixed receiving stations located within the Continental United States managed by the USAF ESC and NRO also exist to receive intelligence conveyed through the ether—with emphasis on E-O imagery and sigint, in support of strategic objectives—virtually in minutes from U-2Rs operating anywhere over the globe. This is made possible by four operational sigint/photint machines (68-10331 and -10339, plus 80-1070 and -1071) which have been fitted with a large dorsal fairing containing a satellite-relay antenna code-named 'C-Span III', capable of bouncing material up to space and thence, via the celestial orbiters, direct to Washington DC.[8] How-

ever, these growths are continuing to chip away at aircraft performance, as the 'Dragon Lady' grows increasingly rotund in its late middle age. As former 'Skunk Works' boss Ben Rich remarked three years ago, 'The U-2 started out at 17,000lb and we're flying at 40,000lb today with the same engine.' Endurance has suffered, and so has altitude: with two and half tons of sensor and relay equipment and nine tons of take-off fuel added to the aircraft's 2,500lb deadweight, the type can only just make it past FL700, at the apex of its constant cruise climb profile. Most Gulf missions were conducted at around FL600–650. Several operational losses have been traced to engine-related problems too. At 7.00 a.m. on 7 December 1977 Capt Robert A. Henderson died with four Cypriot base employees when his machine (68-10330) failed to lift off from Akrotiri and subsequently ploughed into the base's Operations & Air Control Centre and exploded. Two years later, on 6 February 1980, another Det 3 bird crashed into the Black Sea in unknown circumstances. A similar fate nearly befell Capt David Bonsi on 22 May 1984 while with the 'Black Cat' detachment at Osan. The machine blew up shortly after take-off, and he ejected just in time. An identical accident at Beale two months later pointed to structural failure, traced to defective adaptor links joining the engine efflux nozzle to the long tailpipe. Broken, the engine literally blew the tail off. Corrective action was undertaken which grounded the entire force for two months, but the 'Dragons' continued to tumble. Det 2 suffered a further casualty that year on 8 October when an aircraft broke up in mid-air over Korea. Again, the pilot made a lucky escape. More recently, on 15 January 1992, the Osan detachment suffered a third loss, this time tragically killing its pilot. It appears that engine failure forced the pilot to make an unsuccessful attempt at ditching in the Sea of Japan. These headaches, combined with the gradually diminishing performance, have finally prompted a long overdue engine upgrade. Funds have been made available to re-engine the force with the brand new General Electric F101-GE-F29 turbofan (a high-altitude adaptation of the F118 developed for the B-2 Stealth Bomber), shorter and lighter than the existing P&W J75-P-13B yet rated at ten tons static thrust at sea level. The new powerplant, which will be installed during depot overhauls at Palmdale over the course of the next four years, will permit the

---

[8]There may exist only two or three of these machines. The U-2R's complete tail empennage (the only portion of the aircraft bearing an exterior tail number) may be removed, facilitating a quick change of registration to foil 'spotters'. One of the four sighted so far (-10339) has recently been flying eight-hour sorties on alternate days since 5 September 1992 from Aviano AB, Italy, in support of Operation 'Provide Promise' over the Gulf region. Support has been furnished by the 95th RS.

Above: U-2R 10336 on finals at Palmdale. This machine served as test-bed for the Hughes ASARS-2 radar. Note the split flaps (which were continuous prior to the advent of the 'super pods') and the ribbed tail. The latter is a beef-up feature unique to the original FY68 models. For work with the ASARS-2, the relevant aircraft received a new Northrop astro-inertial navigation system, which replaced the old LN-33 INS. (Lockheed)

'Dragon Lady' to cruise at altitudes close to 80,000ft and extend its 3,000-mile operational range by 15 per cent. Test flights began in March 1989, just months before the last U-2R rolled out of Palmdale replete with a commensurately strengthened tail empennage.

DRAGON DESCENT

One facet of U-2 operations which remains fairly constant is the harrowing procedure of gently recovering the delicate machine back on a runway. Getting the beast down safely in the half-hour descent procedure that follows a typical gruelling nine- or ten hour-long sortie is one of most demanding flying jobs anywhere, and Stan/Eval crews pay particular attention to pilots' performance during these manoeuvres. Careful engine management is needed in the descent to avoid flame-out, using a planned Engine Pressure Ratio (EPR) schedule and open engine bleed valves. This cuts EPR from about 2.3 at altitude to 2.08, and eventually to idle, yielding an air speed of between 150 and 170kts (depending on air conditions). A faster descent can be effected in smooth air. Flaps, air brakes and undercarriage are lowered early to generate drag, with the gust control setting operative to reduce elevator load forces on the yoke. The pilot also has to remember the canopy de-icing routine as he re-enters denser, moister air, which typically condenses as an icy glaze also on still-freezing wings—a pointer to a 'Dragon Lady' having just completed an operational excursion. A cockpit fan circulates air, while a canopy heating system prevents the pilot from having to land 'blind'. And 'eyes-out' is critical. At a point about ten miles out at around 2,000ft, the pilot enters the approach glidepath on finals. There now are two crucial operations: calculating landing speed and balancing fuel in the long, see-saw wings. A 'T-speed' formula is used to establish the correct landing speed which the jet should have when it crosses the runway threshold. This is based on the zero-fuel weight of the aircraft plus a knot for every hundred gallons of fuel remaining. In gusty conditions, a further 2–3kts may be added as a hedge against being blown off the

Above: The glass oriel mounted in the 'Q-Bay' of U-2R 10337 denotes a Hycon Type H 66in focal length LOROPS. The aircraft has just completed a high-altitude sortie, as evidenced by the pilot's 'goldfish bowl' pressure helmet and the white icy glaze on the still freezing wings. (John Dunnell via Peter E. Davies)

Below: Like a bird of prey swooping down, TR-1B 01065 heads for the runway at RAF Alconbury during its annual Stan/Eval deployment, back in the days when it continued to wear a glossy white livery. Crews wear standard lightweight flight gear for these low-altitude check-rides. (Peter Foster via Peter Davies)

glidescope. Stall speed is around 10kts below 'T-speed'. As Steve Randle sees it, 'If determining the landing speed of the airplane is a science rather than an art, balancing the airplane for landing is an art rather than a science.' Apart from its small, seldom-folded tip sections (designed for carrier lift compatibility), the entire wing holds fuel. Its vast span, coupled with the poor undercarriage track, makes a finely balanced fuel load essential (and it is made all the more important by the fact that, during a mission, the inboard tanks are used first, enabling fuel in the outer sections to dampen torsional bending moments on the structure). Settling the aircraft to a little above 'T-speed', the pilot judges fuel

Left: 'Dragon Driver' Maj Bob Uebelacker poses for the camera next to TR-1A 01086 in July 1987. He qualified on the type during 1984 after 'transitioning' from the B-52 'Buff'. Only Crew Chiefs are assigned specific 'tails'; pilots fly whatever 'Operations' hands to them, and Bob has flown many different aircraft. (Author)

Below left: The U-2R sits on two tandem undercarriage units, featuring forward pneumatic tyres and this solid tail wheel arrangement. Steering is provided by means of pulleys linked to the pilot's rudder pedals. The 'Dragon Lady' incorporates a minimum of power-assisted controls in order to save weight. (Author)

Below: A 99th RS U-2R under tow, with counterbalancing Crew Chiefs perched on a wing tip. Light winds can cause rolling and weathercocking, even during ground operations. (Frank B. Mormillo)

balance purely by 'feel'. Pumps are activated to distribute the go-juice, 'a tad at a time, until it feels right'. As the aircraft looms into view, the 'mobile' pilot races out in his 5-litre Ford automatic, radio open to the descending pilot who remains dressed with 'goldfish bowl' helmet firmly secured. However, the process is not as difficult as it was during the U-2A/C era: 'At lower altitudes the airplane comes down pretty much like a normal one. We fly standard glidescope. Really, the major difference between landing our airplane and any other is in the last 2–3 feet above the runway. We have to stall it to make it stay on the ground. If you stall from more than about 3 feet there is a great possibility of incurring structural damage. If you midjudge and don't stall, the main gear will hit the runway and then, because you're not out of flying speed, the beast will bound back into the air. If it bounds more than 3–4 feet it will then stall and risk structural damage. That's why we have a mobile officer in the chase car calling off altitude. On the stall, the tail will settle on to the runway, followed rapidly by the main gear.' This time-honoured technique dates back to Tony LeVier's adventurous landing thirty-seven years ago.

The aircraft still needs careful handling as it rolls down the ramp, as aileron and rudder control are negligible. Sometimes a wing tip has to be deliberately 'dragged' to inhibit weathercocking from the tall fin. Maj Bob Uebelacker recalls this occurring at

night, 'generating a magnificent shower of sparks' from the abrasive metal 'skid buttons' built into the wing's tucked-down extremities. After having ground to a halt with the engine remaining on idle, ground crews plug in the 'pogos' to restore stability. Pilots take considerable pride in holding wings-level prior to this, and fuel balance is measured by how many Crew Chiefs it takes to hold down the light wing: 'One Crew Chief balance is very reasonable. Two Crew Chiefs is pretty gross, and if you have two Crew Chiefs and the 'mobile' officer out of his car also jump on the wing, that probably calls for a round of beers some place!' This sometimes strenuous task over, the engines are spooled up and the black jet glider plus inevitably fatigued pilot troll to the assigned parking spot. Following de-suiting and the return of normal bodily sensations, a pilot undergoes debrief before a lengthy period of relaxation. He will not be subjected to the rigours of another high-altitude flight for at least 48 hours. This pattern of events may hold true for another twenty-two years, by which time the 'Skunk Works' creation will have reached its sixtieth birthday. It has already outlived designs intended to replace it.

COMBAT ANGEL

Forming part of the U-2-equipped 100th SRW at U-Tapao at the height of the Vietnam War, and 'hanging tough' in the midst of a barrage of endless flak while the U-2s garnered their data at discreet ranges from altitude, were the air-launched Unmanned Air Vehicles (at the time known as Remotely Piloted Vehicles) of the 350th SRS *Red Falcons*, the only such machines operational anywhere in the world. Built by Teledyne Ryan Aeronautical (TRA) of San Diego, California, the UAV was based on the company's hugely successful Model 124 ground-launched BQM-34A Firebee target drone, which first flew as long ago as 1951. The Model 124 was redeveloped

from 1962 as the Model 147 as part of the USAF's 'Big Safari' elint/reconnaissance programme, to be air-launched and remotely piloted from specially adapted DC-130 'motherships', permitting high-risk reconnaissance jobs to be performed with relative impunity.[9]

Flights over Communist China were conducted from 1964—four downed RPVs were put on display in Peking the following year—proceeding on to SA-2 SAM elint-gathering sorties over North Vietnam as 'Lightning Bug' and 'Compass Cookie' missions which, from 1967, percolated into Laos and Cambodia as 'Buffalo Hunter'. With aircraft flying initially from Bien Hoa AB, South Vietnam, and later from U-Tapao, the programme was a huge success. Not only did the RPVs glean surprise photint and medium-altitude elint on crucial enemy MiG and SAM defences, but they could be ably employed as clay pigeons, permitting manned recce types flying at a distance to determine the precise command detonation codes used by the enemy to set off the 'Guideline' SAMs' warheads. Programmed into QRC (Quick Reaction Contract) countermeasures pods, these kept American fighter-bombers safe from all but the worst ravages of the Russian-supplied radar-directed missiles by jamming them at opportune moments. For photint, the drones sometimes zoomed in so low that their cameras snapped frightened Vietnamese MiG pilots fleeing from their aircraft ladders! Following the reconnaissance pass, the drone would climb to cruise height, steer out to the South China Sea, then enter into a parachute-assisted descent to be 'snatched' in mid-air by a CH-3 or CH-53 helicopter equipped with MARS (Mid-Air Retrieval System). MARS hooks were designed to snag the drones' 100ft-diameter main 'chute, which then disengaged to leave the RPV suspended by the lanyard. It was then gently taxied back to Da Nang AB, South Vietnam, for processing.[10] Altogether, the derivatives comprised no fewer than 22 configurations, though there existed seven primary models: the 'F ECM-jamming version; the 'H 'Combat Angel' ('Litter Bug') bulk chaff- or propaganda pamphlet-dispensing 'Bull**** Bomber'; the 'L and 'M 'Buffalo Hunter' low-medium altitude recce models, the former of which used TV instead of conventional cameras to relay 'real-time' video imagery to the mothership for taping and the latter a Fairchild KS-120A 2.75in (70mm) camera for horizon-to-horizon photography; the 'P

[9]See Chapter 5.

[10]Conducted in RF-4 type Goodyear PPIFs—see Chapter 3. 'Belfry Express' US Navy ships from Task Force 77 also supported the operation, by providing a seaborne base for the MARS helicopters and a back-up RPV pick-up facility if the Sikorsky rotary aircraft missed their catch.

high-altitude photo-recon version with extended wings and a revised powerplant; the 'Q 'Combat Dawn' model with high-altitude 'real-time' TV sensors for 'pushbroom' photint; and, finally, the 'R, an updated 'Q with an extended endurance of up to eight hours' flight time. By the time combat operations had concluded, the 100th SRW had notched up 3,435 AQM-34 sorties for the loss of more than 200 of these 'drones' to hostile fire (it is claimed that as many as 578 were lost to all causes up to January 1973), indicating the burden placed on the unit's shoulders. Yet no motherships were lost, nor any of the 'rotating' 800 personnel that went to form the 'Lightning Bug' community.

In July 1976 TAC took over the force, which was reconsolidated at Davis-Monthan AFB. Operating as the 432nd Tactical Drone Group under the command of Lt-Col Jim Witzel, the unit achieved IOC the following August as two separate squadrons: the 11th TDS, equipped with AQM-34V EW variants, including 44 drones and five DC-130As; and the 22nd TDS, assigned with 37 of the AQM-34M for the photo-recon mission plus four DC-130Es.[11] The RPVs' Continental J69 turbojets provided a cruise speed of 400–480kts at cruise altitudes of between 500 and 50,000ft AGL, depending on the threats; and while flightplan pre-programming was used at all times, the DC-130A/E's microwave Command Guidance System meant that the UAV operator was able to adjust the course or altitude of the 'bug' by pushing just a few buttons. Signals to and from the unmanned craft were dispatched and received via the mothership's curious chin dome. A single DC-130H (65-0979) also flew with the 6514th Test Squadron based at Hill AFB, Utah, designed to carry TRA's follow-on multi-mission BGM-34C model. This was to combine the functions of the 'Buffalo Hunters' and 'Combat Angels' and even added offensive capability in the form of optional AGM-65B/D Maverick missiles, locked on to target by remote control in the mothership. Evaluations began in December 1976, but a major change of heart caused the entire force to be axed within three years. The UAVs were placed in storage, most of the E-model motherships were returned to the cargo configuration and the five DC-130As were transferred to the US Navy for service with Composite Squadron VC-3 (before being contracted out to Lockheed Aircraft Service, and subsequently Flight Systems Inc, in support of target drone launches) at Mojave Airport, California. Killed off by budgeting pressures, the TRA Model 147 UAVs joined

---

[11]The unit also possessed a dozen of the AQM-34M-L (Loran) and AQM-34L craft left over from the war in South-East Asia.

DC-130 UAV MOTHERSHIPS	
DC-130A	**DC-130E**
55-0021 to USN as BuNo 158228	61-2361
56-0491 to USN as BuNo 158229	-2362 ⎫ to 314th
-0514 to USN as BuNo 560514	-2363 ⎬ TAW as
-0527 to AMARC 'boneyard'	-2368 ⎪ C-130E
57-0461 to AMARC 'boneyard'	-2371 ⎭
-0496 to USN as BuNo 570496	
-0497 to USN as BuNo 570497	-2364 ⎫ to 6514th
-0523 to AMARC 'boneyard'	-2369 ⎭ Test Sqn

Below left: This dramatic night-time exposure taken in 1971 shows the TRA Model 147 AQM-34 and its DC-130A mothership of the 350th SRS *Red Falcons* being prepared for action. The partnership endured for fifteen years and the 'Lightning Bug' programme remains one of the most enigmatic 'spyplane' stories of the past three decades. (Teledyne Ryan Aeronautical)

Top right: With thirty mission markings painted on its flank, 'Tomcat' embarks on another mission over North Vietnam. The AQM-34 series flew 3,435 combat sorties for the loss of 578 UAVs to hostile fire, accidents and 'operational causes'. (Teledyne Ryan Aeronautical)

Right: AQM-34 'El Wop a Ho' had already flown 38 missions when it was photographed departing from its mothership. Extensive repairs also appear to have been made to the sporty little vehicle. (Teledyne Ryan Aeronautical)

Below: Twilight of the drones. This marvellous perspective view depicts a TRA AQM-34T high-altitude version, 33 of which were supplied to Israel in 1984. (Teledyne Ryan Aeronautical)

the 'Compass Arrow' AQM-91A and 'Compass Cope' YQM-98A, which had similarly been abandoned following the revitalization of the TR-1/U-2R production run. Thirty-three refurbished 'stealthy' AQM-34Ts went to Israel, but the bulk remained in storage, unless pulled out to act as occasional 'enemy' cruise missiles during tests of coastal OTH-B (over-the-horizon backscatter) defensive radars.

Thinking has once again gone full circle. The dramatic performance exhibited by drones and small land-launched UAVs during Operation 'Desert Storm' has rekindled the Pentagon's interest in TRA's multi-mission UAVs, the reconnaissance versions of which—such as the transportable, ground-launched Model 324—continue to sell overseas to Egypt, among other clients. Enter the BQM-145 target drone, which has been further refined into a medium-range reconnaissance platform, with certain stealth features incorporated into its airframe. With a maximum gross weight of 1,910lb (comparable to a one-ton bomb), it can readily be air-launched from fighter-category aircraft to extend its autonomous 700nm range. The first of what is likely to become a large production run was rolled out of

TRA's San Diego facility in September 1991 and it is intended that this be equipped with the 'real-time' Martin Marietta ATARS (Advanced Tactical Airborne Reconnaissance System), being procured for joint USAF and US Marine Corps use, for ground and pylon launch.[12] Imagery generated by the UAV would be transmitted in 'real time' to ground stations and airborne command posts such as the EC-130E ABCCC III. This feat was recently demonstrated at the 'Green Flag 92' integrated electronic exercise by two specially modified and flamboyantly decorated 'Argus' AQM-34s nicknamed 'Brown Eyes' and 'Blue Eyes', launched from a 6514th Test Squadron DC-130E and equipped with interim target-tracking colour video systems. 'Real-time freeze frame' imagery was conveyed over 150 miles at a time in relay, providing commanders with target data within 30 seconds of its collection! Subject to funding, 'Argus' may be procured as a gap-filler pending the service introduction of the ATARS/BQM-145 combination in 1997. Additional systems under development for the new TRA UAV include 'Thirsty Saber', designed by Martin Marietta and General Dynamics. This is a recce-strike package that will employ automatic target recognition techniques to hunt and then *destroy* mobile targets such as missiles, rockets and even taxying aircraft. The chief advantage of all these pilotless aircraft is that they are relatively easy to operate and provide 'real-time' reconnaissance for field commanders. Meanwhile, for high-altitude snooping, Boeing unearthed its work on its old 'Compass Cope' contender the YQM-94A 'B-Gull' and from 9 October 1988 test-flew a huge all-new UAV built from composites and nicknamed the 'Condor'. With a wing span of 200ft and powered by a pair of fuel-efficient Teledyne Continental liquid-cooled 175hp piston engines, the craft has a mission endurance that is measured in *days* rather than hours. It already holds two altitude records for piston-powered aircraft, including the maximum altitude record of 67,028ft. On one occasion it cruised aloft for 2½ days! The demonstration effort was completed after eight test flights, but backroom work will continue to fine-tune the technology until a new application can be found for its inevitable successor.

Following the recent announcement that the fledgeling ACC will reduce its U-2R force to two dozen aircraft and mothball the remainder at Lockheed Palmdale, the doors have been opened to permit cheaper unmanned reconnaissance aircraft to re-enter the fray and show their worth. The battle between the 'Dragon Lady' and the long-suffering UAV is reaching new heights.

<hr>

[12]ATARS is discussed more fully in Chapter 3.

Opposite page: The AQM-91 'Combat Arrow' was a long-range stealthy UAV designed for covert flights over China and first flew in 1969. Equipped with a 24in Itek camera plus elint sensors, it had a 48ft wing span and its economical GE J97 turbojet gave it a ceiling of 70,000ft. Its mission ended with the Nixon accords three years later. (Teledyne Ryan Aeronautical)

Below: TRA built two YQM-98A 'Compass Cope' UAVs for high-altitude operations. The project, along with Boeing's YQM-94A 'B-Gull', was axed in July 1977 in favour of a second batch of U-2Rs. Twenty-four-hour duration sorties had been demonstrated over Cape Canaveral in 1975. (Teledyne Ryan Aeronautical)

Bottom: A 'Combat Arrow' and its MARS HH-3E companion demonstrate the mid-air snatching technique. (Teledyne Ryan Aeronautical)

2. TRISONICS

LURKING OFF-STAGE and poised to make a dramatic entrance while the little U-2 and 'Lightning Bugs' plied their trade over Cuba, China and Russia was the the glamorous Lockheed Blackbird series. As the late Clarence 'Kelly' Johnson recalled, 'From April 21st, 1958, through September 1st, 1959, I made a series of proposals for a Mach 3+ reconnaissance aircraft to Richard Bissell [of the CIA].' The original U-2 was becoming too vulnerable to the new Soviet-designed SAM missiles—a suspicion that was all too sadly confirmed during the following two years. On 30 January 1960 the proposals were firmed up with an order for twelve of the Project 'Oxcart' A-12 design. It was an immense engineering challenge, but one confronted by the Lockheed Advanced Development Project office—the famous 'Skunk Works'—with typical enthusiasm. New materials, new engineering methods and even new fuels and lubricants had to be designed for the Mach 3 reconnaissance jet, yet the 'Skunk Works' achieved its objective, on budget, in under thirty months! The first flight of the breed (60-6924) took place at the 'Ranch' on 26 April 1962 with Lou Schalk at the controls, paving the way for six years of test trials and covert spyplane operations that remain classified to this day.

Perhaps the A-12's greatest accomplishment is that it laid the groundwork for the superlative SR-71, the USAF's Mach 3 'hot-shot'.[1] Funds appropriated in Fiscal Year 1961 were issued to Lockheed during the course of the ensuing calendar year to build an initial six SR-71As—the first of 29 operational models, two 'humpback' SR-71B trainers and a solitary SR-71C outwardly identical to the 'Bravo' but constructed from salvaged parts and appropriately nicknamed 'The Bastard'. As 'Kelly' Johnson described this version of his masterpiece, 'It looks much like the earlier models, but the structure is considerably improved.' In the SR-71, gross weight increased by ten tons to 140,000lb, the fuselage was lengthened by over five feet to 107.4ft, including the forked pitot, and a second cockpit was added to house a specialized Reconnaissance Systems Officer (RSO) or instructor pilot, depending on the model. Avionics, including a completely revised Stability Augmentation System (SAS) and autopilot, advanced the state of the art of the series' flight controls. Moreover, the airframe was beefier but less complex, drawing on titanium-forging machinery which in one instance replaced 96 separate hand-crafted parts with a single forged and milled airframe member. This was typical of the SR-71 series. The prototype 64-17950 first roared down the runway on 22 December 1964, flown by Robert J. Gilliland and accompanied by a trio of Lockheed F-104 Starfighter chase planes. The vast experience built up during the A-12 effort enabled '950 to be taken to Mach 1.5 and FL500 on its first excursion, and as early as 22 June 1966 the 'Blackbird'-equipped 1st SRS of the 9th SRW (originally the 4200th SRW) was declared operational with Col Douglas T. Nelson in charge—an unparalleled achievement for such a high-performance machine. 'Category' testing followed while crews wrote up procedural manuals and technicians absorbed modifications to the engine/inlet and autopilot systems, ready for combat in troubled South-East Asia. CIA A-12 operations then ceased shortly after 'tail' '932 was lost off Kadena, Okinawa, on 5 June 1968, with pilot Jack Weeks aboard, and the fleet was 'mothballed' at Palmdale shortly afterwards. SAC's SR-71As, with their two-man crews, were already in place to take over the job, having flown their first combat sortie on 10 April with none other than Maj Jerome F. O'Malley at the helm. He later went on to become a fully fledged four-star General (in charge of Tactical Air Command, before his untimely death in a freak accident in an Air Force 'biz-jet' on 20 April 1985) and witnessed the unofficial christening of his steed—'Habu', named by the local Japanese (leered at on finals, the long slender American spy-plane seemed to them to resemble the poisonous pit viper which lurks on the Ryuku Islands). The name stuck. Some idea of the intensity of these pioneering 'Giant Scale' missions can be gauged from the combat hours

---

[1]The A-12 went through a painful development programme precipitated by an inlet/J75 powerplant mismatch that was later resolved with the J58/JT11D-20. Its operational history remains a closed book, the aircraft having been flown exclusively by the CIA. The first SR-71 ('Bravo' '957)—né RS-71, but its designation was transposed by President Lyndon B. Johnson when he publicly announced its existence on 24 July 1964—was delivered to the 4200th SRW at Beale on 7 January 1966, 53 weeks after the parent Wing was formed.

Above: Precursor to the SR-71 Blackbird was the CIA's A-12, developed by the Lockheed 'Skunk Works' under Project 'Oxcart'. It was neither slow nor clumsy, being eventually capable of sustained Mach 3 flight. The first of a dozen flew amidst great secrecy on 26 April 1962 and operations ceased six years later after the bigger and better SR-71A came on line. (Lockheed)

logged by the high-timers—400 hours were amassed by Lt-Col Robert Powell alone. Originally, 'Senior Crown' was to comprise two squadrons of twenty crews and ten aircraft each; however, by the time Col John H. Storrie had taken over the 'Velvet Black' 9th SRW establishment in July 1976 it was apparent that ten machines could handle the job. This set a pattern which endured virtually throughout the type's twenty-one-year operational career. Aircraft would be 'cycled' in and out of storage to preserve airframe integrity (and to ensure that scarce engine spares for the type's unique Pratt & Whitney J58 turbojets were always available), on an eight-year basis.

GOING TACTICAL

As remains the case with its high-flying stablemate the U-2R, mission preparation for the 'Habu' was a lengthy process that consumed up to 36 hours of painstaking work. For the SR-71A aviators there were two types of mission assignments: general trolling or specific target area coverage at the behest of the National Command Authorities and JCS and passed down to what was the 14th Air Division of SAC at Beale and, thence, to the domestic squadron or its detachments, as part of the continuing PARPRO (Peacetime Aerial Reconnaissance Program); or periodically revised 'sealed-envelope' assign-

ments drawn up in Washington in accordance with Emergency War Order provisions, as part of the strategic SIOP (Single Integrated Operations Plan). The latter mission was basically 'nuclear BDA' in the aftermath of the unthinkable, and 'mission tapes' were suitably prepared on a contingency basis and filed. For day-to-day work, flight-planning was vested exclusively with the Squadron, based on times and areas handed down in support of the PARPRO. This was drafted using a series of waypoints or 'destinations' which together formed the critical legs of the 'black line'. The first SR-71A back-seat RSO to qualify, Lt-Col Albert N. Pennington, summed up its importance early on during 'Senior Crown': 'We have to be totally aware of where we are at any given moment, as we cover *thirty miles every minute*.' Straying from the 'black line' resulted in anything from mild embarrassment to a crew reprimand, accompanied by acrimonious exchanges at the diplomatic level which could ruin a aviator's career. In the very early days, a mere sixteen waypoints were 'punched' into the jet's nav panel prior to take-off. By the mid-1970s the manual process had given way to a big trolley which would feed the torrent of data— later comprising up to 1,535 'control', 'destination' and 'fix' points—direct into the 'guts' of the system via a punched paper-tape ribbon. (By the end of the aircraft's career, technology on selected machines had permitted pocket-sized data-loading modules to become available, whereby an RSO's own '40 List' could be shoved into a suitable orifice in the rear instrument panel like a video-game cartridge. This permitted him to effect quick changes to the pre-

Left: Bob Gilliland took the first SR-71 up on its maiden hop on 22 December 1964. It was the best of the Blackbird 'family' in terms of its structure, avionics and performance, building upon new engineering tools and a two-year 'learning curve' with the A-12. (Lockheed)

Below left: Lockheed pilot Bill Weaver poses for the camera from the cockpit of his SR-71A. Note the chunky canopy hoods and 'bat-wing' sunshades. It must have been an extraordinary experience flying at Mach 3.17–3.30 in that machine. (Lockheed)

Right: SR-71 production in full swing in 1966, with five aircraft visible here. Some 90 per cent of the aircraft was fabricated from high-strength, lightweight titanium alloys. However, a fifth of its skin comprised radar-transparent plastic, including the radar-trapping zigzag wedges in the leading edges of the delta wing, clearly visible on the machine second from the front—which has its outer panels folded up (a design feature, used for engine changes). (Lockheed)

cluding tanker rendezvous co-ordinates, ascent, mission requirements, speeds and bank angles, and descent, were pre-planned down to individual knots, degrees, minutes and seconds. Diversionary fields also had to be carefully ingrained: it took 200 miles to descend from trisonic flight, even (perhaps especially) in emergencies, and that gave little time in which to fiddle about with notes. 'Hands-off' flight meant that the pilot had to maintain a constant vigil, ready to take over at a second's notice, while the RSO actually guided the aircraft through the air in the horizontal axis via its astro-navigation system (ANS).

As with the 'Dragon drivers', diet was another physiological consideration. With only a 'pee tube' to get rid of body substances, air crews had to stay well away from 'booze' and high-residue foods for at least a day prior to a scheduled sortie. Crews normally stuck to water leading up to the mission and then ate a high-protein, low-residue repast of steak and scrambled eggs prepared by the PSD just prior to kitting-out. That stage involved half an hour suiting up followed by a minimum of 55 minutes' pre-breathing oxygen (allegedly excellent at curing lingering hangovers or the 'blues'), to purge the bloodstream and fatty portions of the body of nitrogen which all too easily could cause deadly gas embolisms to form in the event of cockpit and suit depressurization.[3]

programmed flight plan at the push of a few buttons.)[2] This would then 'tell' the Blackbird where to fly, in a 'hands off' manner, all the way from launch to recovery. The whole mission, including anticipated autopilot turning commands, could thus be stuffed into the SR-71's comparatively dinosaur-sized computer brains in minutes, freeing the RSO tucked away behind the chunky rear canopy hood to up-load the system, check for faults and go through his entire navigation check-list in under an hour, while the pilot confirmed that the engine, inlet and flying portions were satisfactory. However, it was anything but a carefree process. Planning was meticulous and extensive mental preparations were necessary. Back-up crews were called upon for important missions but, as a 'Habu' pair normally were welded by 'Air Force marriage', each could usually depend on the other to keep out of trouble and turn up fit for duty. The missions were heavily 'canned' and had to be trusted to memory: everything, in-

[2]Including 1,023 control points, 256 fix points and 256 destination points. CPs were used exclusively to initiate and deactivate the sensors; FPs were prominent terrain features along or off the navigation track which could be used for sensor cueing or to check that the aircraft was on course and update the ANS; and DPs were a series of point-to-point co-ordinates that formed the various 'legs' of the 'black line', in a join-the-dots fashion. The grand total of 1,535 points embraced the primary and back-up flightplans, which could be tapped into by the RSO by means of entering the appropriate digits on the nav panel. 'Skip To' and 'Direct Steer' sequence-interrupting was also commonly employed, to bypass certain points—for instance, to go from A to D directly and miss out on B and C. Thus, in the completely automatic mode, it was the RSO who actually 'flew' the aircraft, leaving the pilot to perform only take-offs, refuellings and landings.

With the crew settled in the cockpit and with initial checks completed, engine-start was the first move towards independence, usually conducted half an hour prior to take-off. The normally viscous oil had to be pre-heated to 86°F to enable the turbines to be turned, which, on a cold winter morning in Okinawa or England may have taken up to 3½ hours. An air drive unit coupled to both nacelles was used to spool the P&WA J58/JT11D-20s up to a screaming 3,200rpm, engaged from the starting system built into the hangars (supplementing the Buick, and later Chevrolet V8, 600hp 'huffers' which remained in use for launches from austere locations). When the correct rpm were reached the pilot advanced the first throttle from cut-off to idle, which automatically squirted TEB (tri-ethyl borane) into the spinning system to ignite the low-volatility JP-7/LF-2A kerosene; with a positive start, signified by an electric-green flash in the free-floating nozzles, the procedure was repeated with the other powerplant, at which

point the service lines were unclipped. Pre-taxi checks consumed a further quarter of an hour as the hydraulics were cycled and the flight control surfaces flexed. With the heavy metal canopies clanked shut and secured and a final 'thumbs-up' from the Crew Chief floor-managing the show, the boarding steps were wheeled away and the growling SR-71A became a self-contained matt black capsule of men, sensors and fuel, dripping JP-7 from its cool, loosely fitting wet delta. With 'all systems go', the pilot advanced the throttles up from idle to push the pointy end of his jet out of the 'barn', with nose wheels and rudders moving simultaneously in sympathy with his rudder pedal inputs, as 90° turns were made on to the taxiway and again on to the pre-take-off hold the

[3]See Chapter 1 for a fuller account of pre-high-altitude flight PSD requirements and suiting-up procedures. SR-71A/B crews went through an identical process prior to dressing up in their almost identical S1030 spacesuits. Early Space Shuttle crewmen also wore these life-saving garments.

'hammerhead'—with brake checks while on the move. Wheels were momentarily chocked again at this stage so that the J58s could be revved up to full military power, permitting the pilot to monitor exhaust gas temperature (EGT) and to adjust throttle settings. Auto-trim was then engaged, to take care of symmetry. The onboard ANS would already be plotting position based on the 61 stars catalogued in its memory, taking constant sextant shots through the flush dorsal peephole and feeding position into the pre-aligned SKN-2417 INS in the astro-inertial mode, while the big black beast trembled, the awesome organ-like suction from its intakes reverberating around the base. Back-up 'mobiles' watched over the proceedings in their station wagon as ground crewmen ambled down the runway in a pair of pick-up trucks to check for FOD debris. It was an event waiting to happen, and observers were seldom disappointed. With clearance from the tower, at the appointed time the pilot advanced the throttles to initial afterburner position. The warmed-up J58s responded quickly. With a positive 'burn light' shining on the console, the twin levers were pushed to maximum power, authorizing a combined 65,000lb of thrust from the engines. At fifty tons, the partly fuelled Blackbird would lunge unexpectedly fast, punched forward by the 'burners, leaving a cloud of unspent 'gas' in its wake. It was something akin to a roller-coaster ride for the crew. As Maj Burk describes events: 'On take-off the whole airplane is trembling. The afterburners rarely light together, and we're 107 feet forward on the monsters. At that point I feel I'm merely a passenger; I'm just aiming it down the runway.' Maj Dan House, another former 'Habu' piloting-passenger, added: 'What gets one's attention in the front' cockpit is that the afterburners seldom light at the same time. Since the engines are quite far apart, this causes an asymmetric thrust that pushes the nose toward the side of the runway. If the pilot puts in a rudder correction to straighten the plane, he can be assured that the other 'burner will decide to light at the same time, compounding the correction and pushing the nose toward the other side of the runway!'. NASA pilots still face this phenomenon. Speed built up at a dramatic pace. Seconds later, with 180kts on the indicator, the pilot hauled gently back on the stick to bring the angry trident up to 10 degrees alpha

Above: When SR-71B '956 clocked up its 1,000th USAF sortie it was suitably decorated for the occasion. This aircraft, which now flies with NASA, was one of three twin-seat trainers built but carried out the lion's share of the workload; its companion '957 was written off in January 1968 while '981 ('The Bastard') went into deep storage at Palmdale in the early 1970s. (Lockheed)

Below left: A 'Habu' in its 'barn' at Beale AFB, California, being readied for a mission. Electrical power was applied well before the sortie, permitting the nav computer to 'hold' the flightplan,

composed of up to 1,535 points. The corrugated skin enabled the beast to expand in 'hot-and-high' flight, and the outlet at the tip of the 'boat-tail' was used for dumping excess fuel. (USAF via SSgt David Malakoff)

Below: Majs Ted Ross and Brian Schul model the David Clark S1030 full-pressure suits, less gloves. These suits were mandatory for all flights above FL450. The 'Habus' in the background seem to be on good terms too! A mere 152 pilots qualified on the SR-71 throughout 'Senior Crown'. (Lockheed)

(pitch), unsticking the titanium and plastic bird at 210kts, 4,000ft down the runway, its fleeting departure marked by thunder and the tell-tale orange shock diamonds shooting out of the jet nozzles. The gear was tucked up into its fuel-cooled 'buckets' as soon as possible, to avoid over-stressing the sturdy but 300kts-airspeed-limited undercarriage legs. Climb at the initial 10° pitch pulled the half- to two-thirds-fuel laden beast up in excess of 10,000ft/min, while distant thunder and the smell of burnt JP-7 still lingered at the home-drome.

The three-axis SAS, one of five subsystems which made up the DAFICS (Digital Automatic Flight and Inlet Control System), was engaged soon after take-off to dampen pitch, roll and yaw instabilities, in a true control-configured vehicle mode. The SR was anything but an unfeathered arrow, but did possess—and still does—some inherent instability which had to be checked, especially as trim requirements altered with speed and altitude. Previous 'Blackbirds' in the series featured prominent ventral strakes or a fold-down fin, but the SR-71A ditched these in favour of the SAS and the pilot's unique trim button, which was configured to provide pitch and yaw trim rather than the more conventional pitch and roll. The SAS remained engaged throughout the flight whether being flown by hand or by autopilot. In the former instance 'surface limiters' cut in to prevent him from over-controlling the sensitive

machine, physically limiting manual stick roll elevon inputs and rudder pedal yaw limits. In the automatic piloting mode, this was part and parcel of the programmed flight plan. Only 200 seconds into the flight, the pilot retarded the throttles to just under maximum military power and trimmed for Mach 0.9 cruise at 26,000ft, where everything stopped for a drink. By this time the skin of the 'Habu' had begun to warm, expand and seal the 'wet wing' fuel tanks, ready for a top-up. Typically, the KC-135Q tanker and SR-71 would approach head-on, assisted by encrypted ADF (automatic direction-finding) signals which provided bearing. Twenty miles out but closing, the tanker turned on to a reciprocal heading ready for the Blackbird to join up behind. The union usually took place at 350kts, during which time some thirty tons of fuel was greedily drunk by the SR-71A's tanks, bringing stored fuel to the maximum 80,280lb and the Blackbird's all-up weight to 220,000lb—its heaviest state.

Following the fifteen-minute fuel top-up, the birds broke contact and the heavily laden SR-71A was ceremoniously hauled up to FL330 at 10ft/sec, ready for the famous 'dipsy doodle' manoeuvre dive down

Below: With rudders and nose wheels moving in unison, an SR-71A lines up on the 'hammerhead'. Often, the aircraft barely stopped after leaving their hangars, snaking down the taxiways and roaring off into the sky. (John Dunnell via Peter E. Davies)

Above: Aircraft '955, with 'Skunk Works' badge (and nicknamed 'Flower'—a derisory play on the 'fragrant' attributes of a skunk), joins with its KC-135Q 'go-juice' donor. Up to thirty tons of fuel was transferred over quarter of an hour before the SR-71A broke free and performed the 'dipsy doodle' manoeuvre. No '955 spent much of its life at Palmdale, acting as the validation aircraft for the endless Technical Orders that progressively updated the type. (Lockheed)

to FL280. This 'unloaded' the aircraft, permitting rapid acceleration through the sound barrier, with the autopilot and the SAS replacing manhandled flight as the beast tucked through 510kts. However, transition to higher Mach numbers presented a whole new set of demands on the pilot, who had to orchestrate the inlet, engine and bypass doors as the machine transformed itself into a ramjet. This was a purely automatic function handled by the Honeywell DAFICS, but an eager eye—and ear—was necessary to ensure that all was functioning according to the manuals. DAFICS also compensated for the dreaded 'unstart' phenomenon, when the supersonic shock-wave popped out of one of the inlets, turning tons of thrust into tons of drag with one of the 'suckers', creating a momentary violent yaw before corrective action was initiated. Originally corrected by the IARS (Inlet Automatic Restart System), 'unstart' was an unpleasant experience despite the spontaneity of

Lockheed's ingenious systems. Pilots tended to note the symptoms. As Maj Dan House explains, 'The inlets are the heart of the propulsion system. They consist of movable spikes to control the shock wave, and bypass doors to control pressure. When things are not quite in balance the inlet doors will "talk" to you. If they are bouncing off the stops, the limits of travel, they generate a rumbling sound similar to propellers out of synchro. When this happens, the pilot can try to eliminate the sound by adjusting the doors manually, or he can elect to sit it out and hope it goes away. Sometimes, this will result in an "unstart", causing considerable yawing moment. Depending on altitude, attitude, speed and power setting, this can be quite gentle—or violent enough to bounce your helmet off the canopy!' Old stories from the A-12 and early SR-71 days of 'Habu' handlers dismounting with cracked visors were not based on myth. 'After the initial head-banging we have definite proecdures to follow,' recounted Maj House during his tenure on the beast, 'which include maintaining positive aircraft control, monitoring the autopilot "restart" function and checking the affected engine for proper indications—EGT, ICT [inlet compressor temperature], nozzle position, fuel flow, rpm. We will also check appropriate hydraulic and

SR-71A SERIAL NUMBERS

Serial no	Notes	Model
60-6924		
-6925		
-6926	Written off 24 May 1963	
-6927	Twin-seat 'Titanium Goose'	
-6928	Written off 5 Jan 1967	
-6929	Written off c1966	
-6930		
-6931		
-6932	Written off 5 June 1968	A-12
-6933		
-6937		
-6938		
-6939	Written off c1965	
-6940	Converted as M-12 mothership	
-6941	Converted as M-12 mothership and written off 30 July 1966	
-6934	Damaged during landing and rear half later used to construct SR-71C 64-17981 'The Bastard'	
-6935	At Wright-Patterson USAF Museum	YF-12
-6936	Written off 24 June 1971	
64-17950	Written off 9 Feb 1966	
-17951	Became NASA YF-12C and new serial 60-6937	
-17952	Written off 25 Jan 1966 near Tucumcary, New Mexico; first SR-71A accident.	
-17953	Written off 20 Jan 1967	
-17954	Written off 11 Apr 1969	
-17955		
-17958		
-17959		
-17960		
-17961		
-17962		
-17963		
-17964		
-17965	Written off 25 Oct 1967	SR-71A
-17966	Written off 13 Apr 1967	
-17967		
-17968		
-17969		
-17970	Written off 1970	
-17971		
-17972	Transatlantic record-breaker To NASM March 1990	
-17973		
-17974	Written off 21 Apr 1989	
-17975		
-17976		
-17977	Written off 10 Oct 1968	
-17978	Written off May 1973	
-17979		
-17980		
-17956		
-17957	First SR-71 delivered and written off 12 Jan 1968	SR-71B
-17981	Hybrid aircraft built from spares	SR-71C

electrical systems, including numerous circuit breakers [trusting that the IARS or DAFICS would work, and talking over if necessary]. The only thing worse than a manual inlet is no inlet at all, because that meant you stayed in subsonic configuration.' An unstarted engine would also continue to ingest a rich fuel-only intake and burn itself out. All going to according to plan, however, the machine would continue to climb into the stratosphere.

At FL600 the RSO would deactivate the AN/APX-108(V) IFF 'squawk' box. From that point onwards, the 'Habu' was flying a strictly classified route and its presence was kept a well-hidden secret. Fuel would continue to be guzzled at a rate of up to 8,000 US gal/hr, gradually lightening the aircraft and enabling it to soar higher yet. Cruise profile parameters were always a trade-off between height, speed and range, based on desired Mach number, aircraft weight and ambient temperature (which affected CIT). Speed decreased slightly with altitude, range with speed, and so on. Usually a 'maximum range cruise' offered the best compromise, which meant dashing along at a mean FL800 at Mach 3.17. At those velocities, the 'spikes' had translated the full 26in aft, increasing the inlet capture area by 112 per cent. Much of this bypassed the big P&WA J58s, which provided as little as 17.6 per cent of the thrust. Instead, the whole nacelle became a ramjet, with the inlet producing a staggering 54 per cent of the thrust and the after-burning ejector the remaining 28.4 per cent. As one pilot commented, 'With all running smoothly, the bird sort of sucks its way through the sky'!

From the rapidly heating back seat—at speed, the SR-71 would have expanded by up to 11in as temperatures reached 1,100°F in places—the RSO would monitor the way the mission tape was running the show, via the ANS. A pair of 'control head course error windows' furnished him with slant-range and along-track drift in nautical miles. Three zeros meant that all was well. If not, the RSO could update the ANS by means of the viewsight (featuring a wide, 136° FOV with a demagnification ratio of 6:1 and a narrow, 56° FOV with a 2:1 demag ratio). The viewsight presented an optical display of the terrain below on a curvacious 9in tube at the top of the navigator's instrument panel (later replaced on selected 'tails' by a square, metal-hooded E-O video display), laced with a cursor grid. Visual fixes could thus be used to correct 'present position', which would in turn command a gentle shift from the autopilot to put the aircraft back on course. (Alternatively, the pilot could press the 'disconnect steering' button on the control column and employ extremely subtle inputs to manhandle the beast back on track, within the controlled-configured restraints imposed by the surface limiters, based on instruc-

Above: An eerily lit Blackbird awaits its next mission. The three-wheeled main-gear 'trucks', unique to this aircraft, featured 22-ply aluminized rubber tyres pressurized with inert nitrogen at up to 415psi. (Lockheed/Eric Schulzinger)

Below: With everything ticking over as planned, Crew Chiefs wheel away an SR-71A's boarding steps; seconds later the 'pointy end' of the machine will have lunged out of the 'barn'. (Lockheed/Eric Schulzinger)

tions from the RSO and the ADI course deviation bar.) The projected film map display could also be cross-referenced, based on a 25ft long, 35mm roll film that laid out crucial parts of the intended flight plan as it unfurled. Turns on to a new leg were effected automatically by the autopilot, based on either planned 'auto range to turn' (limited to 32° bank angles, when airframe dynamics were the primary concern) or a 'fixed range to turn' (at full limit, when the flight plan was sensitive and the beast was not permitted to waddle about). Meanwhile, the dorsal star-plotter would go about its business unaided, feeding its extrapolated 'fix' to the navigation computers. Checking that the ANS was on track was a full-time job for the RSO, who would be rewarded with digital read-outs pertaining to present position, groundspeed and steering, as well as en-route *time* to ten selected 'destinations' and three 'mark points'. With all ticking over correctly, reconnoitring could begin as planned—that is, on

schedule. Timing was a key ingredient, practised for the purposes of co-operative reconnaissance and so as to maintain an edge in the event that the 'Habu' had to fly 'nuclear SIOP'.

CUE SENSORS
Mission equipment could be tailored for various duties, housed in up to ten compartments. Initially these comprised only cameras, but they soon grew into a mixed 'bag of tricks' which included optional SLAR and elint systems. At the sharp end was the detachable nose, 'Compartment A', which could be fitted with either a high-resolution 24in focal length horizon-to-horizon OBC (optical bar camera, easily distinguished by the presence of a large oriel) or one of two sideways-looking radar packages (made obvious by the blank electromagnetic-transparent panel lines on the nose, though difficult to differentiate at a distance from the ballast-filled training version) which generated a ground map display at the bottom

Top left: With 'Tiger Tails' signalling its departure, SR-71A '972 soars away, bound for 80,000ft over who-knows-where. At FL600 the transponder was deactivated and the mission became top secret, though ATC (Air Traffic Control) staff were often able to monitor its fleeting radar 'blip' across their screens—or, more likely, the false returns created by the aircraft's luxurious 'Def' systems. (Lockheed)

Above left: This marvellous shot of aircraft '968 (nicknamed 'DBX') was taken just before the SR-71A fleet was retired from military service in early 1990. Today's little boys and girls don't enjoy the sight of such inspiring hardware in action. Neither the US Air Force nor the US Congress really grasped the public-relations value of the aircraft. (Lockheed)

Top: SR-71A '972 was originally delivered to the USAF on 12 December 1966, and it ended its career on 6 March 1991 when it broke the transcontinental US speed record in a run from California to Maryland that averaged 2,110mph. (Lockheed)

Above: SR-71A '959 featured this unique 'Big Tail' modification designed to house cameras and data-link devices, thereby permitting the nose to be used for radar at all times. The programme was allegedly cancelled in 1976 and the aircraft was never seen operating in daylight afterwards. (USAF via Peter E. Davies)

of the RSO's instrument panel in addition to providing true all-weather reconnaissance products which would be radar-filmed. Built by Goodyear Aerospace (which was absorbed into the Loral Corporation in March 1987, and which thereafter assumed new responsibilities for field support), the 'two' radars began life as a 1968-vintage SLR known by the acronym CAPRE, which was revisited seven years later and adapted into the follow-on ASARS-1 (Advanced Synthetic Aperture Radar System), capable of producing variable swaths of near photo-quality images at oblique ranges in excess of 50nm. All of this nasal equipment could be cued left or right of the navigation track for oblique work at a discreet range.[4]

---

[4]The SR-71A's CAPRE and ASARS worked on identical principles to the similar Loral SLAR and SAR radars described elsewhere in the context of U-2R and RF-4C sensors—see Chapters 1 and 3.

The remainder of the recon gear was carried in four parallel bays located in the left and right chines aft of the cockpit, each of which was further divided laterally into two compartments. At the advent of 'Senior Crown', these were used almost exclusively for 'techs' (technical objective cameras, of 48in focal length) but gradually gave way to more surreptitious reconnaissance gear as the technology emerged. Indeed, by the time the SR-71A was undergoing its final updates (a continuing process), the far aft compartments ('S' and 'T') had been given over to sophisticated passive EIP elint interrogative sensors and three of the four forward ones ('L', 'M' and 'N') to a bank of mission-, radar- and EIP-related digital and ARI700 recorders, leaving only the two intermediate left and right aft compartments ('P' and 'Q') for 'techs'—and even then 'Q' was often stuffed with additional radar-recording equipment in lieu of a camera! In its mature years, it was a misnomer to describe the SR-71A as a 'photo-reconnaissance' platform, even though the contemporary press releases continued to lavish praise on the jet's ability to 'photograph 100,000 square miles an hour'. The official storyline was surveillance, which naturally failed to make specific mention of the other equipment. Nevertheless, it gave the SR-71A four times the photint area coverage of the U-2R on a minute-for-minute basis, which was particularly crucial over heavily defended zones. The two EIP elint receivers, designed to plot GCI and SAM radars, covered left or right (or both) flanks while the 'techs' could be used for overflight or oblique work, at bank angles of up to 40°. Warm-up times for the sensors ranged from 20 seconds for the 'techs', to six minutes for radar. If fitted in lieu of radar, the OBC was kept in standby mode from the moment the aircraft was powered-up and trundling swiftly to the 'hammerhead'. Just like the U-2R, choices had to be made as to whether SAR or photint equipment was carried in the optional nose.[5]

Sensor cueing was customarily fully automatic (with manual override assisted by the viewsight), based on the 'control points' and/or 'fix points' entered into the ANS computers via the mission tape. These co-ordinates 'bracketed' the pre-planned area to be covered on a start-stop basis to ensure adequate coverage (specific 'target' co-ordinates, as such, were not used), while the ANS also took care of sensor-pointing angles and annotated film and tape with co-ordinates and additional data relating to relative 'look' angle, height and aircraft attitude to assist with the interpretation of the raw information following aircraft recovery. The programming was complex. Getting the right 'photos' while staying firmly on the 'black line' demanded constant attention from the RSO, particularly when ad hoc modifications were made to the 'canned' flight plan by means of 'sequence interrupting' (i.e. skipping 'legs' or way-points). This was made all the more demanding during multiple sensor operations, though the skilled navigator-RSOs provided a 'man-in-the-loop' over the target which U-2s never have, permitting significantly greater flexibility over high-threat areas. For more gentile 'blue water' tasks, multiple sensors were often employed as a means of providing a near-complete analysis of a new 'enemy' vessel—its where-abouts, its design and performance, its offensive and defensive radar systems and so forth—all from the one sortie. In fact, the old 'Habu' was particularly effective at 'fused' maritime reconnaissance and, in the latter years, monitoring the Soviet Fleet in the Baltic, Black and South China Seas on behalf of the US Navy accounted for some 90 per cent of its operational assignments! The swift probe by the 'Habu' was often the only means by which the Soviet vessels could be caught unawares or tuned into full action for tell-tale moments; had slow-moving platforms like the U-2R (or the US Navy's own 'Aries' Orion) been employed for such high-priority tasks, the ships' sensors would have been alerted in good time and would have reverted from 'hot' to 'warm' status, thereby denying to the US satisfactory intelligence data. The finer aspects of sigint are discussed elsewhere, but suffice it to say that the US Navy has recently embarked on an extensive ES-3A Viking retrofit programme to fill this gaping hole in their capability in the aftermath of the demise of the glamorous 'Blackbird' and obsolescent, sea-going ERA-3 'Whales'.[6]

PARPRO assignments also frequently tasked the SR-71A to the edges or midst of hostile airspace, to map Soviet, Cuban, North Korean and Middle Eastern radar defences and key military installations.

---

[5]Radar warm-up took over ten minutes (and could not be initiated on the ground, owing to microwave-radiation hazards to the ground crew and nearby civilians. In many military aircraft this is an ancillary function of the nose-gear landing lights, which act as 'lighthouses' during the taxi and take-off/landing phase of operations. Enthusiasts should stay clear of the take-off and landing approach paths). The final compartment, 'K', located in the forward port position, housed the 'Def H' self-protect countermeasures system at all times. Oblique photography by means of banking was used only during carefully prescribed fixed-range-to-turn manoeuvres incorporated into the flightplan. A trailing-end, eight-foot-long 'Big Tail' housing which was designed to accommodate additional photint sensors, allowing the nose to be used for SAR at all times, was tested on '959, replete with a 'near real-time' satellite link to boot; however, the project was allegedly cancelled in 1976, though the author believes that the aircraft may have been retained for covert long-legged missions from the US West Coast, which would have benefited from a combination of optical and radar sensors. It would have been relatively easy to hide the machine behind the closed doors of one of Beale's many 'barns'. Aircraft '959 was never sighted during daylight hours after the 'mod'.

[6]The ES-3A is described in Chapter 5.

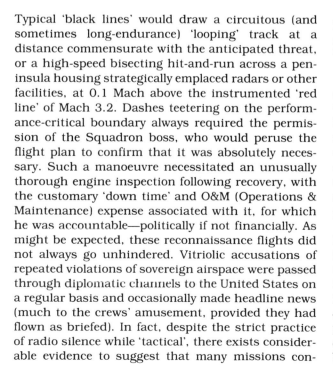

Above: A fabulous Mildenhall 'fireball' shot, taken when SR-71A '960 from Det 4 treated her audience to a 'wind tunnel' aerodynamic vortex and a flaming mass of excess fuel. (John Dunnell via Peter E. Davies)

Typical 'black lines' would draw a circuitous (and sometimes long-endurance) 'looping' track at a distance commensurate with the anticipated threat, or a high-speed bisecting hit-and-run across a peninsula housing strategically emplaced radars or other facilities, at 0.1 Mach above the instrumented 'red line' of Mach 3.2. Dashes teetering on the performance-critical boundary always required the permission of the Squadron boss, who would peruse the flight plan to confirm that it was absolutely necessary. Such a manoeuvre necessitated an unusually thorough engine inspection following recovery, with the customary 'down time' and O&M (Operations & Maintenance) expense associated with it, for which he was accountable—politically if not financially. As might be expected, these reconnaissance flights did not always go unhindered. Vitriolic accusations of repeated violations of sovereign airspace were passed through diplomatic channels to the United States on a regular basis and occasionally made headline news (much to the crews' amusement, provided they had flown as briefed). In fact, despite the strict practice of radio silence while 'tactical', there exists considerable evidence to suggest that many missions con-

ducted adjacent to old Soviet borders were designed to 'taunt' the defences into action, so that they could be monitored by both the SR-71A and its slow-moving RC-135 'Rivet Joint' companion (which would have been lurking at a considerable stand-off distance and eavesdropping on the ground transmissions with more finely tuned listening apparatus, carefully co-ordinated to coincide with the SR-71's provocative probe).

Blatant overflights of Cuba, China, North Vietnam, North Korea and the Sinai peninsula also were not an irregular feature of the crews' month-to-month itinerary, particularly during the extremely turbulent first half of the 1970s, when the machines were flying from FOLs at Kadena, Okinawa, and Seymour-Johnson, North Carolina—the origins of the semi-permanent Detachment 1 in Japan and the *raison d'être* of Detachment 4 at RAF Mildenhall, England, both within 3½ hours' flying time of the key trouble spots in their respective theatres. By the time President Nixon had suspended operations over the 'Bamboo Curtain' as part of his rapprochement with Peking in 1971, there had already been nearly 500 Chinese protests at overflights by the Lockheed 'spyplane' families! Tail '974, nicknamed 'Ichi Ban' ('Number One') was one of the South-East Asian high-timers, sporting at least 44 white 'hissing snake' mission markings on its flank before the practice—which obviously provided a pointer to 'Habu' activities—was discontinued. North Korea repeatedly spoke of 'provocative acts of espionage by American imperialistic aggressors' and ten years later in August 1981 lost its patience and shot off a volley of SAMs from Chokta-ri at an SR-71A going about its business in *international* airspace, though with the customary lack of results. In the 1980s, when attention focused more towards North Africa and the troubled Persian Gulf, Det 4 became the true 'Home of the Blackbird' and flew up to 450 hours of monitoring flights annually right through to its last operational sortie. The cat-and-mouse game endured for twenty-two years and became deadly on occasion. The high-flying SR-71A's regular opponents included the SA-2 and SA-5 surface-launched missiles, bearing the respective NATO code-names 'Guideline' and 'Gammon'. Of the two, the 'Gammon', with its 155-mile range, active terminal guidance and 100,000ft ceiling, presented the biggest threat. Yet none of these found their mark. RSOs would monitor the threats and 'switch on the music' (prompt the 'Def A', 'C', 'M' or 'H' defensive countermeasures systems into action) when the warning lamps shone. The 'Def' devices could work autonomously or rely solely on manual intervention—though a combination of the two, with the emphasis on chunky, golden-gloved digits initiating an appropriate automatic response, was the customary procedure. Activated, the 'Defs' confused and confounded the opposition's acquisition and tracking radars by means of range-gate and repeater mode deception jamming. As an added bonus, the systems' allied receivers featured a dedicated recorder from which further elint could be garnered. The counter-measures did their job. In September 1979 *Aviation Week & Space Technology* reported that, up to 1977, when President Jimmy Carter suspended the 'Giant Plate' Cuban overflights (ten days after taking up office), the 9th SRW trisonic community had drawn and evaded no fewer than 810 SAMs! The crews' recollections usually revealed the same sequence of events. After the initial excitement of realizing that they were being shot at and responding coolly with the 'Def' systems, they would watch the missiles exploding harmlessly behind them like rapidly receding fireworks, visible in the 30° cone reflected on the aircraft commander's pop-up rear-

view periscope and the RSO's two rear-view mirrors. It was an almost surreal form of combat, battling with the laws of nature and the huge SAMs while cocooned in a pressure suit.

Then there were the fighters to contend with. A carefully vectored 'Foxbat' or 'Foxhound' was perfectly capable of 'zoom climbing' to catch a fleeting 'Habu', and of engaging it with radar or long-legged heat-seeking missiles before ducking back down, short of energy. Speed, altitude and a modicum of stealth all played a role, as did the countermeasures. The Soviets' Achilles' heel was their rigidly run, radar-based ground control network, which spent too much time tracking flocks of birds, with little else to do. By fooling the GCI radar controllers into vectoring their fuel-limited MiGs on to spurious targets (whose height and speed could be differentiated from migrating storks and snowbirds), the 'Habu' successfully denied the opposition a chance to rattle its tail—although the MiGs undoubtedly forced the big black titanium snakes to keep their distance.

One aspect of 'combat' the SR-71A crews are not reticent to discuss is what was their biggest fear of all: difficulties with the aircraft (inlet or engine temperature, or the 'unstart' phenomenon). The crews were well briefed and trained in terms of safety, and thus such contingencies would force them to fly manually or semi-automatically. With this came the obligatory throttling-back and descent, making them comparatively easy prey, even at FL500–600. The SR-71 carried no self-defence armament, and with reason: neither the opposing MiGs nor the Blackbirds were capable of 'mixing it' at those tremendous heights and closing velocities. Although at light weights at low level the Blackbird could perform 3.5g aerobics at bank angles of up to 70°, at the edge of the envelope, at Mach 3.2 and at 85,000ft, its operational limit load factors were narrowed to $-0.1g$ to $+1.5g$, while a simple 180° turn at a maximum 45° angle of bank guzzled up 100 miles of sky! And that was with everything working according to the book. Reversion to manual inlet control or high CIT or some other unforeseen requirement spelled potential danger for the crew both from the 'enemy' and from their own trisonic steed—a classic case of Hobson's choice. 'Tactical limits' acknowledged the need to override airframe considerations and go hell-for-leather for up to ten minutes' flight time, in make-or-break fashion, though it is not known if this was ever put into action in a combat situation.

As it happened, all twelve SR-71 losses were self-inflicted, mostly as a result of mechanical problems or pilot error during the early days of 'Senior Crown' when the procedural manuals were still being written and the performance graphs being tabulated. Remarkably, there were no *operational* crew fatalities,

BLACKBIRD OPERATING LOCATIONS

Unit	Base	Equipment
5th and 99th RS	Beale AFB, California	U-2R/U-2R(T)
95th RS	RAF Alconbury, England	U-2R
1704th RS(P)	Taif RSAB, Saudi Arabia	U-2R
Det 1	Kadena AB, Okinawa	Former A-12/ SR-71A
Det 2/6th RS	Osan AB, Republic of Korea	U-2R
Det 3	RAF Akrotiri, Cyprus	U-2R
Det 4	RAF Mildenhall, England	Former SR-71A
Det 5	Patrick AFB, Florida	U-2R
Det 6	Norton AFB, California	U-2R

in contrast to the speckled career of the demonic 'Dragon'.[7] Indeed, this safety record remained unblemished for seventeen years following the demise of '978 'Rapid Rabbit' in May 1973, until '974 (the Vietnam-era Kadena ground crews' former beloved 'Ichi Ban') made a big splash in the Sea of Japan on 21 April 1989, following engine problems. As Lt-Col Dan House remarked two years before he and his RSO went 'feet wet' after successfully ejecting from 'Number One', 'The improvement in safety compared with the first few years is the result of the learning curve and training. We have had a number of fairly serious emergencies and continue to have them, as is normal for any high-performance aircraft. What saves us is excellent planning and supervision . . . and vigorous preparation in the simulator. A typical comment after a safe recovery of a serious emergency is "No big deal. I've done it, seen it or heard of it in the simulator".' This stringent attention to detail was applied equally to the post-recon legs of the mission, where the dangers of crew fatigue—brought about subconsciously by the sophoric trance of whirling instrument dials—might have all too easily set in. To offset vertigo during operations at night and in twilight, the pilot was provided with a Peripheral Vision Director (PVD), a laser which drew a harmless red line across the instrument panel to denote the horizon. However, the opportunity seldom presented itself to take a respite prior to the taxing descent, as few 'legs' were straight enough to give the crews more than momentary respite from the chart- and instru-

ment-scanning routine, with the result that adrenalin levels could drop owing to unperceived boredom. Energy-sustaining squeeze-bottle rations, identical to those to which 'Dragon Lady gourmets' continue occasionally to subject themselves, were steadily made more appetizing but often had to be guzzled. The gravy-based dinners were warmed by being placed on the hot canopies for a few seconds ('which could burn the heck off your gloves if held there too long'), as there was neither the time nor the space to fiddle with food warmers in the sophisticated 'Blackbird'. The other distraction SR-71A crews glimpsed and welcomed was the beauty of the speckled dark blue celestial mural above, or the blue-green tapestry of the Earth below, when night missions permitted the 'batwing' sunshades to be skewed down. Ferry flights provided the best time and calm to enjoy the relaxing vista. In 1988 Dan House confided, 'It is easy to see things on the ground like lakes, rivers, main highways, and on a clear day you can literally see for hundreds of miles to the front and side. I made a turn over Des Moines, Iowa, one day at about 75,000ft. As I looked to the west I was looking down at Omaha, Nebraska, and could see Colorado. In instances like this it helps to have a working knowledge of geography and an active imagination.' Above them, the pilots could become mesmerized by everything from shooting stars to the dazzling lights of the aurora borealis. The RSOs had less of a grandstand view through their small rectangular windows but could watch the terrain unfold below in the big viewsight display and 'update' an on-track ANS simply for amusement. There was also the satisfaction that they traversed more ground in an average month than a 'gold card' business air traveller would cover in a year, and the smug knowledge that an otherwise normally laborious jetting journey could be completed in a quarter of the time. However, dreams would be quickly discarded as new automatic turns were effected by the ANS, jolting the crew back into the real world of the arduous process of descent.

DESTINATION HOMEPLATE

To come down from bullet speed (in fact, slightly faster: a .30-06 rifle bullet decelerates from a muzzle velocity of 3,000ft/sec when it leaves the barrel whereas the SR-71A *sustained* a 3,100ft/sec true air speed in cruise), the throttles were retarded gradually through minimum afterburner to military power until they were 'half way back at Mach 2.5'. The

---

[7]The exception was Maj James W. Hudson, who lost his life in an unsuccessful ejection from a T-38A companion trainer on 23 March 1971. Two aircraft losses have been attributed to pilot error, including that of 64-17970 which was involved in a tanker collision in 1970. Unfortunately, the primary source records may well be shredded and thus not enter the public domain.

process lent the SR-71A its alternative nickname the 'Sled', as much could go awry in microseconds and pilots had to respond by instinct during the tobogganing. The descent rate was typically 400ft/min in a 5° nose-down attitude. The inlet and bypass systems reversed their motions under the management of DAFICS, while the auto-fuel transfer pumps again shifted the SR-71A's centre of gravity, all under the watchful eye of the pilot, as speed and height were gradually bled off. Below FL600, radio communication was resumed and the RSO would reactivate the IFF transponder to keep the friendly air defence forces happy. The process was a roller-coaster ride all the way down to FL260, when a fuel top-up was often scheduled. The precision required for a successful rendezvous with the 'GLOB' in three dimensions after an exhilarating but tiring excursion into the stratosphere, given the pressing need to follow a 'canned' or strictly prescribed noise-abating descent profile, presented its own demands. To top it all, during night-refuelling operations pilots often reported powerful sensations of vertigo brought upon by reflections of the tanker's belly line-up lights in their 'goldfish-bowl' visors. (SR-71 trainees underwent what was known as a 'hot departure' to familiarize them with the phenomenon, which involved taking a fuel-laden Blackbird direct from the tarmac up to Mach 3 at altitude then straight down to practice hook-ups, while they were still fresh.) Again, the Stratotanker made most of the advances while the SR-71A pilot lined up on a tanker's ADF signal and looked out for the refueller, preparatory to the plug.

Mid-sortie top-ups were also called for on long-endurance missions, at two-hour intervals between the successive reconnaissance 'loops' at altitude, when the whole rigmarole of ascent and descent was repeated. Such seemingly endless missions—more in the vein of 'Dragon Lady' excursions—were limited only by crew fatigue, film remaining and stocks of onboard NO_2 and LOX. (As fuel was burnt off, NO_2 nitrogen gas was fed into the tanks from a pair of 105-litre thermos flasks to purge them of their explosive mix of JP-7 and air, and to reduce fuel-sloshing. This would in turn be expelled by new stocks of JP-7 squirted into the tanks, and so on, until the dewars were expended. The crew oxygen limit is self-explanatory.) Indefatigable crews were known to stay at the helm from sunset to sunrise. The technique was first demonstrated on 26 April 1971 by Mackay Trophy winners Lt-Col Thomas B. Estes and Maj Dewain C. Vick, who flew 15,000 miles in a loop over the United States outbound from and returning to Beale, equivalent to a non-stop flight from San Francisco to Paris and back. They were airborne for 10½ hours! The first such operational missions were staged out of Seymour-Johnson AFB in North Carolina two and half years later, to monitor the Golan Heights and Sinai at the height of the Yom Kippur War. Crews returned too fatigued even to enjoy a post-debrief beer. Among them was Lt-Col George T. Morgan, the first RSO to amass 1,000 hours (a fifth of it combat time) in a career which saw him perform a record-breaker in 1976 and later move on to become Chief of Flight Test Operations at Palmdale. While at Beale he had the distinction of actually wearing out one of his custom-tailored David Clark pressure suits (each crewman had two), which had fourteen velcro patches sewn on the outer garment by the time it was binned.

On the correct vector for 'homeplate' the pilot retarded the throttles to produce 350kts indicated air speed, and reduced speed further to 275KIAS in the traffic pattern. Downwind, more air speed was bled off and the undercarriage lowered, until on finals the still-hot machine was rumbling along at 230–175KIAS at 1,500 ft. Riding at 10° nose-up attitude (most landings were 'composite', using ILS pitch-steering on the ADI with quick visual cross-references through the split windshield), pilots further toyed with the throttles to bring their steed down to T-speed. Threshold speed under normal conditions was calculated at 155kts plus 1kt for every 1,000lb of fuel remaining over a 10,000lb reserve. Viewed head-on, the sink rate appeared dramatic, as huge wisps of cloud vortexed from the wing, marking the low-pressure suction of the upper surfaces of the delta planform. As the runway markers loomed into view, the pilots would raise the nose to 12° pitch to flare the machine, aided by a massive pillow of ground effect. As one pilot noted, 'It's *almost* impossible to perform a hard landing.' Dan House added: 'Our flare and landing technique is similar to most high-performance fighters. The difference is that we are going much faster, so we look like we are sinking and being saved by ground effect. The large delta wings push a cushion of air in front of the plane and we get into ground effect at about 25ft, so the plane is actually very easy to land acceptably. It is very difficult to land on speed at a specified point though—spot-landings are tough.' The maximum sink rate for USAF operations was 10ft/sec at 10,000lb fuel. With 40,000lb still on board, taking the great steaming trident up to sixty tons, pilots executed a dramatic, 185kt landing at a maximum 7.75ft/sec drop-down. However, no matter how

Top right: 'Sled ride' over, an SR-71A settles into the traffic pattern and its final approach to Beale AFB, California. (USAF)

Right: Screech! Palmdale's 'Flower' touches down, assisted by its 40ft diameter drag parachute. The orange blossom, which slowed the 'Habu' down to 100kts in a second, was released when the ground speed reading fell to 60–55kts. (Lockheed)

Left: 'Like a snake swallowing three mice' was how 'Kelly' Johnson described his Mach 3 masterpiece when the aircraft was viewed head-on. The aviators are leaving their still broiling steed while wary ground crews perform the final shut-down procedures. After a 'hot and high' mission, the skin of the machine remained too hot to touch for over half an hour. (Frank B. Mormillo)

Below left: Mission complete, but still on a 'high', the spacesuit-clad pilot and RSO stroll briskly to the PSD van, to be whisked away for a debrief and a well-earned rest. (USAF)

Right: The smouldering wreckage of SR-71B '957 being doused down on 11 January 1968. The aircraft crashed on approach to Beale, its crew—comprising instructor Lt-Col Robert G. Sowers and student Capt David E. Freuhauf—having successfully ejected. (Appeal Democrat/Bob Magnetti)

routine it seemed to its pilots, observers would always be awed by the majesty of the process. Rubber tyres squealing, power chopped to idle and the 40ft-diameter orange blossom 'chute deployed, the 'Habu' was anchored back to 100kts in a second. The 'sled ride' continued. Only after some 5,000ft of runway had been consumed, and a lot of noise made and kinetic energy spent, could the crew slacken their harnesses. 'De-planing' took up a further forty-five minutes as the correct shut-down procedures were followed in the cockpit and by ground technicians, who would assist the numbed crew in their sometimes jelly-legged, ungraceful egress. The 'gold suiters' were then driven to the PSD and intelligence for 'out-processing', prior to some well-deserved R&R. Meanwhile, a six-hour inspection of the reconnaissance jet followed, during which time hydraulic juices were reclaimed before they returned to a near-solid state, each and every spot-weld on the airframe was checked, the computerized maintenance report (based on a Central Airborne Performance Analyzer known by its aconym CAPA) was down-loaded and the vital sensors were interrogated for the contents of their film magazines and magnetic tapes. This latter function was performed at Beale by the 9th Reconnaissance Technical Squadron (and at the two 'Dets' by detached personnel working in security-tight, cordoned-off portions of a hangar given over to the Mobile Processing Center cabins), permitting high-resolution glossies and elint graphics to be made available to higher authority within a few hours of touch-down—anywhere up the line to the President and his aides. It was a time-honoured process that endured for two decades, and which earned the flyers their coveted 'Habu' patches.

Sadly, most of the airframes will now be cold for a long time, with left-over blobs of solid lubricating grease blocking their arteries to sustain the coronary until one day, hopefully well into the future, their svelte carcasses are inevitably reclaimed for their exotic metals. To enthusiasts and crews alike, the 'Blackbird' epoch ended all too soon, and far too

abruptly. While high-speed 'tempering' of the airframe actually improved its strength—meaning that it could go on virtually for ever—O&M costs became gradually more prohibitive. Det 4 flew its last operational sortie on 20 November 1989 and two months later bade farewell to England and fourteen years of 'Busy Relay' operations in a gloomy sky charged with emotion: SR-71A '964 (call-sign 'Quid 20'), crewed by Maj Tom McCleary and RSO Maj Stan Gudmonson, roared into the sky at noon on 18 January; and the following day, at 11.56 a.m., '967 ('Quid 21'), with Maj Don Watkins and back-seater Maj Bob Fowlkes dressed in standard gold regalia, lifted off, flew one circuit in salute, then swept past the airfield bound for California. Det 1 had already ceased all operations by 22 December, and the establishment at Beale was formally deactivated on 26 January. However, the trusty old 'Habu' did not end its career with a whimper. On 6 March, while en route to the East Coast for disposition to the Smithsonian National Air and Space Museum in Washington DC, '972, crewed by Lt-Col R. Edward Yeilding, pilot, and Lt-Col Joseph T. Vida, chief of SR-71 flight test ops, made a 68min 17sec cross-country run from California to Maryland, averaging 2,110mph over the 2,404.05-mile course. It was one of four records established during the sortie. Originally delivered on 12 December 1966, '972 was the same machine which, in the hands of Maj James V. Sullivan and Maj Noel F. Widdifield, set the 1 September 1974 New York-to-London transatlantic record of 1hr 56min, slashing nearly three hours off the previous run made by a Royal Navy Phantom crew in 1969. All records still stand. It was a fitting end for a fantastic military aircraft. Tail '976, with more combat sorties than any other survivor, has since been handed over to the Air Force Museum at Wright-Patterson AFB, Ohio, while the bulk of the remainder have found similar homes dotted around the United States. All that still flies at the time of writing is the twin-seat 'tub' ('956), currently on charge with NASA's Ames-Dryden Research Facility in California. This aircraft is

being flown on training missions to ensure that the institutional knowledge gleaned in terms of piloting and maintenance skills is not completely squandered, in preparation for several (but as yet undetermined) high-speed research projects.

FOXBAT

Cold War protagonist of the trailblazing 'Habu' (yet still operational, unlike its American counterpart) is the Mikoyan-Gurevich MiG-25, NATO code-name 'Foxbat'. Since its first flight as the Ye-155 test-bed on 6 March 1964, this hefty fighter has grown into a formidable 'family' of dedicated reconnaissance, counter-reconnaissance and interceptor variants—including the derivative twin-seat MiG-31 'Foxhound', which is able, while flying in fours, to employ data-linked look-down radars to 'broomsweep' a sector 600 miles wide and brush away any target at arm's length with long-range AAMs. China and at least one other undisclosed customer have the latest models on order, posing a major threat to unwary reconnaissance aircraft. It remains the only credible adversary for Lockheed's high-flying velvet-black menagerie (and, although the subject is now a moot point, it is probably doubtful that the SR-71A could

have survived the predatory instincts of the latest of this Russian breed).

A year after Mikoyan's chief test pilot Alexander Fedatov pushed his frightening new amalgam of welded titanium and steel skyward to reveal the type's 22,000m (72,000ft) ceiling and Mach 3.0 dash speed, the Russian design team were confident enough to file for, and obtain, official absolute speed and time-to-climb records, which it continued to stack up in abundance during the course of its development. Some of these records remained unchallenged for six years. The follow-on E-266/M test-bed pushed the boundaries further by attaining 98,430ft in a 4min 4sec zoom climb, together with a peak altitude of 118,900ft (records which held firm until January 1975, when the Americans eventually managed to top some of the time-to-climb figures with a series of F-15 Streak Eagle 'Aquila Maxima' sorties in the cold air over Grand Forks AFB, North Dakota). Rocket-assisted zoom-climb records, which were never properly filed, remain unique for its class.

By 1969 the MiG-25 had been ordered into series production, but not before aileron roll and stabilator flutter problems had been eradicated. These anomalies claimed the lives of NII V-VS (Soviet Air Force Flight Test Research Institute) pilot Igor Lesnikov on 30 October 1967 and the NII (Ministry of Aircraft Flight Test Research) organization's top 'stick' Oleg Gudhov, who, with the sort of heroism more typically exhibited in motion picture sagas, radioed-in crucial handling reports seconds before their untimely deaths. Further flight-test work carried out by Boris Orlov led to a design 'freeze' the following year, from which the now well-known outlines of the racy 'Foxbat' were settled upon. Initial production concentrated on the MiG-25P *Perekhvatchik* interceptor version, code-named 'Foxbat-A' by NATO, which began to equip front-line squadrons straight off the production line. Its performance—'red-lined' at Mach 2.93—soon became the yardstick against which every Western fighter was measured, despite the type's relatively poor quality missile armament and limited manoeuvrability. Yet its large size and stable high-speed cruise characteristics at altitude offered the perfect platform for reconnaissance work, and during 1971 a dedicated MiG-25R *Razvedchik* (recce) variant, NATO code-name 'Foxbat-B', began to trickle from the top secret production facility at Gorky into frontline V-VS (*Voyenno-Vozdushnye Sily*, or Air Force) service. Equipped with a SLAR, a vertical viewfinder and three technical objective cameras, the type made its operational début in Egypt in the autumn of 1971, several months before the model had achieved full IOC at home, flown and maintained by select Soviet crews who enjoyed the luxury of an endless stream of technicians and spares ferried in to Cairo West airfield by a procession of An-22 'Cocks'. *Ab initio* missions were flown for a trial period of six months (later extended to fully fledged operations, similar to American 'Dets') over the northern stretches of the Israeli-occupied Sinai Peninsula, unchecked by *Heyl Ha'Avir* F-4E *Kurnass* fighters, which simply could not catch the fleeting Russians. In exchange for their assistance, the Egyptians became privy to the considerable intelligence amassed by the 'Foxbat' squad, which was subsequently used during the drawn-out War of Attrition which predated the bloody pan-Arab assault

against Israel in September 1973. The successful combat evaluation was the brainchild of Alexy Minaev, Deputy Minister of Aircraft Production, an accomplished designer with a keen eye for proving his wares who had been intimately involved with the development of the superlative MiG's critical flight control system. This timely evaluation prompted further orders, together with development roubles for a MiG-25PU 'Foxbat-C' twin-seat trainer, a -25BM 'Foxbat-F' defence-suppression mark (based on the 'vanilla' 'Bravo' mark and outfitted with specialist 'Iron Hand' elint gear plus provisions for up to four AS-11 'Kilter' anti-radiation missiles, honed primarily for counter-AWACS) and a completely revised 'dash-Papa-Delta' 'Foxbat-E' interceptor variant, which packs state-of-the-art RP-25 'Spfir' radar, IRSTS and a new air-to-air missile kit based on transistor as opposed to valve technology. Much scoffed-at by the United States (which, at the time, was suffering some electrical interface anomalies with the solid-state air-to-air systems stuffed into its newest fighters, while valve-equipped 1950s-era technology soldiered on to provide the backbone of its own air defence system!), over 300 of the 'Foxbat-Es' were eventually manufactured (MiG-25PD) or con-

Below: A pair of MiG-25 *Razvedchiks*, known in the West as 'Foxbat-Bs', squatting on the ramp ready for their next mission. The radar and camera sensor fit are contained in the sharp nose. (*Flying Colours*)

Above: 'Red 53', a MiG-25RB 'Foxbat-B' from the 931 *Razvedchik Aviasonniy Polk*, displays its glamorous fighter lines, plus nasal triple camera and radar sensor fit, while in the landing pattern at Welzow air base. (M. D. Tabak via Frank Visser)

verted from old stock (MiG-25PDS) and assigned to the IA-PVO (*Istrebitel'naya Aviatsiya Voyska-Protivovozdushnoy Oborony*, or Aviation of Air Defence), obliging the Americans to confine their reconnaissance missions to skirting snoops around the vast Soviet borders, or anywhere other than where 'Foxbats' were eagerly awaiting 'trade'. As pure interceptors, these aircraft were not in the 'turn and burn' category, but they presented a deadly threat to high-flyers wandering off track. Contrary to Western fighter pilot mythology, these 'metallic amalgams' could be 'bent' in hard-pulling turns of nearly 11g, subject to GLOC (g-induced pilot loss of consciousness), to bring their steadily improved quartet of R-40 AAMs to bear. (One test example and its suffering pilot was inadvertently subjected to 11.5g but still made it back to base, having only 'popped' a few rivets.) The Russian design team acknowledge that the aircraft was 'grossly overengineered' and relied more on brute force than finesse, but its inherent simplicity meant it has always been relatively easy to maintain. Defecting pilot Lt Victor Ivanovich Belenko, who 'crash-landed' his powerful MiG-25P at Hakodate, Japan, on 6 September 1976, told US officials that his fourteen-strong 'Foxbat' outfit located at Sakharovka had *one* primary tasking—'to check photography over Vladivostok by the two-to-three SR-71s the United States has based on Okinawa.' Other such squads were stationed in the Baltic in the north-west, along the East German border and adjacent to the Black Sea (some on 'Det' near Varna, Bulgaria), with a similarly narrow specialist role. Belenko, apparently, exhibited the same colourful style and salty language as Western fighter pilots and was reputed to have revealed to his CIA debriefers that he had had 'an ambition to shoot down an SR-71 reconnaissance plane'. Skilful navigation by the Americans—who also, perhaps, had more than their fair share of luck—meant that none of Belenko's peers succeeded either. But updated models of those long-legged monster fighters are now optimized to hit vital Western intelligence-gathering machines using home-on-radar missiles in hit-and-run manoeuvres, and will not hesitate to do so if the need arises. The fragile 'Dragon Lady', in particular, announcing its position with ASARS-2 radar, could quite easily be chewed up and spitted out by AA-9 'Amos' missiles.

Following close on the heels of the basic 'Romeo' recce aircraft came the MiG-25RB (*Razvedchik Bombardirovtchik*, or recce-strike) 'Foxbat-D', designed for exclusive use by the V-VS at home and on special detachments overseas, thus freeing a quantity of the simpler 'Foxbat-B' for export. Pushed by a pair of massive Tumansky R-15-B-300 turbojets, each rated at 22,508lb s.t. with afterburner, 'Foxbat-D' is capable of sustained supersonic cruise at 70,000ft for up to 750 miles. Its equipment fit includes no cameras but advanced SAR and elint sensors similar to those previously employed on the Blackbird; however, it also possesses the capability to lug a nuclear bomb for high-altitude strike (and is often seen flying with practice bomb racks, designed for 'nukes' and 'slick' high-capacity chaff dispenser

pods). Production of all models ceased at Gorky (now again named Niznhi Novgorod) during 1984, when attention shifted exclusively to the substantially redesigned MiG-31 twin-seat 'Foxhound' interceptor variant. However, some 130 MiG-25RB and BM examples remain on the inventory. Until very recently these were distributed at the 'cutting edge' of the V-VS's *Razvedchik Aviasioniy Polk* (Air Reconnaissance Regiments) at Welzow (with a detachment at Werneuchin) in former East Germany; at Osla (plus a detachment at Kolobrzeg) in Poland; at Kabul and Shindand in Afghanistan; and at least two other undisclosed domestic bases in the Far Eastern TVD (*Teatr Voyennykh Destivy*, or Theatre of Military Operation) on the Sino-Soviet border. Remarkably, none were authorized for acquisition by fellow signatories to the now- defunct Warsaw Pact, with the exception of Bulgaria's *Bulgarski Vozdusny Vojski*, which received four 'Foxbat-Bs' in 1981 for use on long-range reconnaissance from Dobritch (formerly Tolbukhin).[8] Indeed, there existed few true overseas 'customers' during the first decade of service; instead, Soviet crews carried out their surreptitious duties under foreign flags as part of four-ship detachments assigned to Egypt, Libya, Syria and the Yemen. By the start of the 1980s several Arab countries had procured fighter models and had ostensibly absorbed the recce detachments into their own ranks, flown and maintained by composite cadres of Soviet, pan-Arab and domestic crews. Egypt, Iran (which, ironically, prior to the collapse of the Shah's regime and subsequent shift towards trade with the Soviet Union, had previously been subjected to V-VS MiG-25RB overflights, beginning

Above: The MiG-25R relies on the brute force generated by its Tumansky R-15 turbojets to achieve its 'red-line' speed of Mach 2.93. The well-worn 'Foxbat-B' model depicted here made its operational début in Egypt in the autumn of 1971, flown and maintained by a select Soviet detachment. (*Air Forces Monthly*)

in January 1973), Iraq, Libya and Syria (the last two alone accounting for the procurement of some 90 'Foxbat' interceptors), are each reputed to operate four reconnaissance aircraft. The exception to this pattern is India's *Bharatiya Vayu Sena*, which has enjoyed greater autonomy from the outset. The Indian Air Force possesses six 'Foxbat-Bs' and two 'Foxbat-C' trainers, gradually introduced from 1981 to replace its aged Canberras. Operated by No 102 Squadron, aptly nicknamed *The Trisonics*, these have been heavily engaged in sky-spy operations against its neighbours Pakistan and the Republic of China, supported by the indigenous manufacture of a steady stream of spare parts (the bane of other 'Foxbat' operators, who are facing stop-go's in supply on account of a fractured Soviet logistics system).

As might be expected, the performance of the recce 'Foxbat' was for a long time a source of considerable embarrassment and concern to both the Israelis and their technological mentors the Americans, who, between them, conjured up myriad unsuccessful plans to 'bag' a 'Foxbat' on the wing, the object of which was to heal hurt pride as much as to thwart enemy operations. This was eventually made possible by the *Heyl Ha'Avir*'s acquisition of the new F-15A

[8]Of the three remaining jets—one was written off in heavy fog when its pilot was ordered to eject—none is operational. Their high fuel consumption has kept them grounded since the beginning of 1991, and negotiations are under way to swap them for simpler fighters.

Above: 'Foxbats' are capable of nuclear and conventional strike, as evidenced by the empty low-drag bomb racks slung under this camouflaged MiG-25 *Razvedchik Bombardirovtchik*, a veteran of the Afghan War. (*Air Forces Monthly*)

Baz equipped with the tailor-made medium-range Raytheon AIM-7F Sparrow III missile, for use in ambush tactics. By 1981 the 'glitches' had been worked out of the weapon system and the plot was hatched: at 1319Z on 13 February that year, a brace of RF-4E 'Photo-Phantoms' entered Lebanese airspace at supersonic speeds at a height of 40,000ft, serving as decoys for a *Baz* which zoomed in at low altitude beneath them. A pair of Syrian MiG-25Ps were duly launched to make contact with the 'Recce Rhinos' but, while closing rapidly at a range of sixty miles, the RF-4Es unexpectedly broke formation and released clouds of radar-cluttering chaff in their wake. The MiGs pressed home their attacks, only to encounter the F-15, which popped up unexpectedly through the chaff to 'bag' one of them in a head-on missile attack. A further Syrian MiG-25 fell foul of an F-15 over Akura on 29 July, but the reconnaissance mark's sorties continued unchallenged until 31 August 1983, when one of their number was dam-

aged by an MIM-23B Improved Hawk SAM while overflying Beirut, making it easy prey for a marauding Eagle. It was a lucky kill in the sort of scenario which SR-71A crews used to dread most—incapacitation (by shrapnel from an inanimate SAM, or a gross technical malfunction) which would force them to throttle back and descend into the clutches of enemy fighters. There have been other close calls. To avoid missile interception, MiG-25Rs have, on occasion, been tracked flying over the Sinai peninsula at speeds of Mach 3.2—in excess of the operational restriction—and it has been reliably reported that the aircraft concerned required a complete engine change after performing such strenuous antics! However, at the time of writing, the Beirut shootdown stands as the only confirmed loss of a MiG-25R to hostile fire, despite thousands of combat sorties clocked up over Middle Eastern and Chinese borders, not to mention the treacherous landing patterns over Shindand and Kabul, where lesser breeds of MiG were downed by co-ordinated pot-shots from Mujahideen elephant guns. Unless, of course, there is substance to the rumoured American Project 'Aurora', a mysterious diamond-shaped hypersonic high-altitude vehicle which allegedly creates contrails akin to 'doughnuts on a string' by means of an air-breathing rocket impulse motor, then the MiG-25R/RB remains king of the stratosphere, and will reign supreme for the remainder of this century.

Below: 'Red 50' shows off the 'cleaner' radar-mapping and elint systems carried aboard the MiG-25RBK 'Foxbat-D'. (M. D. Tabak via Frank Visser)

3. ALONE, UNARMED AND UNAFRAID

O R SO the story went! Photo-reconnaissance has for a long time been the means by which tactical air forces and army commanders obtain their vital pre- and post-strike target intelligence, and the enemy has always done his best to deny them this information. Considering the fact that tac-recce crews customarily fly machines whose armament capability has been seconded to reconnaissance hardware, to penetrate the most heavily defended target areas (the only ones worth taking a peek at) on a 'first in, last out' basis, it is hardly surprising to discover that they have to endure more than their fair share of 'flak'. Modern computer mission-modelling and satellite reconnaissance spacecraft have gradually eroded their role over the past three decades, while 'near real-time' reconnaissance technology has added the unsavoury ingredient of crews not being required to return home in order to provide a complete 'picture', since their vital 'products' are obtained well in advance of tyres thumping on tarmac. However, there are few who would decry the value of 'wet film' pictures—black and white, colour and infra-red—ingrained on silver-based emulsions: no other medium provides the same degree of clarity, or is as much coveted by politicians and the popular media alike.

Of all the 'tac-recon greats' of the past three decades, there is none which has seen as much combat service in so many different theatres of operation as McAir's RF-4. When Bob Little pushed the first Phantom into the skies above Lambert Field on 27 May 1958, designer and company boss James S. McDonnell foresaw a requirement for a mere 376 Navy fighters with a nominal 1,000-hour warranted fatigue life. Little did he or his test pilots know then that production would eventually total 5,201 airframes, of which a significant 719 would be built purely as photo-reconnaissance aircraft, excluding additional conversions. There exist few fundamental differences between the RF-4—variously known as the 'Photo-Phantom' and 'Recce Rhino'— and the high-flyers of the same epoch such as the 'Habu' and the 'Foxbat', except in one crucial regard: the sensor-equipped Phantom was designed to get down 'in the weeds' and brave the flak-filled skies above an integrated air defence system which those machines were designed assiduously to avoid. While a medium- to high-altitude driftsight formed the standard equipment on all RF-4s, crews usually perfected the art of coping with the cockpit-saturated task of map-reading while whizzing over roofs and tree-tops. As, at the beginning of the Phantom era, 10th TRW commander Col Spain put it, the RF-4 'has no place as an area surveillance aircraft'. His crews were taught to fly in search of pin-point targets for their cameras—bridges, vehicle concentrations, airfields and other tactical sites, snapped at about 500ft and 500–550kts. Images were recorded by their clutches of Chicago Aerial Industries (CAI) KS-87 framing sensors in the forward oblique/vertical and sideways-facing stations at around six frames per second. Below these, the No 2 station held a Fairchild KA-56 panoramic camera producing transverse strips possessing very fine detail up to 1½ miles each side of the aircraft's track. British residents in the more rugged, rural areas soon became used to fleeting, smoking Phantoms winding in pairs through valleys and around mountains as crews searched out the landmarks ringed in grease pencil on their 1:50,000 scale maps. The 10th TRW also pioneered the infra-red and radar sensors which were capable of 'seeing in the dark' and through the harsh, weather-prone European environment.

However, it was in South-East Asia where the type truly came of age, reaching its zenith in the late 1960s with four squadrons stationed at Udorn, Thailand, and Tan Son Nhut, South Vietnam.[1] Udorn was a composite Phantom fighter-reconnaissance base and the placards near the squadron ops buildings proudly stated: 'Bring Back the Pictures . . . and Kill MiGs'! Lt-Col John Taylor, who flew 48 'Recce Rhino' combat missions from Udorn at the height of the 'Rolling Thunder' campaign in 1967–68, recollected the ferocity of the enemy's defences,

---

[1] The first aircraft assigned to the theatre came from Shaw AFB, South Carolina. The force later became established in 1966 as the the 460th TRW (12th TRS, code 'AC', operational until July 1971, and the 16th TRS, 'AE', operational until March 1970) at Tan Son Nhut, South Vietnam; and the 432nd TRW (11th TRS, code 'OO', operational until November 1970, and the 14th TRS, 'OZ', operational until 1975) at Udorn, Thailand. It peaked in 1968 with sixty jets and again during the 'Freedom Dawn' and 'Linebacker' operations conducted between May 1972 and January 1973.

US RECCE AIRCRAFT LOSSES TO HOSTILE FIRE IN SOUTH-EAST ASIA, 1964–1973											
Type	1964	1965	1966	1967	1968	1969	1970	1971	1972	1973	Total
US Navy & Marine Corps											
EA/EKA/RA-3 Skywarrior			2	3	1	11					17
RA-5C Vigilante		4	3	4	3	1			3		18
EA-6A Intruder									1		1
EA-6B Prowler											0
E-2 Hawkeye											0
RF-4B Phantom				1	2						3
RF-8 Crusader	1	7	6	2	2				2		20
OV-10 Bronco						3	5	4	2		14
P/OP-2 Neptune						3					3
P-3 Orion						1					1
S-2 Tracker			1								1
USAF											
RB-57 Canberra		1				1					2
EB/RB-66 Destroyer		1	2	1	1				1		6
RF-4C Phantom			7	20	24	8	9	4	6		78
RF-101C Voodoo	1	9	13	8	2						33
O-2 Skymaster				1	8	6	4	4	14		37
OV-10 Bronco						1	11	8	14	1	35

Losses include those destroyed by ground attack but exclude those ascribed to operational causes and O-1 FAC Birddog losses.

and the tactics used by the 'Peepin' Phantom': 'Our prime duties consisted of BDA (bomb damage assessment), exploratory recce, or just trolling—you know, randomly seeking out targets. A good way of doing this was just to find out where any shooting was coming from. Like Yen Bai, about 30–40 miles northeast of Hanoi and right on the Red River, or Banana Valley, just south of Hanoi. Plus anything east of "Thud Ridge", anything in town itself, of course, and anything south of the Haiphong Ridge.' All missions were two-ship. On his second excursion Lt- Col Taylor recalled that 'We were two RF-4Cs, up near the Chinese buffer zone at about 22,000 feet—as high as I've ever been over there. We were coming back and got some "Bandit" calls just as we were finishing up our targets. It was obvious that they were coming in on us. We were staying high like that to conserve fuel but then we picked up some weak strobes [enemy radar signals on the RHAWS, or radar homing and warning system scopes] and went down—got *right down to the weeds*. I kept an eye on my six o'clock, making weaving turns to check from time to time.' By unloading the airframe with negative *g* and piling on the thrust, the Phantoms would accelerate rapidly, leaving most opponents way behind them. Having dropped the tanks, and being unhindered by bombs or guns, the 'Photo-Phantoms' had an impressive transonic dash capability at low-level: 'The best tactics you could use were to go low, because the MiGs were limited to 560 knots, maybe 570 knots, below 10,000 feet. We were always low; I used to fly 500 to 1,000 feet AGL (above ground level) and there were a lot of guys who used to go even lower—100 to 500 feet kind of thing. But that can be damn' dangerous! I would keep to 500 minimum.'

Above right: 'Photo-Phantoms' on the wing in April 1967. The aircraft customarily flew in pairs, though usually in trail, using threat-reaction 'jinking' over the target area. (McAir)

Right: An RF-4C's perspective of the Lang Giai Bridge in North Vietnam during Operation 'Freedom Dawn'. The bridge was dropped by one-ton 'smart' bombs on 25 May 1972 and 'Recce Rhinos' followed this up with the pictures to prove it—one of several million taken over the flak-filled skies of North Vietnam. (USAF)

These altitudes provided detailed photographs of gun emplacements and a host of other targets. Fuel was eaten up voraciously on such high-speed low-level runs, but it gave the crews that 'edge', tactics also espoused by their combat peers flying the 1950s-vintage RF-101C Voodoo. 'We would hit 420 to 480 knots at the pre-IP [pre-Initial Point] and at the IP (the co-ordinates at which the recce-run begins) we'd be at 550–580 knots. Over town [Hanoi, smack-bang in Route Pack IVA], of course, you couldn't go low because of the intense gunfire. So we would pop up to medium altitude just before running-in. Over town, they would throw up a real barrage and if the wingman was following behind he could get in real trouble. The safest place to work was 8,000 feet—at the most, 14,000 ft—to avoid the SAM-2s and triple-A. You could spot the SAMs by the smoke and flame when they left the ground, but the big problem for the pilot was that he's so busy looking at the target that there's no time to look for stuff like that. My 'gator [navigator] would call the flak too—37- and 57-millimetre, and some 85-millimetre stuff as well. Very black puffs, that 85. It was all radar-controlled and they knew just when to stop firing if the MiGs were coming in. Those gunners on the 85s, if they hit your altitude and got you once ahead and once behind,

they'd just walk the stuff up to you and you were finished. They were really *great* gunners. The best way, though, to beat the enemy threats was to g-load the aircraft, positive and negative, while you were popping up to locate the target (which had to be done visually from the IP onwards). This threat reaction manoeuvre drew a sine wave through the air. Downtown, we'd probably be picking the target at 10,000 feet or so. Standard targets included POL [petrol, oil and lubricants storage areas], the MiG fields, or the Paul Doumier Bridge just north of town.' Once the photographs had been taken, a quick egress was in order. '[A] kid named John Ward came up with something we termed "The Slice". This was the fastest way to get out of this high-threat area, into the weeds and home. It was just to pull 135 degrees right or left, nose down and split for home at full power.'

For night-time work, the aircraft featured an AN/ AAS-18 infra-red line-scanner (IRLS, later replaced by the variable-swath AN/AAD-5 IRLS with an optional 60° or 120° FOV) tucked under the navigator's seat, capable of producing swaths of imagery based on the infra-red electromagnetic energy emanating from the terrain below. In this manner, the aircraft could track vehicles, troop bivouacs and arms caches through light foliage. Anything that moved or had moved recently was 'warm' enough for the IRLS to

pick up and record on film. Photoflash cartridges were also available for pure photography, ejected from LA-429A units in the Phantom's empennage (in the same compartments that were turned over to chaff 'tinsel' for daytime flights). Their combined one billion candlepower was enough to light up the entire vista below. Often, the back-seat navigator would use his set of throttles to keep the aircraft at around 580kts during the 'lo' part of the mission profile, freeing the pilot to concentrate on steering and observation: the AN/APQ-99 ground-mapping radar in the nose provided an E-scan display to assist with manual terrain-clearance, not 'hands off' automatic

Right: The Alabama ANG were the first part-time outfit to receive RF-4Cs, beginning in 1971; two decades later the 117th TRW formed the backbone of tac-air photo-reconnaissance assets committed to the Gulf. This shot of a 'be-chuted' machine was taken in the early 1980s, when the jets wore 'Vietnam wraparound' camouflage finishes. (USAF)

Below left: A delightful study by ace photographer Frank B. Mormillo of a 192nd TRS, Nevada ANG 'High Roller' RF-4C banking to reveal its clean, aesthetically pleasing lines. (Frank B. Mormillo)

Above: Nevada ANG crews flew Alabama Guard jets from Sheikh Isa, Bahrain, during the Gulf War. Seen here during peacetime training over the NAS Fallon range in Nevada, the aircraft are making a formation run over road junction and bridge 'targets'. In combat, the aircraft fly solo or in pairs: formation flying is merely used to pass on the skills of tac-recce to novices. (Frank B. Mormillo)

flight, and crews only very rarely flew below 500ft AGL during these manoeuvres—something akin to a role-reversal. On the completion of a mission, the aircraft's cameras were rapidly unloaded for attention in the Goodyear WS-420 Photo Processing and Interpretation Facility (PPIF) trailer. The crew's debrief would result in a mission report ('MisRep') for planners and commanders to act upon and, about two to three hours after touch-down, finished products from the PPIF would be conveyed up and down the command channels to the relevant authority. All film was annotated with co-ordinates pertaining to aircraft position, furnished by the navigation computer. Combat was a scary business—especially so by night. One McAir tech-rep recollected a novice crew ready to throw in their wings after drawing and evading no fewer than *sixteen* SAMs on their first combat mission in the 'slot' position over North Vietnam! However, there was a price to be paid for all the millions of images obtained: 74 USAF RF-4Cs and three USMC RF-4Bs were lost to hostile fire (excluding four destroyed on the ground at Tan Son Nhut during the Tet Offensive), of which 21 were destroyed in 1967, and a horrifying 26 the following year, during the course of 70,000 combat sorties. An additional seven were stricken in 'operational accidents' in that theatre alone, mostly as a result of 'manual TF-ing'—something which today's top-of-the-line recce crews need not lose sleep over.

True all-weather reconnaissance was made available by the Goodyear AN/APQ-102A sideways-looking airborne radar (SLAR), which was packaged into the Phantom's cheeks (and which also served as additional armour-plating!). As explained by 'Recce Rhino' boss Maj-Gen Gordon Graham in his 1966 report to the 7th Air Force shortly after the sensor's combat assessment, 'SLAR can detect a variety of targets under day or night conditions, and can penetrate haze, smoke, and most clouds. It is claimed that it can record targets such as convoys on open sections of road, trains, airstrips and support facilities, parked aircraft, bridges, boats, and missile sites. Its high-resolution mapping mode can be used in conjunction with its Moving-Target Indicator (MTI) mode to clearly show moving vehicles against a high-resolution background. The minimum speed at which moving vehicles can be detected and recorded is a direct function of the altitude, speed, and angle between the aircraft and vehicle movement, with targets moving at 90° to the aircraft flight path giving the best returns. The SLAR offset capability allows it to cover targets as much as 30 miles to one side of the flight path, providing the aircraft [with] safe separation from defended target areas. Optimum altitude for SLAR flights is 30,000 to 35,000 feet, although lower altitudes at times provide better shadows on some targets to improve interpretation potential. Unfortunately, SLAR has many limitations, chief of which is its fixed scale of 1:400,000. This is far too small a scale to provide good interpretation, and special skills and techniques must be developed in order to properly exploit the product. SLAR cannot separate targets closer together than 50 feet, penetrate foliage or water, or detect targets under trees or similar cover.'

The problem related to 'spot size' and was solved by Goodyear engineer Carl Wiley, who invented *synthetic aperture radar*, which proved capable of building up a radar image covering a swath ten miles wide by recording a series of neat synthetic portions of the returning reflected target radar imagery by means of a laser correlator-processor. Back at base, the resultant material could be decoded back into images by a companion correlator-processor to produce photo-quality pictures. Tested in Europe after the cessation of hostilities in South-East Asia during the 1974 annual 'Reforger' exercise, the system—known as the AN/UPD-4—furnished imagery with a *constant* scale of 1:100,000 across and along the film. This permitted the imagery to be magnified to scales as high as 1:2,000, which not only showed up individual parked aircraft, tanks and even oil barrels but also permitted interpreters to classify them by model![2] It was a remarkable breakthrough. Such recce products had only previously been available by means of daring low-level flights over the target, as

---

[2]'Spot size', or a 'resolution cell', is the area covered on the imagery by a single point target. This area is determined by multiplying the across-track by the along-track resolution of the radar. As range increases, real-aperture radar (RAR) cell size expands disproportionately in the along-track mode and creates an asymmetric picture which consequently suffers from a loss of detail. For example, as Goodyear engineer Brian Lynch explains it, the resolution cell size for a typical SAR at a range of 25nm is 100 sq ft; a resolution cell size for an RAR with an even bigger 12ft long antenna and 100ft resolution is 120,000 sq ft at that same distance. The resultant cell shape from RAR is 100ft × 1,200ft for a ratio of 1:12, whereas the SAR cell ratio is 1:1. This *constant* scale in SAR resolution is what makes it so superior. It can be magnified in 'soft copy' and 'hard copy' format and manipulated in all sorts of ways to produce the fine detail required for target recognition. This process has steadily become highly automated, freeing interpreters to sift through the ground station's conclusions rather than having to squint through micro- and stereoscopic eyepieces. SAR is also discussed in Chapter 1, in the context of the ASARS-2, and in Chapter 2, when examining the ASARS-1 fitted to the SR-71A.

RF-4 PHOTO-PHANTOMS

Model	Production block/serials	Numbers	Service
RF-4B 20	151975 to 151977	3	
21	151978 and 151979	2	
22	151980 and 151981	2	
23	151982 and 151983	2	
24	153089 to 153094	6	USMC
25	153095 to 153100	6	
26	153101 to 153107	7	
27	153108 to 153115	8	
41	157342 to 157346	5	
43	157347 to 157351	5	
	Subtotal	46	
RF-4C 15	6212200 and 62122011[1]	2	
16	63-7740 and -7741	2	
17	-7742	1	
18	-7743 to -7749	7	
19	-7750 to -7763	14	
20	64-0997 to -1017	21	
21	-1018 to -1037	20	
22	-1038 to -1061	24	
23	-1062 to -1077	16	
24	-1078 to -1085	8	
	65-0818 to -0838	21	
25	-0839 to -0864	26	
26	-0865 to -0901	37	
27	-0902 to -0932	31	
28	-0933 to -0945	13	USAF
	66-0383 to -0386	4	
	-0388	1	
29	-0387	1	
	-0389 to -0406	18	
30	-0407 to -0428	22	
31	-0429 to -0450	22	
32	-0451 to -0472	22	
33	-0473 to -0478	6	
	67-0428 to -0442	15	
34	-0443 to -0453	11	
35	-0454 to -0461	8	
36	-0462 to -0469	8	
37	68-0548 to -0561	14	
38	-0562 to -0576	15	
39	-0577 to -0593	17	
40	-0594 to -0611	18	
41	69-0349 to -0357	9	
42	-0358 to -0366	9	
43	-0367 to -0375	9	
44	-0376 to -0384	9	USAF (contd)
48	71-0248 to -0252	5	
49	-0253 to -0259	7	
51	72-0145 to -0148	4	
52	-0149 to -0152	4	
53	-0153 to -0156	4	
	Subtotal	505	
RF-4E 43	69-7448 to -7455	8	
44	-7456 to -7462	7	
45	-7463 to -7481	19	Germany
46	-7482 to -7510	29	
47	-7511 to -7535	25	
	Subtotal	88	
44	69-7567, -7570 & and -7576[2]	3	
45	69-7590 to -7595	6	
63	75-0418 to -0423	6	Israel
64	-0656 to -0661	6	
	Subtotal	21	
48	72-0266 to -0269	4	
61	74-1725 to -1728	4	
62	-1729 to -1736	8	
68	78-0751 to -0754[3]	4	Iran
	-0788 and -0854[3]	2	
69	-0855 to -0864[3]	10	
	Subtotal	32	
66	77-0309 to -0316	8	Turkey
	Subtotal	8	
66	77-0357 and -0358	2	
	-1761 to -1766	6	Greece
	Subtotal	8	
RF-4EJ 56	47-6901 to -6905	5	Japan
	57-6906 to -6914	9	
	Subtotal	14	

[1] Two prototypes converted on the McAir lines from F-4Bs.
[2] F-4E(S) converted from F-4E fighter-bombers.
[3] These sixteen aircraft were built but not delivered.

Below left: A *Luftwaffe* RF-4E makes a 'dirty' flypast with everything—hook, wheels and flaps—down for the camera. The Service bought 88 J79-GE-17-powered examples and assigned them to two Wings, both of which are due to decommission by the end of 1993. South Korea, Turkey, Greece, Spain, Israel and Japan (which is converting an additional seventeen F-4EJ fighters to the reconnaissance task, equipped with Thomson-CSF Raphael SLAR) will continue to operate the 'Photo-Phantom' through to the end of the century. (Tim Laming)

Right: Quick-release latches provide ready access to the RF-4E's film magazines and cameras, for quick dispatch to the Photo-Processing and Interpretation Facility (PPIF). (Author)

related earlier. By 1976 the 38th TRS flying the trials had added a 'near real-time' data-link facility so that the images (all suitably laced with UTM, lat/long and Loran co-ordinates) could be made available within a quarter of an hour from the ground-based TIPI (Tactical Information Processing & Interpretation) cabin. Moreover, automatic target recognition functions were made available, by means of comparing old and new imagery. Following the successful QRC76-01 demonstration, eighteen USAF RF-4Cs were re-equipped with the 'near real-time' AN/UPD-8, while the US Marines bought several AN/UPD-9s for their RF-4Bs, and the *Luftwaffe* (and, later, the *Heyl Ha'Avir*) procured AN/APD-6s for select numbers of its RF-4Es. The Goodyear/Loral systems were the first 'real-time' reconnaissance sensors to be introduced into the world's tac-recon community. No longer was the RF-4 just a 'Photo-Phantom'; instead, it had blossomed into a round-the-clock, all-weather surveillance platform. The advances in technology also meant that forward-deployed forces could be shrunk without any adverse affect on the quantity and quality of recce products generated. By 1981 the USAF establishment had been split down the middle with eight full-time and nine Air National Guard (ANG) 'weekend warrior' squadrons, flying 328 aircraft. Training was handled at Bergstrom AFB, Texas, and by the ANG at Boise, Idaho, with the active forces concentrating on 'instant intelligence' gathering and the ANG on traditional photint and BDA. Little mention has been made so far of the RF-4C's high-altitude capabilities, and this is where the Guardsmen have always excelled.

While the vintage T-11 mapping camera and KA-1 formed part of the optional high-altitude kit of the 'Recce Rhino' for over a decade, they were seldom used. Both demanded adventurous overflight at altitudes which placed the crew in serious jeopardy. Replacing them with newer systems, the Alabama 'Recce Rebels' of the 106th TRS, 117th TRW, kept the tradition alive with more optically advanced clear-weather CAI Recon Optical KS-127B 66in focal-length LOROPs, capable of generating photographs featuring 1–2ft resolution when exposed at oblique slant ranges of up to 25nm! Six of their machines

deployed from Birmingham, Alabama, to 'Phantom-town' at Sheikh Isa in Bahrain during the Gulf War—the only such 'game in town', commanded by Col (now Gen) Jim Brown. Pushed on 50-mile sorties into Iraq well before hostilities formally began, they bore the brunt of missions that formerly would have been assigned to types like the SR-71A—and at a cost. Maj Barry Henderson and Lt-Col Stephen Schramm lost their lives on 8 October 1990 in sharkmouthed RF-4C 64-044 during the 'Desert Shield' work-up while performing long-range photography deep in Iraq, their stricken machine plummeting into the Persian Gulf on the return leg. A second Alabama jet (64-1056) was lost on 31 March the following year while performing mop-up reconnaissance in the aftermath of the campaign. Happily, this time both crew members (including a Nevada 'High Roller' Guardsman at the helm) successfully ejected in their zero-zero Martin Baker Mk 7 seats. The unit handled its job magnificently and will continue to fulfil this task until the last few remaining ANG 'Photo-Phantoms' are withdrawn from service during the course of 1993–94, leaving only a handful of export models in service overseas with the air arms of Greece, Spain and Turkey and some other select users.[3]

---

[3]Spain received twelve ex-USAF RF-4Cs and the Republic of Korea eighteen such examples. RF-4E new-builds for export included those to Israel discussed below, eight to Greece, sixteen (of 32 built) for Iran, fourteen (designated RF-4EJ) to Japan, eight to Turkey and a hefty 88 (about to be retired) to Germany. Greece and Turkey also employ LOROPS on selected machines.

'Two out of three ain't bad', as the saying goes, and the *Heyl Ha'Avir* well knows it. Client for eighteen RF-4E J79-GE-17-powered versions of the photo-snapping *Kurnass* ('Hammer', as part of some 204 Phantoms which were bought or scrounged on various Foreign Military Sales deals), Israel has seen its 'Photo-Phantoms' embroiled in numerous actions ever since the War of Attrition at the beginning of the 1970s; one-third of the aircraft have been stricken from the inventory in combat and related operations. The beleaguered but highly respected Israeli air arm has always placed reconnaissance amongst its top-priority defence programmes, and 'Scout' UAVs and RF-4Es have been instrumental in assisting with the service's better-publicized successes (the extraction of civilian hostages in Uganda in 1976, code-named Operation 'Thunderbolt', and the annihilation of Syrian anti-aircraft defences in the Beka'ar Valley in 1982 counted among the greatest). Far less is heard about its F-4E (Specials), comprising a trio of 'Phantom Phighters' (69-7567, -7570 and -7576) which were gutted by General Dynamics and fitted with its HIAC-1 in brand new, 1ft-extended gunless noses turned over to the task. Offering 3ft resolution at ranges of sixty miles in the clear Middle Eastern skies, the project originally called for the installation of water-injection saddle tanks to boost engine performance to a steady-state cruise capability of Mach 2.7. However, only the HIAC portion of the retrofit was eventually completed, and two of the beasts remain operational to this day (one having been shot down on 24 June 1982, the sole F-4 casualty suffered during the Beka'ar operation; its sensitive wreckage was the attention of a follow-on rocket strike, which demolished its remains, along with eleven Soviet engineers engaged in dismantling its equipment.)

'CLICK A**'
While RF-4s battled their way over Hanoi *et environs* in search of increasingly elusive lucrative targets, carrier-borne jets operating with Task Force 77—the

Above: 'The goods' arriving at the Goodyear PPIF for processing. The resultant negatives are then printed, the film is checked for density and data are gleaned from the imagery—a process which may take several hours and which is combined with air crew 'MisReps' and 'SitReps' (Mission and Situation Reports) before being conveyed to the 'end user' (typically Air Force and Army theatre commanders). (USAF/A1C Andy Rice)

Far right, top: The original TARPS pod was jury-rigged from a fuel tank and mounted on the Tomcat's intake trunks. It was first test-flown in 1977. (Grumman)

Below right: TARPS training is handled by the two Fleet Replacement Squadrons, VF-101 *Grim Reapers* at NAS Oceana, Virginia (Atlantic Fleet) and VF-124 *Gunfighters* at NAS Miramar, California (Pacific Fleet). This example belongs to VF-124 at Miramar, home of the 'Top Gun' school made famous in Tony Scott's movie. (Grumman)

'Tonkin Gulf Yacht Club'—went about their business in the equally hazardous skies above Haiphong in Route Pack IVB, monitoring shipping and the steady stream of supplies being imported from the Soviet Union. At the leading edge were Rockwell/North American's RA-5C Vigilante—the 'hottest' jet ever to have been embarked on carriers—and RF-8G adaptations of Ling-Temco-Vought's venerable Crusader, which braved 'Injun' country' to get the pictures before returning home to pound the carrier decks with their sleek airframes, filled with quality photo-recon imagery. Processed and assessed below deck by PIIs (Photo Intelligence Interpreters), the material was duly passed on to the Carrier Air Group's mission planning department in support of Navy daylight 'Alpha Strike' packages and night-time intrusions by A-6s (whose crews relied on a steady stream of target photos, BDA images and knee-board snapshots to assist them in their strikes). This frenzy of round-the-clock recce operations was maintained until 1979, when the US Navy bade farewell to its last beloved 'Vigi'. The last vestiges of the 'Camera Crusader' with its Korean War-style 'PP' photo-plane tail code followed not long afterwards. The post-Vietnam climate had not only reduced the tempo of US Navy reconnaissance operations but had also placed increasing reliance on US National Reconnaissance Organization files which could be conveyed by satellite, direct to ship.[4] In the meantime, the decision was made to make increasing use of strike cameras and E-O targeting systems being fielded on the latest models of Navy strike machines—chiefly the KB-18 strike camera fitted on A-7E Corsairs and the A-6E's TRAM (Target Recognition Attack Multisensor), which tended to obviate the need for handy-size photos—while pre- and post-strike target assessment would be relegated to a 'strap-on' recce pod. Scratching around for funds for a replacement for the epoch-making 'Vigi' was a lost cause given the renewed emphasis on EW and sigint.[5] Instead, the US Navy dipped into the USAF inventory and its own decommissioned sensors and repackaged them in a pod, to be slung under its air superiority fighter, the F-14A Tomcat.

Contractor engineering studies for an 'RF-14' originated in 1974, and TARPS followed three years later, created jointly by Grumman and the Naval Air Development Command. The team originally looked at mounting the package on the intake duct (a standard drop tank station) in order to avoid compromising the fighter's missile capability, and initial flight trials proceeded along these lines. However, this proved to be unsatisfactory because of trim and power requirements, and a standard bomb rack adaptor was jury-rigged to hold the 1,700lb pod on the starboard aft Phoenix missile station. The installation was deemed successful and the order to

[4]A major step in the automated exploitation of available recce imagery was the USN's Integrated Operational Intelligence Centers (IOIC) installed on board several 'super-carriers' during the 1960s. IOICs included a number of IBM systems and were designed to provide rapid exploitation of mission data. As in many early attempts to automate, the overall packages did not perform as desired, mostly because of the unacceptable 'downtime' associated with many of the shipborne mainframe computers. Photo-interpreters often preferred to return to manual modes, and made insufficient use of the photo film plot and viewer machines. Carriers of the smaller *Midway* class performed equally well without IOIC during the Vietnam War, though the statistics were distorted by these ships' inability to compete with the larger carriers' capacity to provide fleetwide 'intel'. The early 1980s also witnessed shortfalls in sea-going tac-air photo-recon imagery (not that this mattered much during pure peacetime operations). Imagery was obtained by satellites, and by USAF U-2Rs and SR-71As flying PARPRO missions on behalf of the NRO. Refer to the Introduction, and Chapter 2, for a fuller development of the arguments.

[5]Sigint is described in the final chapter of this book. The US Navy honed its efforts and spent its spare cash on developing advanced models of the Grumman EA-6B Prowler, E-2C Hawkeye and F-14 Tomcat, with rewarding results.

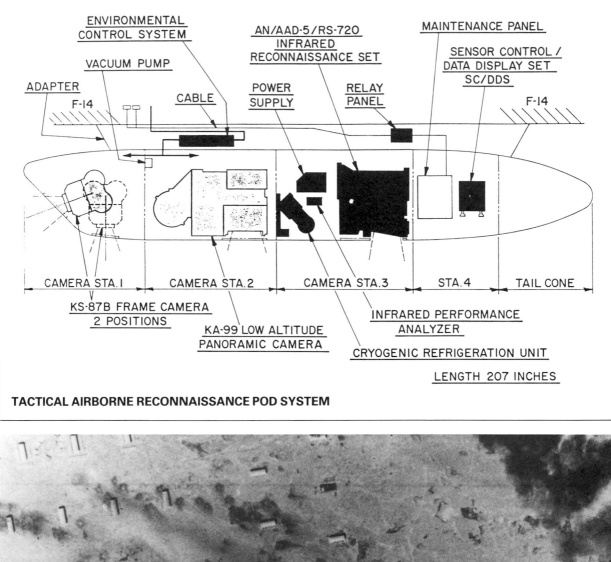

ENVIRONMENTAL CONTROL SYSTEM

VACUUM PUMP

AN/AAD-5/RS-720 INFRARED RECONNAISSANCE SET

MAINTENANCE PANEL

SENSOR CONTROL / DATA DISPLAY SET SC/DDS

ADAPTER
F-14

CABLE

POWER SUPPLY

RELAY PANEL

F-14

CAMERA STA.1

CAMERA STA.2

CAMERA STA.3

STA.4

TAIL CONE

KS-87B FRAME CAMERA 2 POSITIONS

KA-99 LOW ALTITUDE PANORAMIC CAMERA

INFRARED PERFORMANCE ANALYZER

CRYOGENIC REFRIGERATION UNIT

LENGTH 207 INCHES

TACTICAL AIRBORNE RECONNAISSANCE POD SYSTEM

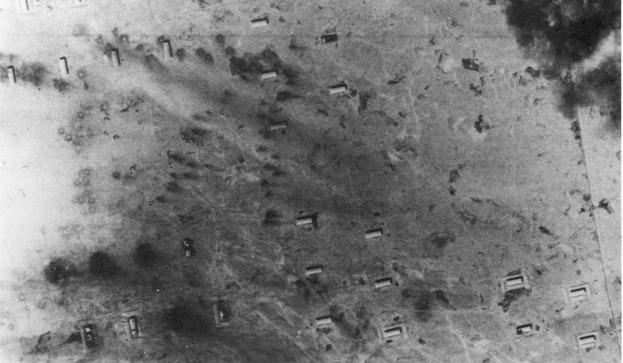

Above: The clean TARPS pod stands out clearly against this well-weathered F-14A from VF-102 *Diamondbacks*. The AIM-7M Sparrow and AIM-9M Sidewinder missiles under the starboard 'glove' pylon are carried purely for self-defence. (Raytheon)

Left: This TARPS BDA shot of 'Scud' storage bunkers at Quebaysah, Iraq, was taken by Lt Kuhn and Lt-Cdr Parsons flying with VF-32 *Swordsmen*. (US DoD)

proceed with production followed during 1979. This was undertaken by the Naval Avionics Center at Indianapolis and incorporated 'off the shelf' sensors comprising a forward oblique/vertical CAI KS-87B framing camera, a Fairchild KA-99 low-altitude panoramic camera and a Honeywell AN/AAD-5A IRLS. Modifications to 64 F-14As (all drawn from production 'tails' 138 to 504) to bring them to TARPS standard called for simple alterations to the wiring harness and the addition of a 'recon control' panel fitted to the left rear cockpit console, and the application of a TARPS logo in parentheses adjacent to the Bureau of Aeronautics number sprayed on the engine trunks. The back-seat Radar Intercept Officer (RIO) is the primary sensor manager, though the front-seater is furnished with a simple 'on/off' switch on the control column for back-up. In its all-up configuration, the aircraft's INS is used to furnish steering instructions on the pilot's head-up display (HUD) and auto-cueing of the sensors. The simplicity of the system has been the key to its success and all the latest F-14D Tomcats now joining the Fleet incorporate provisions for TARPS.

The first of 48 production and four refurbished development pods entered operational service in May 1981 when VF-84 *Jolly Rogers* deployed aboard the *USS Nimitz*. Every sea-going Carrier Air Wing (CVW) was subsequently equipped with a minimum of two TARPS Tomcats—appropriately nicknamed 'Peeping Toms'—and three fully qualified crews, which fly the unofficial mission of 'Clickin' A**'! The aircraft first saw action with VF-31 *Tomcatters* aboard the USS *John F. Kennedy* during CVW-3's Mediterranean cruise of 1983–84, where the unit clocked up 39 reconnaissance sorties over the Lebanon. Some drew hostile fire from anti-aircraft batteries but none received attention from Syrian MiGs. As the TARPS Tomcat still routinely carries a reasonable complement of weapons for self-defence (including a loaded M61A1 20mm 'Gatling' gun, plus four shoulder-mounted AIM-7M Sparrow and AIM-9M Sidewinder missiles), the machine is undoubtedly not a reconnaissance aircraft to tangle with! More recently the TARPS force, flying with live missiles plus an ECA

Above: The 'rear office' of the Grumman Tomcat is inhabited by a Naval Flight Officer, skilled at radar interception and, in some instances, the use of TARPS. The TARPS modification was applied to 64 F-14As and involved a new wire harness, additional circuit breakers and a new recon control panel on the side console. (Grumman)

(Expanded Chaff Adapator) and AN/ALQ-167 ECM pod for added protection, operated with six squadrons in support of 'Desert Storm', flying off the salty decks of five of the eight carriers deployed to the Persian Gulf and the Red Sea. One aircraft was brought down on 21 January: F-14A(Plus) BuNo 161430 (call-sign 'Clubleaf 212') was hit by a SA-2 SAM, prompting the additional ECM fit. Its pilot, Lt Devon Jones, was rescued by AFSOF, but RIO

Randolph 'Rat' Slade was captured and spent the rest of the war interned in Iraq.[6] Photo 'targets' included the traditional assortment of BDA tasks, and 'Scud' hunting according to requirements handed down in the ATO (Air Tasking Order), gearing up with a gradually increasing intensity as attention shifted away from full-time MiGCAP duties.

The US Marines, devoid of a dedicated recce machine since it retired the last of its El Toro, California-based VMFP-3 RF-4Bs on 1 October 1990, is looking to the new Advanced Tactical Airborne Reconnaissance System. Supplied by Martin Mari-

---

[6]Air Force Special Operations Forces (AFSOF) are described in Chapter 4.

F-14 TARPS SQUADRONS

Designation/nickname		Call-sign	First TARPS cruise
VF-31	*Tomcatters*	Bandwagon	1982 *John F. Kennedy*
VF-32	*Swordsmen*	Gypsy	1982 *Independence*
VF-84	*Jolly Rogers*	Victory	1981 *Nimitz*
VF-102	*Diamondbacks*	Diamondback	1982 *America*
VF-103	*Sluggers*	Clubleaf	1984 *Saratoga*
VF-111	*Sundowners*	Sundowner	1984 *Carl Vinson*
VF-143	*Pukin' Dogs*	Taproom	1985 *Dwight D. Eisenhower*
VF-154	*Black Knights*	Black Knight	1985 *Constellation*
VF-202	*Superheats*	Superheat	1988 *America*[1]
VF-211	*Checkmates*	Checkmate	1983 *Ranger*
VF-213	*Black Lions*	Blacklion	1982 *Enterprise*
VF-302	*Stallions*	Stallion	1988 *Enterprise*[2]

[1] USNR. Carrier Qualifications (CARQUAL) only.
[2] USNR. CARQUAL and two-week exercise, August 1988.

GULF TARPS UNITS

VF-32	*Swordsmen*	*John F. Kennedy*
VF-84	*Jolly Rogers*	*Theodore Roosevelt*
VF-102	*Diamondbacks*	*America*
VF-103	*Sluggers*	*Saratoga*
VF-143	*Pukin' Dogs*	*Eisenhower*

F-14A TARPS TOMCATS, BY BuNos

159951	161134–161135	161164–161165	161621–161622
159606	161137–161138	161167–116168	161624–161626
159612	161140–161141		
	161143–161144	161270–161273	161864
160696	161146–161147	161275–161278	161866
160910–160911	161149–161150	161280–161283	161868
160914–160916	161152–161153	161285–161286	
160920–160921	161155–161156		
160925–160926	161158–161159	161604–161605	
160930	161161–161162	161611	

All 49 new-build and converted F-14Ds are TARPS-capable, and have been omitted as they are easily distinguished. Data courtesy Grumman Aerospace.

PRIMARY RF-4 AND TARPS CAMERA SYSTEMS

Camera designation	Primary use	Image format (in)	Optical angular coverage	Focal length (in)
KS-87A/B CAI-Recon Optical	Day/night	4.5×4.5	73°44'	3
			41°06'	6
			21°14'	12
			14°14'	18
KA-56 Fairchild	Lo-alt day	4.5×9.4	73°44'	3
KA-1 (CA-13b) Fairchild	Med/hi-alt day	9×18	41°06'×73°44'	12
			21°14'×41°06'	24
			14°14'×21°14'	36
KA-91B CAI-RO	Med-alt day	4.5×18.8	14°14'×60°	18
		4.5×29.2	14°14'×93°	18
KA-82A-C Fairchild	Med-alt	4.5×29.3	21°×140°	12
KA-99A Fairchild	Day	4.5×28.3	28°×180°	9
KA-102A Itek	Day stand-off LOROP	4.5×4.5	3°54'	66

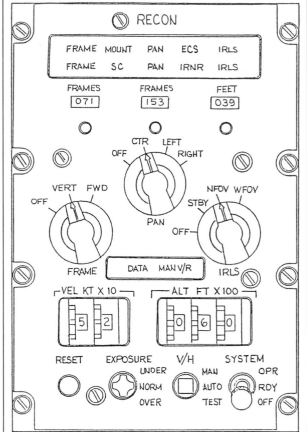

Above: VF-84 *Jolly Rogers* TARPS imagery depicting hardened aircraft shelters at Ahmed Al Jaber Air Base, Kuwait, shows the degree of resolution that can be obatined with traditional cameras—albeit at low level. (US DoD)

Above right: F-14 TARPS recon panel detail.

etta of Orlando, Florida, ATARS is a US joint-service project designed to upgrade all tac-recon assets with a common, modular integrated E-O sensor which will provide round-the-round reconnaissance directly to combat commanders through ground and shipborne Joint Services Imagery Processing System (JSIPS) terminals. Contractor flight tests are under way at Eglin AFB, Florida, on board an RF-4C Phantom II, while full sensor suites have been delivered for trials at NAS Patuxent River, Maryland; full-scale Development Test & Evaluation was scheduled to begin late in 1992. However, domestic American Phantoms are not being considered for the role, and in its operational guise ATARS will be packaged as a pod for carriage aboard RF-16s and as a pallet to be stuffed into the nose of the F/A-18D(RC) and TRA Model 234 UAV.[7] The package comprises two Chicago Aerial Industries (low- and medium-altitude) E-O sensors and an IRLS, with options (subject to space in the user aircraft) for a LOROPS and SAR radar. The heart

of the modular system is the Reconnaissance Management System (RMS), a 32-bit processor which handles all image-formatting and the interface with the host aircraft. For use in the UAV, a pre-planned mission is stored and executed by the RMS, ensuring that the correct sensor configuration is selected for each 'target'; in manned aircraft, the RMS provides live or recorded imagery for in-flight editing by the crew. It is a completely digital 'dry film' system using only Charged Coupled Devices (CCDs) tied to tape recorders. While this approach has not advanced to provide the same degree of image acuity as traditional 'wet film' reconnaissance, the system works in 'near real-time' and so has speed on its side: commanders can anticipate a delay of a quarter of an hour as opposed to anything up to four hours, as related earlier, for photo images. The other advantage is that it is environmentally sound . . . yes, even the

[7]The Model 234 UAV is described in Chapter 1. An RF-18 nose configuration was test-flown several years ago on on BuNo 160775. The equipment was subsequently transferred to BuNo 161214, which still flies at NAS Patuxent River, Maryland, and will shortly serve as ATARS test-bed for the US Navy and Marine Corps. The operational F/A-18D(RC) twin-seater will carry ATARS and a centre-line SAR pod, and the first such examples are destined to be allocated to VMFA(AW)-225 *Vagabonds*.

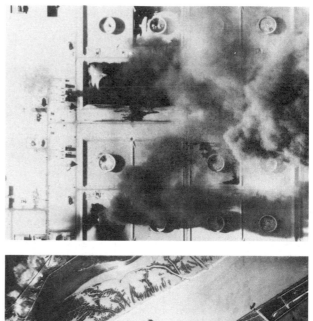

military are under pressure to conform to modern trends! The all-electronic process eliminates the logistics burden for film processing, which traditionally involves large quantities of water, acids, bleaches and silver-based chemicals, creating waste products which necessitate special handling. International orders for the modular system will probably follow its entry into US service later this decade. Low-rate initial production is planned for 1994, with the US Marine Corps kicking-off operations.

Above left: An intelligence specialist evaluates TARPS aerial photographic images aboard the USS *John F. Kennedy*, a time-consuming affair which requires considerable attention to detail. (US Navy/PH2 Charles W. Moore)

Top right: Smoke tends to obscure the target, as evidenced by this TARPS BDA shot of the Al Basrah petroleum refinery taken on 29 January 1991. (US DoD)

Above right: TARPS was kept busy long after the cessation of hostilities in 1991 as part of the continuing monitoring of Iraqi forces. This oblique photograph reveals cargo ships just south of Umm Qasr, Iraq, and demonstrates how shadows can assist by providing an instant pointer to objects of interest. (US DoD)

MIRAGE

Another contender for most widely used reconnaissance jet of the twentieth century is the best-selling high-performance Mirage 'family', produced by France's Avions Dassault-Breguet. In fact, there exist three distinct types—the single-seat III/5 (and two-seater trainer derivatives), the strategic, two-of-everything (including engines) Mirage IV and the more recent F1CR. The Mirage III/5R series, based on a sub-scale interceptor test-bed which was first flown in 1955, spawned a production run of no fewer than 1,422 examples of the famous delta-winged fighter. The purpose-designed Mirage IIIR first flew on 31 October 1961, paving the way for a production run

of fifty for *l'Armée de l'Air*, initially equipped with OMERA Type 31 cameras and progressively updated with Type 33 and 40 sensors, plus a SAT Cyclope IRLS. This equipment similarly formed the basis of the 109 export examples, with the exception of the Belgian and Pakistani variants, which employ Vinten cameras. Many nations fly the Mirage IIIR and 5R as direct-sales or hand-me-down operators: the aircraft still fetch a high price in the second-hand arms market. Among the key operators are Pakistan (thirteen Doppler-equipped IIIRPs, assigned to No 20 Squadron at Rafiqui), South Africa (four IIIRZs and four IIIR2Zs with uprated SNECMA Atar 9K50

Above: Belgium's 42nd 'Mephisto' Squadron celebrated its seventy-year-old tradition with this startling colour scheme. The Mirage 5BRs remain in service but are likely to be ousted during 1993 as part of the nation's massive cuts in defence expenditure. (Via Tim Laming)

Below: Belgian and Pakistani Mirage 5s utilize Vinten cameras instead of the *en suite* OMERA systems used elsewhere. The aircraft are operational around the globe under various flags and continue to play an important role. South Africa, in particular, makes good use of its similarly equipped Mirage IIIRZs assigned to No 2 Squadron at at Hoedspruit. (Tim Laming)

turbojets), Switzerland (eighteen IIIRSs assigned to *Fliegerstaffel* 10 at Dubendorf, built under licence by the Swiss Federal Aircraft Factory at Emmen, from which the blueprints were covertly stolen instead of being destroyed during their transfer on to micro-film, permitting Israel to manufacture its illicit Kfir) and France (which retains a token force of IIIRD trainers for 'recce familiarization' duties). Of the 5R operators, whose aircraft are based on the simplified Mirage V series, Belgium ranks top with 27 Mirage 5BRs assembled by SABCA (eighteen remaining, assigned to the 42nd 'Mephisto' Squadron, 3rd Wing, at Bierset and scheduled to be phased out in 1993 as part of Defence Minister Leo Delcroix's latest cuts), followed by Abu Dhabi (three 5RADs based at Maquatra), Colombia (two 5CORs flown under *Grupo Aéreo de Combate 1* at German Olano) and Libya (ten 5DRs at Gemal Abdel Nasser air base). Although teetering on the obsolescent and a little dog-eared, the aircraft are likely to remain in service into the next millenium in limited quantities. As spares are readily available on the black market, even Dassault can no longer keep tabs on all surviving airframes and the numerous III/5 pure fighters percolating down into Third World air force use which can be jury-rigged with limited reconnaissance hardware. The Israeli Aircraft Industries batches and South African 'production' lines have further complicated any such efforts.

Strictly supervised for safety and security are the eighteen updated Mirage IVPs (selected from the survivors of an original production run of 62 IVAs produced up to March 1968), which equip two squadrons of France's go-it-alone nuclear *Force de Frappe*: EB 1/91 *Gascoigne*, and EB 2/91 *Bretagne*, each with seven machines and based at *Base Aérienne* (BA) 118, Mont-de-Marsan, in Cazaux, south

Above: A trio of *Force Aérienne Belge/Belgische Luchtmacht* Mirage 5BRs show the flag. The camouflage scheme is a NATO left-over originally introduced by the USAF in the late 1960s. (Christian Gerard)

Below: Sporting its conventional grey camouflage, the slick Mirage F1CR shows off its Dassault COR-2 optical pod, one of several that may be strapped to the centre-line point to gather additional reconnaissance. (Dassault Aviaplans)

of the Bassin d'Arcachon, respectively, with *Escadre de Bombardement* 91 (with detachments at BA115 Orange and BA125 Istres, distributed in this manner to reduce its vulnerability to a pre-emptive attack). An additional trio were assigned to Bordeaux/Merignac with the operational conversion unit 1/328 CIFAS (*Centre d'Instruction Forces Aériennes Stratégiques*), nicknamed 'Aquitaine'.[8] The aircraft's primary assignment is nuclear attack, using ASMP (*Air-Sol Moyenne Portée*) missiles fitted with 300 kilotonne warheads, but reconnaissance—usually a long-legged affair—is an important part of the crews' brief. At any one time four of the Mirages are plumbed in with Dassault CT52 pods toting OMERA Type 35 and 36 cameras and SAT 'Super Cyclope' IRLS. Most missions are flown from the domestic BAs for training purposes, though the crews enjoy 'first call' on the service's Boeing KC-135FR Stratotankers, and training detachments have winged their way around the globe on various excursions, including joint exercises in the Continental United States with ACC's 'heavies'.

The final member of the Mirage family to enter *le domaine de la reconnaissance optique et infrarouge* is the dart-like F1CR. This exclusively equips the *Escadre de Reconnaissance* 33 at BA124 Strasbourg/Entzheim in north-east France, split into three flights: ER 1/33 *Belfort* and 2/33 *Savoie*, fully operational with an authorized unit establishment of eighteen aircraft apiece; and ER 3/33 *Moselles*, a conversion unit with fourteen F1CRs and four Mirage IIIRD twin-seat trainers. The sensor equipment is integrated with the central SNAR navigation computer, Uliss 47 INS and Cyrano IV-MR ground-mapping radar and optimized for low/medium-altitude reconnaissance work using an internal fit of OMERA-33 vertical and -40 panoramic cameras and the aptly named 'Super Cyclope' WCM 2400 IRLS (which replaced the starboard DEFA cannon). A 'near real-time' capability is made possible by means of SARA (the *Système Aérotransportable de Reconnaissance Aérienne*), composed of nine portable shelters complete with provision for NBC (nuclear, biological and chemical warfare) protection. For higher altitude and stand-off work, one of three pods may be strapped to the centre-line station, air-conditioned by the fighter's SNECMA Atar 9K50 engine: the COR-2 (*Conteneur Optique de Reconnaissance*) which employs variable-angle day/night OMERA cameras of up to 600mm (24in) focal length; the Dassault *haute altitude, grande distance* 'Harold', fitted with a 1,700mm (66in) focal length LOROP which is capable, in clear weather, of classifying objects as small as 1m (3ft) at a slant range of 50km (30 miles); and the Thomson-CSF/Raphael-TH *nacelle radar de photographie aérienne*, a SLAR which works very much like the Loral systems installed in the 'Photo-Phantom'. The options are shortly to be increased when the Thomson-CSF

[8]CIFAS 1/328 disbanded on 1 September 1991 but the aircraft remained in place with the training job administered by EB 91 until the task was transferred to the operational bases on 1 July 1992. A grand total of nineteen Mirage IVPs were adapted from IVA stock, the final aircraft acting as an attrition replacement for one of the main batch of eighteen (delivered between 12 February 1985 and 9 December 1987) which was written off only a week before the programme was completed.

Above: A crisp, almost toy-like study of a Mirage F1CR wearing a fresh coat of 'Chad sand and brown', later employed with equal effect over Kuwait and Iraq. Assigned to the 33e *Escadre* at Strasbourg/Entzeim, the force is destined to move to Colmar/Meyenheim within the next two years. (Dassault Aviaplans)

Below: A stalky undercarriage is one of the F1CR's characteristic features. Forty-five aircraft remain operational at any one time, dispersed at the 'home drome', Chad, the Gulf and various training venues. (Christian Gerard)

ASTAC elint pod is issued. Capability is also being bolstered by the addition of the Dassault TRT Intertechnique FLIR pod. This features wide and narrow FOVs ('Grand Champ' and 'Petit Champ'), automatic search and target-tracking and recording facilities, as an aid to low-level night-time reconnaissance.[9]

Despite its comparatively small size (measuring up at just over 50ft long, with a 30ft wing span), by means of twin external tanks the F1CR can muster sufficient fuel capacity to conduct patrols of up to two hours' duration, including dashes at up to Mach 2.2. Its low approach and 125kt landing speeds, STOL characteristics and medium-pressure tyres also

make it ideal for forward-based operations from roughly prepared fields. Unlike many of the other machines described in this chapter, the F1CR can also be 'turned around' extremely rapidly using integrated maintenance techniques: it takes six minutes to 'gas it up' using a single-point pressure refuelling system and no more than ten to turn around the recce pods and internal systems. Its 4.5 maintenance man-hours/flight-hour is also impressive, making it popular with overseas customers, many of whom have procured the 'vanilla' fighter variant wired up for the COR-2 and other off-the-shelf reconnaissance pods. However, the F1CR purpose-built model is unique to *l'Armée de l'Air*, which received all 64 production examples following the maiden flight of the test-bed F1CR-200 on 20 November 1981. Operations, as part of the FATac (*Force Aérienne Tactique*), have seen it committed to combat in two theatres. First came Chad. A pair of F1CRs have been maintained there since early 1987, to

---

[9]ASTAC is described in Chapter 5, in the context of elint.

Above left: Vaulting from the bow of the French aircraft carrier *Foch*, an Etendard IVP takes to the air with OMERA cameras tucked in its angular nose and belly pack . . . (Dassault Aviaplans)

Below left: . . . and another *Flotille* 16F Etendard IVP drops its hook on approach to the bow of the carrier *Clemenceau*. The dozen remaining Dassault-Breguet Etendard IVPs are land-based at Landivisiau between cruises. (Dassault Aviaplans)

Above: Two recce versions of the Viggen serve in the cool

Scandinavian region: the SH37 maritime reconnaissance mark housing Ericsson PS-37/A radar and the chisel-nosed SF37 photint version. Saab manufactured twenty-six of each type for the *Svenska Flygvapen* and these serve with three Wings, *Flygflottilj* 13, 17 and 21, based at Bravalla, Ronneby and Lulea-Kallax respectively. Seen here is the SF37 model, complete with FFV 'Red Baron' reconnaissance pod housing additional cameras and TI IRLS. (Saab-Scania/A. Anderson)

Below: Typical IRLS imagery from a 'Red Baron' pod.

monitor Libyan incursions and provide BDA for such manoeuvres as the big showdown of 5 September, when 22 Libyan aircraft were destroyed on the ground by hit-and-run Chad army forces. The cease-fire that followed did not curtail reconnaissance operations, which continue to this day from the newly constructed base at Faya. It was for these missions that the two-tone desert tan and sky blue camouflage was introduced to selected machines, which later proved perfect for Operation 'Daguet', France's contribution to the Gulf War Coalition forces. An initial squad of eight machines left Strasbourg on 3 October 1990, deploying to Al Ahsa in Saudi Arabia to reconnoitre Iraqi forces in Kuwait during the 'Desert Shield' build-up, using mainly SLAR and LOROP pods. Operations were suspended at the outbreak of hostilities: fears existed that the aircraft could not be adequately differentiated from Iraqi Mirage F1EQ fighters, although IFF (Identification Friend or Foe) 'fixes' later permitted six of them to enter the fray. Making full use of their superior radar systems and back-up strike capability, they were tasked as pathfinders in support of Jaguar As on combined strikes beginning on 26 January, and they ended the war with a respectable 114 sorties/264 hours under their belts before returning home to France in March. With ASTAC and updated ECM pods, the aircraft will soon branch out into elint. There are no plans to retire the force this century, even though attrition continues to chip away at numbers. The most recent tumble occurred on 1 June 1992. The pilot abandoned his jet after it encountered severe engine problems near Arbil over northern Iraq, while taking part in the continuing UN-sanctioned watch.

FISHBEDS, FITTERS AND FENCERS

The former Eastern Bloc has also been prodigious in the development of tactical reconnaissance aircraft, so vital for keeping track of events around its huge borders. The Russian Mikoyan-Gurevich design team continues to support the out-of-production MiG-21R (version 94R, NATO code-name 'Fishbed-J'). Just as with the Phantom and Mirage, the abundant MiG-21 began its life as a pure interceptor and its lineage can be traced to the Ye-2, which first took to the air as long ago as 14 February 1955. The reconnaissance model, the tenth in the series, introduced a semi-permanent ventral recce pack housing an AFA-39m sideways-looking camera with synchronized photo-flash port for night-time work (in lieu of the traditional 'strap-on' GSh-23L twin-barrel cannon fit), optimized for low-altitude optical photography. The more specialized MiG-21RF (version 96R, NATO code-name 'Fishbed-H') was fielded with a more powerful Tumansky R-13-300 turbojet rated at 6,600kg

Top: RF-104G Starfighters equip the Italian 28° and 132° *Gruppi* of the 3° *Stormo* at Villafranca. The Orpheus recce pod is one of their trademarks. Half a dozen of the aircraft deployed to Turkey in January 1991 as part of Italy's contribution to 'Desert Storm'. (Via Tim Laming)

Centre: The spectacular Saab RF35 bowed out of service on 31 December 1991 when the sole remaining Danish Draken squadron of the *Kongelige Danske Flyvevabnet*, *Esk* 725, formally disbanded. However, any book on 'spyplanes' would be incomplete without a last glimpse at the cranked-wing supersonic machine. Closest to the camera is a TF35 recce-capable trainer (one of eleven received by Denmark between 1969 and 1973), while the tail of a standard RF35 (one of twenty procured) lurks behind. (Author)

Above: Portugal's *Force Aérea Portuguesa* remains the last full-time operator of the famous Aeritalia G.91R-3/4 'Gina' (the *Aeronautica Militare Italiane* force at Treviso having flown its last sortie on 9 April 1992) and one of its number wears these flamboyant feline markings. The aircraft is popular with its pilots, even if it is a little short on performance and systems by today's standards. (*Flying Colours*)

(14,550lb) and a bigger pod containing provisions for IRLS. Both types can be readily distinguished from the ubiquitous fighter variants by the presence of ESM pods on the fin tips, although they are becoming increasingly scarce as their withdrawal from front-line service is hastened. The Commonwealth of Independent States still has some sixty copies on strength (excluding fifteen which have been on permanent 'loan' to Afghanistan, where the type saw considerable combat action flying from Kabul under the 263rd Independent Tactical Reconnaissance Squadron, V-VS, and subsequently the Afghan Air Force), while client nations include Czechoslovakia, with some 40 'Fishbed-Hs' divided between two regiments, and Poland, with 35. However, their days are numbered, as the former Warsaw Pact nations scratch around for scarce operating and maintenance funds and consign obsolescent equipment to open storage or the fire dump in favour of newer,

more capable machines which can switch roles by means of 'strap on' recce pods: in the East also, specialized reconnaissance and electronic support aircraft, of which the V-VS alone boasted a mighty force of 600 jets, are rapidly becoming a luxury reserved for special operations. Within this new framework, the smaller MiGs and the aged and esoteric fleets of Yakolev Yak-28 'Brewers' and Sukhoi Su-17 'Fitters', are being gradually supplanted by a more streamlined swing-role force, which in turn is being pulled back within the new borders of the CIS.

Foremost among the newcomers is Sukhoi's formidable Su-24MR (*Modifikatsii Razvedchik*), NATO code-name 'Fencer-E', capable of conducting long-range nuclear or conventional strike as well as all-weather reconnaissance by means of Efir-1M and Shpil-2M pods, an internal IRLS fit comprising two scanners and a nose turned over to SAR radar; and its stablemate the 'Fencer-F', which features similar arrays of flush dielectric nose panels, in this instance dedictated to elint and ESM operations.[10] These specialized models are relatively recent acquisitions, having first entered service with the Baltic Regiments at the beginning of 1987, honed to interdiction and maritime support. Current estimates indicate that over 100 examples are serving in the key military

Above: A mighty Su-17M-4 'Fitter-K' at rest at Kunmadaras. Ten of these machines flew from the Hungarian base, alongside a trio of Su-17UM 'Fitter-G' twin-seaters. (Ka'Roly Gere via Ga'bor Szekeres)

Left: 'Fitter-H/Ks' garnered their recce by means of the hefty centre-line KKR multiple-sensor reconnaissance pod. (Ka'Roly Gere via Ga'bor Szekeres)

Below left: Su-17UM-3K twin-seaters flew countermeasures support using a pair of wing-mounted SPS active jammers. (Ka'Roly Gere via Ga'bor Szekeres)

districts adjacent to the Baltic, Atlantic and Bering Sea. Closer to the heart of Europe, 'Fencer-E/Fs' can be observed operating under tight security with 11 RAP at Welzow air base near Dresden, where they will remain operational throughout 1993. Until very recently, the base oozed reconnaissance capability: Welzow was also home to a squad of MiG-25 'Foxbats' belonging to 931 RAP which, with the 'Fencers', formed the bulk of the former Soviet Union's forward-deployed tactical reconnaissance machines facing NATO. However, despite the winding-down process under way there, spotters are advised not to spend too much time with their noses pressed against the perimeter wire![11]

---

[10]See Chapter 5.

[11]See Chapter 2 for a fuller account of the MiG-25R/RB 'Foxbat'. A third recce regiment, 294 RAP, was based at Allstedt and operated the Su-17M3 'Fitter-H' and some dual-seat Su-17UM3 'Fitter-G' models until it returned to Russia in early 1991.

Above: Su-24MR (*Modifikatsii Razvedchik*) 'Fencer-Es' serve with 11 RAP at Welzow in the recce-strike role. In size and performance they closely match the RAAF's RF-111C 'Photo Pig' but are operational in significantly larger numbers. (M. D. Tabak via Frank Visser)

Below: With ground crew on the intercom, the crew of an Su-24MR prepare to launch from Kunmadaras, east of Budapest. The Hungarian station housed a large Soviet reconnaissance force which included two dozen 'Fencer-Es' and 'Fitter-H' reconnaissance jets and a number of MiG-27 'Floggers'. The base was officially closed on 21 April 1991 as part of the general retreat of CIS hardware in the aftermath of the collapse of the Soviet Union. The conspicuous main undercarriage doors of the 'swinger' also serve as air brakes, another feature 'borrowed' from its US counterpart the F-111. (Ka'Roly Gere via Ga'bor Szekeres)

SWING-WING SWING-ROLERS

With its two-man side-by-side crew arrangement, variable-geometry wings, maximum take-off weight in the vicinity of 90,000lb and ability to fly 'hands off' at low-level at speeds of up to Mach 1.2 using terrain-following radar, the 'Fencer' bears a remarkable similarity to its American counterpart the General Dynamics F-111 'Aardvark', the West's first 'swing-wing' operational fighter jet.

The much-maligned 'Vark', alias the 'Earthpig' (and plain and simple 'Pig' to its antipodean operators the Royal Australian Air Force) first saw combat as an interdictor in March 1968 when Col 'Ike' Dethman led his six-ship 'Combat Lancer' detachment to Takhli in Thailand to prove the concept of autonomous low-level bombing under the cover of

Above: The Su-24MR's twin infra-red scanner fit is evident here, along with belly-mounted ECM, as a crew amble to the runway with further 'Fencers' in attendance. (Ka'Roly Gere via Ga'bor Szekeres)

Below: Soaking up the sun between 'Red Flag' excursions from Nellis, RAAF RF-111C A8-146 sits with its red tarpaulin protecting its sensitive static pressure sensors from the ravages of the Nevada heat. (M-Slides via Peter E. Davies)

darkness. Although the F-111's baptism in Vietnam met with mixed results (three machines were lost during 55 combat sorties, one to hostile fire while in a holding pattern over Laos, another to pilot error and a third whose demise was traced to structural failure), the groundwork was successfully laid for a production run which eventually totalled 562 strike aircraft and lasted until November 1976. It was

during this troubled teething stage that the F-111's manufacturers began to explore the possibilities of a reconnaissance derivative: the 'Vark' was the first tactical aircraft to feature a totally self-adaptive flight control system and this rendered it 'as smooth as glass' throughout the performance envelope. Coupled with fully automatic 'hands off' TFR, a capable ground-mapping radar, unmatched range and pay-load and a state-of-the-art cockpit (for its era), it made an ideal candidate for reconnaissance duties. In all, GD attempted to sell three recce versions of the Texan 'do-it-all' bomber to the Pentagon, but the programme repeatedly stumbled on stony ground while being driven roughshod by three successive Secretaries for Defense.[12] Instead, that honour lay with the RAAF, the sole export customer for the pioneering 'Pig' under Project 'Peace Lamb', which had from the outset expressed interest in the RF-111A effort and, upon its cancellation, announced a clear intention to convert a selected number of its custom-built F-111Cs—built, but at that time not yet delivered—for the task.

Project definition was established initially in 1975, two years after the aircraft had begun to settle into their new domain at RAAF Amberley, 50 miles west of Brisbane. Government approval followed in July 1977, and F-111C A8-126 was flown back to its birthplace at Fort Worth to be gutted and remodelled. The converted aircraft was rolled out again on 18 April 1979, initial flight-test work being performed by Sqn Ldr Kevin Leo and Flt Lt Andy Kemble, who confirmed the machine's excellent handling qualities before follow-on trials with the new array of sensors took place 'down under' at RAAF Darwin, Northern Territory. By December the programme had received a full 'thumbs-up' and during the following year three additional aircraft, A8-134, -143 and -146, were modified to the task by RAAF personnel from No 482 Squadron and No 3 Aircraft Depot, drawing on retrofit kits fabricated by GD. The main historical feature of this programme is that it represented the first true application of the 'swing role' recce-strike concept. Unwittingly, the RAAF set a trend which has now become the norm: that of using high-perform-ance fighter-bombers equipped with an internal

complement of sensors for dual-role tactical recce-strike. The RF-111Cs did lose their weapons bay capability (which had seldom been used for the optional M61A1 'Gatling' gun but rather for lugging aircrew baggage), but the machine's overall strike capability was in no way compromised. The full Mk 1 nav-and-attack system was retained for all-weather radar-bombing, matched to up to twelve tons of bombs and fuel, carried snugly underwing on

Below: Four RF-111Cs were converted from standard 'Charlie' stock between 1979 and 1981 and form the most potent reconnaissance force in the Pacific Rim. The weapons bay was modified into this hinged pallet to house the cameras and IRLS, but up to eight tons of bombs and missiles may still be carried underwing on snug streamlined racks. (RAAF)

Bottom: Gulf veteran Capt Craig 'Quizmo' Brown in his ground-based 'office', the ops room of the 494th *Panthers* at RAF Lakenheath in Suffolk. 'Quizmo' now flies the same Pave Tack F-111Fs with the 524th *Hounds* at Cannon AFB, New Mexico. The mission planning room is stuffed with fresh maps, cursors and flight-planning tables, plus a portable Mission Modelling System computer . . . and the essential bottomless coffee pot. (Author)

---

[12]The $118 million programme (expensive by 1960s standards) involved re-working Research & Development F-111A No 11 (63-9776) to accept a dedicated reconnaissance pallet housing Hycon KA-55 12in high-altitude and Fairchild KA-56 low-altitude panoramic cameras, Texas Instruments IRLS, framing cameras synchronized with flares for night-time operations and a twin set of Westinghouse Electric AN/APD-8 SLARs mounted in slim radomes facing abeam of the pallet, all managed by a Rockwell digital control system. Flight-test operations commenced on 17 December 1967 and plans were mooted for a force of sixty RF-111Ds for the USAF and an unspecified number of RF-111Bs for the US Navy. The programme was axed by Secretary for Defense Laird two years later.

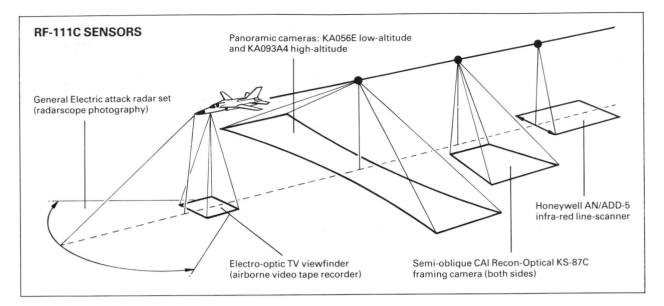

RF-111C SENSORS

Panoramic cameras: KA056E low-altitude and KA093A4 high-altitude

General Electric attack radar set (radarscope photography)

Honeywell AN/ADD-5 infra-red line-scanner

Electro-optic TV viewfinder (airborne video tape recorder)

Semi-oblique CAI Recon-Optical KS-87C framing camera (both sides)

streamlined BRUs (Bomb Release Units) and in 'slick-finned' tanks.

The sensor suite comprises a familar array of devices bought off-the-shelf from the US and mounted on a swing-down pallet fitted to the belly of the 'Pig': two CAI recon-optical KS-87C day and night framing cameras, which take semi-oblique snap-shots using 3in, 6in, 12in or 18in focal length lenses, depending on altitude and required area coverage; and the bigger Fairchild KA-56E low-altitude patch and KA-93A4 high-altitude, horizon-to-horizon panoramic cameras, contained in the ventral 'dog house' and forward bay. These produce excellent results in the clear, idyllic antipodean skies. For night-time work a Honeywell AN/AAD-5 variable-swath IRLS peeps from behind a shutter during overflight manoeuvres, while the final piece of hardware is an E-O viewfinder matched to a related cockpit display and tied to an AVTR. The fit is very similar to that employed on the old RF-4 'Photo-Phantom' and is used in much the same manner. Additional intelligence may be garnered from the nose-mounted KB-18A strike camera (which pro-duces a nose-to-tail perspective of the ground track) and GE AN/APQ-113 Attack Radar Set (ARS), which, by means of radarscope photography, provides a useful forward-scanning substitute for a SLAR sensor as well as being the 'big eye' for navigation and ground attack. Assigned to No 6 Squadron, who fly with the call-sign 'Falcon', this modest-size force is considered to be one of Australia's greatest military assets. Range and flexibility are considered to be the aircraft's finest virtues. As one senior RAAF officer remarked, 'You know, you can get into an F-111C in Brisbane on a black and nasty night and fly south through the Great Dividing Range, down through the

Perisher Valley and deliver bombs on a target in, say, Melbourne—all at 200ft AGL without ever seeing the ground. You can use it on an anti-shipping strike in the morning against a target in the vicinity of Cocos Island and conduct recce of a land target 2,000 miles distant from that on the same evening.' Typical profiles call for take-off and climb to FL270 for optimum cruise, a drop down to low-level TFR at 200ft AGL over a 400nm radius, with pop-up to the required altitude for the reconnaissance pass, and then a return home at cruise height using a mirrored profile. This can embrace an impressive 1,000nm radius in tropical conditions—more if AAR support is available. The RF-111C has never gone to war. However, exercises have proved this capability beyond doubt. Detachments of up to three machines have been assigned to New Zealand for 'Triad' events; west to the Indian Ocean and north beyond the Timor Sea to Indonesia and Malaysia in support of No 82 Strike Wing's 'blue water' tasking; to 'Coral Sea' frolics with the American Pacific Air Forces; and on further adventures to Bergstrom AFB, Texas, for participation in RAMs (Reconnaissance Air Meets), where its night-time prowess topped the billboard. 'Red Flag' integrated wargames at Nellis AFB, Nevada, have also pushed crews to the edge, where they have consistently acquitted themselves well by scoring top honours for 'night-time snooping'.

Mission assignments are handed down by HQ Operational Command (continental), HQ Support Command (overseas) and Defence, Air Force Office ('Defair'). Flight planning is based on maps and charts and rulers, to provide a list of navigation 'legs' for point-to-point flight, drawing on situation reports ('SitReps'), radarscope photography (RSP) and pre-dictions. Post-mission, the goal is to get the film out of the aircraft and processed as fast as possible. This is an art which has changed little in several decades and customarily entails a delay of a few hours before it lands on the desk of the end user—be it the Department of Defence or a Hornet strike unit. Support is transportable, provided by crews from the the semi-mobile PIC (Processing and Interpretation Cabin) complex, who can forward-deploy overseas or to any of the country's six 'bare bases' and live under bivouac between sessions with the chemicals and hot lines. The RF-111C's only real drawback is its vintage Litton AN/AJQ-20A Mk1 NCU/INS (navigation computer unit/inertial navigation set), which forms the core of its aged avionics. This is responsible for guiding the crew to their target in all weathers, for 'bracketing' the sensors during recce-runs and for commanding weapons release during first-pass, low-level attacks. The system requires the navigator to perform the tedious task of entering each and every waypoint and offset as the aircraft plies its way along the pre-planned navigation track, commanding the system to the next 'destination', one at a time. The somewhat long-in-the-tooth analogue avionics are also prone to break down at crucial moments in the proceedings. The same niggles are affecting the remaining eighteen of the RAAF's 'Pigs', which fly interdiction missions.[13] The aircraft have a projected service life of another fifteen years, and the decision has been made to revamp the avionics 'from the belly up' as an adjunct to the USAF/Rockwell 'Pacer Strike' programme (which aims to keep America's surviving F-111Fs at the peak of efficiency for a further decade). The two updates are broadly similar, although the Australians are opting for bigger-capacity 250K navigation computers. Among the new systems are multi-function displays (MFDs), a digital flight plan loading system and a GPS Navstar receiver linked to a new RLG (ring laser gyro) for precision navigation and sensor-cueing. Automation is making waves in mission-planning too. Horizon Technology mission data preparation equipment is on order, and this will permit the flyers to plot routes quickly on lap-top computers and then print them out for reference and upload the information directly into the aircraft. As well as speeding up the often tedious process of mission-planning, the system's Digital Terrain Elevation Data feature takes only about a minute to generate projected radar images like the ones that will appear on the ARS, thus obviating the need for teams of prediction artists to spend hours studying maps and for crews to flick through cabinets full of rolls of previously shot RSP negatives. The US is fielding similar packages as a follow-on to the service-wide MSS mission-planning support system update, able to convert raw 2-D maps into anticipated radar images, even full 3-D graphics for display in the

Above: The Loral Aeronutronic AVQ-26 Pave Tack targeting pod features the biggest man-made crystal put into series production. The resolution of the imagery from its FLIR has to be seen to be believed (DoD releases tend to comprise blow-ups extracted from the whole imagery), and the author knows: he has sat through over an hour's worth of strike imagery recorded during the Gulf War, a compilation jokingly referred to as 'The F-111F's Greatest Hits'! The Taif 'Vark' veteran depicted here shows off Pave Tack's 'beach ball' sensor head to best advantage. (Jim Rotramel)

cockpit. These are a boon to accurate navigation and targeting in adverse weather conditions, with or without E-O sensors and radar to hand. A complete digital land mass file, covering the globe, has been created and is being constantly updated. Two digital 'Varks' are now undergoing flight testing in sunny Australia and California, and all 106 RF/F-111Cs and F-111Fs at present on the inventory are destined to be revamped by the end of 1994.

Further work may see the RF-111C sensor kit upgraded with a 'near real-time' capability. The CAI KS 87 is now available as a dual-capable (i.e. film- and data-link-based) recording device, while the Honeywell AN/AAD-5 IRLS has similarly been tested in a D-500 format which permits the transmission of digitalized images direct to ground receiving stations via existing aircraft HF/UHF radio communications systems. Neither capability would degrade the availability of back-up high-acuity 'wet film', which could be processed following aircraft recovery. The shortfall in 'real time' systems is, to a certain extent, offset by the E-O strike-reconnaissance capability built into its remaining F-111Cs, distributed between No 6 Squadron and the RAAF's premier strike outfit, No 1 Squadron, the 'Supersonic Kookaburras' (call-sign 'Buckshot').

In September 1979, to keep abreast of technology in the Northern Hemisphere, the RAAF initiated a study of new 'smart' weapons systems which led to

---

[13]At the time of writing, four of the F-111Cs had been stricken in accidents (A8-136 in April 1977, A8-133 in September 1977, A8-141 in October 1978 and A8-137 in August 1979). These were replaced by four ex-USAF F-111As (67-109 and 67-112 to -114 inclusive) which were modified to Australian specifications, thus maintaining the 24-strong force of four recce-strike models, seventeen quick-strike interdictors and one full-time test article.

Above: F-111Fs from the 493rd TFS *Roosters* head for the target range with inert 'dumb' bombs during a weapons training deployment (WTD). Pave Tack has been rotated into the weapons bay, and all that is visible is the slight bulge on each aircraft's belly. (Jim Rotramel)

Below: Taif in Saudi Arabia became home for sixty-six F-111Fs belonging to Col Tom Lennon's 48th TFW(P), which conducted operations deep into Iraq using the superlative Pave Tack. From this perspective, the aircraft is barely distinguishable from the RAAF's twenty-two RF/F-111Cs, except for its 63ft (as opposed to 70ft) wings. (John 'Bear' Daughtry via Jim Rotramel).

the acquisition of American 'Pave' (Precision Avionics Vectoring Equipment) hardware. Central to this upgrade was the Loral Aeronutronic AN/AVQ-26A Pave Tack FLIR/laser targeting pod. The first test-bed was remodelled in January 1983 and the programme was completed during the course of the ensuing four years as aircraft became due for major overhauls. While much ado was made about other E-O 'smart' targeting systems' performance in the Gulf War, most

experts agree that Pave Tack is by far the best. It reigns supreme because of its enormous gallium arsenide crystal FLIR 'window', the largest single man-made crystal ever put into series production. Pilot Capt Craig 'Quizmo' Brown, who flew Pave Tack F-111Fs out of Taif, Saudi Arabia, during 'Desert Storm' and who continues to rely on its night and under-the-weather sensor capability in New Mexico and on TDY to Turkey while flying with the 524th FS *Hounds*, reckons that it was definitely what gave the F-111F its sparkling edge in performance during the Gulf War: 'That [pointing to its window] is probably the single most expensive piece of equipment on the entire aircraft.' Boresighted with the FLIR is a laser gun and receiver, and, working as a combination, these were instrumental in tracking and marking targets for destruction by means of Paveway 'smart' bombs, released from the same strike aircraft in an autonomous manoeuvre known as the 'Pave Tack Toss'. Col Tom Lennon's 48th *Statue of Liberty* Wing at Taif, equipped with sixty-six jets, obliterated 2,203 targets, achieving direct hits on at least 920 tanks, 252 artillery pieces and 245 hardened aircraft shelters. Lt-Col Tommy Crawford noted that the FLIR was able to pick out dug-in targets, by noting the different heat signatures of surface and subsurface soils which had been scraped away by bulldozers. Pave Tack's AVTR (Airborne Video Tape Recorder) feature also served as a handy BDA tool. In fact, its wide aperture provides such high-quality resolution imagery that crews have to spend an initial three months learning to work with the aircraft's attack radar alone, so that they do not become complacent at target acquisition! RAAF crews work up on No 6 Squadron's 'basic' jets (whose Pave Tack cradles are fitted with a simple drum, frequently given over to golf paraphernalia, or for cooling lager in the −40°C ambient temperatures found at cruise altitude), before learning the refined art of 'Tacking or pure recce duties. The USAF stipulates a similar learning curve, beginning with 'Strike Day' and 'Strike Night' phases on digitally updated F-111Gs (shortly to be replaced by more advanced AMP-modified F-111Es) under the 429th FTS *Buccaneers*, before novices progress to the Pave Tack, TF30-P-100-powered, gunship grey F-111Fs (the most powerful of all 'Varks') flown by the 27th FW's two operational fighter squadrons, the 522nd *Fireballs* and the 524th *Hounds*, all of which reside at the high-plains 'Vark Town' in New Mexico.

EUROPEAN WHIRLWIND

The RAF boasts a similar force within its multi-role Tornado establishment. The tasks comprise both pathfinding in 'real-time' and the collection of high-resolution IRLS imagery—the ideal blend of old and new technology. The Tornado may be short on range compared to the 'Fencer' and 'Vark', making it more dependent on AAR support and drag-inducing external tankage, and it requires considerably greater support than the 'rough field' Mirage, but it makes up for these disadvantages in other ways, including a state-of-the-art cockpit using MFDs and a nav-and-attack computer which can be fed with the complete flight plan in minutes using pocket-size, digital CPGS (Cassette Preparation Ground Station) tapes drafted in the ops room by simply running a cursor over maps. It also boasts a sharpened TFR which is a generation ahead of the F-111's antiquated system, and even this is shortly to be replaced under the Mid-Life Update programme by startling new technology—a stealthy GEC Avionics Spartan terrain-referenced navigation system linked to a 'smart' radar altimeter, which will provide 3-D 'highway-in-the-sky' graphics on the pilot's HUD fused with imagery from a GEC Sensors Thermal Imaging Common Module II, permitting safe terrain-skimming flight without the need to resort to tell-tale radar emissions which have an alarming tendency to advertise an attacking aircraft's presence. Backed with optional BAe ALARM anti-radar missiles and a GEC-Marconi TIALD (Thermal Imaging and Laser Designator) pod, Tornado is an impressive piece of kit.[14] Add to that the new 'dry film' tac-recce fit—made up of a ventral Vinten 4000 horizon-to-horizon IRLS plus two flanking BAe SLIR (sideways-looking infra-red) sensors, tied to six VCRs (video cassette recorders) stuffed into the bays previously occupied by the interdictor Tornado's seldom-used Mauser 27mm shootin' irons—and the resultant GR.1A is formidable.

The prototype of this select reconnaissance breed (ZA401), adapted from the generic Panavia consortium Tornado IDS (Interdictor Strike), first flew on 11 July 1985. A total of sixteen jets were subsequently modified with the recce suite by No 431 Maintenance Unit and issued to No 2 Squadron at RAF Laarbruch in Germany beginning in September 1988, followed by a further fourteen BAe 'Batch 7' new-builds which were issued to No 13 Squadron at RAF Honington starting in January 1990. Their combat inauguration as part of Operation 'Granby II', comprising six 'Desert Pink' GR.1As, nine crews and the mobile support team that made up the Reconnaissance Interpretation Centre (RIC) that would be deployed to Dhahran, Saudi Arabia, followed a mere twelve months later. The recce hardware had only

---

[14]TIALD features automatic target-tracking and is compact, but its small-aperture FLIR is not in the same class as Pave Tack. Five Tornados and two pods were deployed to the Gulf for Operation 'Granby', serving with No 13 Squadron.

just been installed, and so the half-dozen combat jets drawn from Laarbruch were hastily outfitted with software modifications devised by Computing Devices Company to bring them up to full operational status. By 9 January 1991 the combat crews—including four from Honington with boss Wg Cdr Glen Torpy in charge and five from Laarbruch led by Wg Cdr Al Threadgould—were working up in RAFG,

Above and top right: Two RAF squadrons formed with the GR. 1A recce-Tornado, No 2 at RAF Laarbruch, Germany, and No 13 at RAF Honington, Suffolk. The units have since joined up at RAF Marham in Norfolk. (Tim Laming)

Above right: No 2 Squadron Tornado GR.1As are prepared for a recce tasking. The machines feature a 'dry film' based reconaissance system, including a ventral Vinten 4000 horizon-to-horizon IRLS, plus two flanking BAe SLIRs tied to six video recorders and the navigator's cockpit displays. Imagery may thus be edited in flight. (Author)

flying a minimum of two sorties each to familiarize themselves with the new 'gismos'. Fitted with 495 Imperial gallon 'Hindenburger' endurance-stretching tanks, the first three machines (ZA371–373) and their crews deployed to Saudi Arabia on the 14th of the month, followed by a further trio (ZA370, ZA397 and ZA400) on the 16th, supported by TriStar K.1 tankers for the non-stop eight-hour-long ferry flights.

Like the TIALD and ALARM Tornado detachments deployed to the theatre, the GR.1A force did represent something of a 'rush job'.

Combat assignments made full use of the CPGS. Targets were issued just 2–3 hours prior to take-off (compared with the full day's notice given to strike crews) based on night-time tasking orders handed down by the Recce Cell at Coalition HQ in Riyadh,

Above: Replete with BOZ chaff pod, a 'Desert Pink' GR.1A zooms over England 250ft above the ground. The type was initiated into combat during the Gulf War under Operation 'Granby II' when six recce-Tornados and nine crews deployed to Dhahran, Saudi Arabia. Three of No 2 Squadron's GR.1As (alongside three TIALD pathfinding GR.1s of No 617 Squadron) returned there on 27 August 1992 to support Operation 'Southern Watch', aimed at enforcing the 'no-go' area south of the 32nd Parallel imposed on Iraq the previous week. (Author)

Left: TIALD imagery from the Tornado, just like that from the F-111's Pave Tack, is an extremely useful tool for BDA and crews spend a lot of time poring over replays. The pod features selectable thermal imaging and TV modes, and these have different advantages. In these two photographs of the same power station, note how the boats (the small white flecks to the left on the TV display) disappear on the thermal image while the storage tanks stand out. (GEC Ferranti)

which was responsible for 'fragging' all photo- and E-O-recon assets in the southern sectors. GR.1A 'Granby' missions kicked off with three missile-hunting sorties in western Iraq (primarily near H-2 and H-3, adjacent to the Jordanian and Syrian borders) in hot pursuit of the enemy's militarily insignificant but potentially politically fractious 'Al Hussein' and 'Al Abbas' rocket force poised to strike Israel, which moved from their shelters to pre-surveyed firing positions under cover of night. Within three days of the outbreak of hostilities, the recce detachment had already earned the popular

Above: The 1st *Staffel* of Germany's *Marinefliegergeschwader* 2 based at Eggebeck are outfitted with a centre-line MBB-Aeritalia recce pod housing two Zeiss cameras plus TI RS-710 IRLS. The aircraft fly daily 'Eastern Express' missions over the Baltic. (Author)

sobriquet 'Scudbusters', having successfully located two installations. 'Real-time' editing in the cockpit permitted the Tornados' navigators to discriminate the weapons and to convey target co-ordinates over the radio through the well-oiled command and control system to strike aircraft, thus permitting timely bombing. This remained the recce Tornados' primary assignment until the land war diverted attention to the task of reconnoitring enemy Republican Guard and Staff command vehicles, and to post-strike BDA of bridges spanning the Euphrates which had been breached by Tornado laser-bombers. Most crews flew single-ship, and operations were concluded when Flt Lt Mike Stanway and his 'nav' Sqn Ldr Roger Bennett touched down at Dhahran just after sunrise on 26 February. In all, the detachment flew 123 sorties/280 combat hours, without loss.[15]

The GR.1A was originally designed for front-line service with NATO's now somewhat anachronistic 'cutting edge' in RAF Germany, but the United Kingdom Government's *Options for Change* policy has resulted in Laarbruch's GR.1A force being 'pulled back' to within the borders of mainland Britain. The move officially took place on 3 December 1991, and both recce-strike squadrons—No 2 and No 13—are re-grouping at RAF Marham in Norfolk. This leaves

Germany's *Marinefliegergeschwader 2* as the only Tornado unit in place in central Europe with a photo-reconnaissance capability. Stationed with the 1st *Staffel* of MFG 2 at Eggebeck, these are outfitted with a centre-line MBB-Aeritalia recce pod housing two Zeiss cameras plus a Texas Instruments RS-710 IRLS, optimized for photint on daily 'Eastern Express' missions which monitor naval traffic in the Baltic.[16]

---

[15]Tornado GR.1 strike losses included three to operational causes and a further six in combat. Four RAF Jaguar GR.1A tactical reconnaissance jets also saw action during the Gulf while operating from Muharraq, Bahrain. Flying in pairs, the aircraft were fitted with either a podded Vinten LOROP camera or a regular BAe recce pod housing IRLS and an F126 survey camera. In toto, the 'JagDet' machines flew 31 recce sorties. Alongside No 1 PRU's strategic PR.9 Canberras based at RAF Wyton in Cambridgeshire, these provide traditional photo-intelligence.

[16]2/MFG 2, the second *Staffel*, operates with the Texas Instruments AGM-88 HARM anti-radar missile. The use of these weapons as an adjunct to the elint mission, and of similar weapons by other specialized versions of the Tornado, is discussed in the final chapter.

4. ANYTIME, ANYPLACE

SHOULD ANY of today's recce or strike airmen fall foul of hostile fire and successfully 'punch out' over enemy-held ground, their primary goal would be to evade capture for as long as is humanly possible. Apart from the uncertainty of what fate might befall them if captured, not to mention their military and political usefulness to the enemy, there is the morale-boosting lure of being picked up by friendly Combat Search and Rescue (CSAR) forces, which will whisk them away at speed. Responding to this dangerous task are a number of uniquely American squads which specialize in low-level pathfinding, depositing and retrieving special ground forces, reconnaissance and CSAR, under the label 'Special Operations'. During the Vietnam War they rescued hundreds of airmen from Laos and North Vietnam, often operating under intense fire. Other duties included reconnoitring and pounding the enemy Ho Chi Minh Trail in Laos with sensor-equipped gunships on 'armed recce' duties. Flying a motley collection of converted propeller-driven cargo aircraft, Korean War-vintage A-1 'Spads' and newer Sikorsky heavy-lift helicopters, they soon earned themselves the affectionate sobriquet 'The Antique Air Force'! The motto of their parent Wing, stationed at Hurlburt AFB in the steamy microclimate of Florida's swamplands, was 'Anytime, Anyplace'. Like the genie lamp in the insignia, they stood on constant call to pluck airmen from enemy territory or the inhospitable environment of icy-cold or shark-infested waters, deeds which permitted their forward-deployed elements to operate under the official guise of Air Rescue & Recovery Squadron (ARRS). The cloak finally came off during the Reagan era, when the force grew to much bigger proportions: saddened and perplexed by the failure of Operation 'Eagle Claw', the attempt to retrieve American diplomatic hostages from Teheran in April 1980, the new administration poured millions into the airborne element of the Special Operations Force (SOF), which now has considerable justification for its claims as the world's most capable special duties organization, ready to be sprung into action at a moment's notice by the President and Joint Chiefs of Staff.[1] Its hardware comprises purpose-converted Lockheed transporters backed by longed-legged Sikorsky heli-copters, on hand to provide round-the-clock CSAR and to support the US Army's elite forces: the Rangers at Fort Hunter in Georgia, the Airborne based at Fort Bragg, North Carolina, and a nearby spin-off from the acclaimed 'Green Berets', the 'Delta Force'. This aerial element is the key to the United States' more modern, flexible defence posture and has been called upon to test its mettle on many occasions in recent years.

The hub of the Air Force SOF is the Hurlburt (Eglin Auxiliary Field No 6) 1st Special Operations Wing (SOW), a component of the co-located Air Force Special Operations Command created in March 1990, which flies a diverse group of machines bearing the warlike code-names 'Spectre', 'Combat Talon', 'Combat Shadow' and 'Pave Low'. Stealth, in the broader sense, is their trade: to fly deep into hostile airspace under cover of radio silence, night and inclement weather to drop or retrieve their human cargoes, a profession described as 'infiltration/exfiltration'. Globe-trotting detachments are

Top right: Lockheed built 59 F-117A Stealth fighters for the USAF under the 'Senior Trend' programme, and 55 of these remain in service, re-assigned to Holloman AFB, New Mexico. The 37th TFW pioneered their use in combat, at the 'leading edge' of AFSOF operations in Panama. (Lockheed/Eric Schulzinger)

Centre right: With a touch-down speed in the vicinity of 165kts, the F-117A is one of few third- or fourth-generation machines in need of a drag 'chute! The USAF stipulates a 12,000ft runway, BAK (barrier arresting cable) devices and other refinements, yet the complex aircraft provide pivotal support for the more rough-and-ready elements of AFSOF. (US DoD)

Bottom right: Although primarily a bomber designed to hit hardened targets using laser-guided bombs (such as the two one-ton 'bunker-busting' GBU-27A/Bs dangling on the weapons trapezes under this jet's belly), the F-117A can operate as an electro-optic reconnaissance machine. The aircraft are being updated with new all-digital navigation systems under the OCIP (Offensive Capability Improvement Program), and plans have been mooted to install a derivative of the US Navy's TARPS into the aircraft's weapons bay; presumably this would involve new 'peep holes' in the bay doors or a conformal exterior pod relying on the copious use of RAM (radar absorbing materials) so as not to betray the presence of the stealthy 'Black Jet'. (US DoD)

---

[1]The Lockheed F-117A Stealth bomber was originally fielded for use in conjunction with the SOF on the direction of the President and JCS. Only after Congress swelled the order books to 59 aircraft—enough for a complete Fighter Wing—was the aircraft turned over for use by theatre commanders.

Left: F-117As of the 37th TFW got their second taste of action while flying out of Khamis Mushayt, Saudi Arabia, during the Gulf War. Precision targeting and BDA was made possible by a pair of synchronized TI infra-red sensors (a forward-facing FLIR, visible in this head-on view, and downward-looking DLIR, known as the IRADS, for Infra-Red Attack & Designator System) cued to the target using stored co-ordinates and constantly computed positions based on an exotic, electrostatically suspended beryllium gyro known as the SPN/GEANS. The machines flew 1,271 Gulf combat sorties without loss and worked up to the task using passive sensor techniques to gain familiarity with the terrain. (US DoD)

Above: Wearing its Vietnam-vintage matt black decor smudged with olive drab, an MC-130E takes to the air above Rhein-Main AB, Germany. Attached to the fuel tanks are a pair of Northrop AN/AAQ-8 infra-red countermeasures pods, which radiate 'puffs' of intense energy to foil heat-seeking missiles. The remarkably sprightly machine may be fitted with a reconnaissance pallet or command and control module. (MAP)

assigned to such far-flung bases as Panama, South Korea and Saudi Arabia, where the teams go about practising their clandestine business relatively unnoticed.

DE OPPRESSO LIBER

Dominating the flight-lines are the fork-nosed MC-130Es of the 1st, 7th and 8th Special Operations Squadrons, adapted from Lockheed Marietta's venerable 'Herky Bird' which first flew on 7 April 1955 and which is still bred at the company's Georgia aviary just outside Atlanta. The type forms the pivotal element of the SOF's covert long-range ingress/egress machinery and a enjoys a career which stretches back to August 1967 and the bitter days in Vietnam, when an initial batch was assigned to the 15th SOS at Nha Trang AB in support of the 'Green Berets' and Navy SEALs. The aircraft were originally conceived as C-130E-1 covert recce aircraft and were shortly afterwards nicknamed 'Skyhook' and 'Combat Talon

Blackbird'—allusions to their distinctive Robert Fulton Co Surface-to-Air Recovery System (STARS) yokes and sinister green-smudged matt black camouflage. Production eventually totalled twenty machines, the fourteen survivors of which bear the odd Block-related code-names 'Clamp', 'Swap' or 'Yank'. Two dozen brand new MC-130H 'Combat Talon 2' models, adapted by E-Systems from fresh stock and equipped with more modern cockpit multifunction displays, have been funded. These made their first appearance on the inventory on 17 October 1991 and, unlike their portly brethren tasked with pure 'trash-hauling' in low-threat environments, are adapted to fly into the thick of it using nap-of-the-earth (NOTE) tactics to avoid detection.

Avionics comprise the Texas Instruments AN/APQ-122 TFR or newer Emerson multimode AN/APQ-170 system, which permits 'hands off', earth-hugging operations down to 250ft AGL; and an infra-red detection set linked to dual INS which may be updated by AN/ARN-92 LORAN C, Doppler or GPS/Navstar (managed by no fewer than two navigators!) to ensure that the 'Combat Talon' does not drift from its intended flight-plan. With suitable training, the eleven-man crews are permitted to assume full manual control and take their thirty-five-ton 'cloud splitter' down lower—which in extremely hostile airspace would include switching off the mapping radar and flying solely by IDS, INS and radar altimeter. It is hair-raising stuff: 'the ground kills every time' (as does the sea), as the old saying goes, but heat-seeking SAMs can be more than a nuisance too. To decoy these devices, the lumbering beast is fitted with a hefty load of Tracor ALE-27 or newer -40 flare dispensers which can put on a fireworks

Above: The MC-130E 'Combat Talons' still feature Robert Fulton Co STARS forks and have a beefed-up rear cargo hatch, enabling it to be opened at low level at speeds of up to 250kts—100kts faster than the basic cargo Hercules. The aircraft specializes in infiltration/exfiltration missions where it can snatch, drop or offload payloads, including human 'cargoes' of Delta Force, Ranger, SEAL or SAS special operations troops. (MAP)

display able to match the best Fourth-of-July performance. Working in harmony with these are wing-tank-mounted Northrop AN/AAQ-8 infra-red counter-measures (IRCM) pods, which blow out invisible 'puffs' of distracting energy by means of caesium lamps.

The structure is all beef, and it can take a lot of punishment. During the ill-fated Operation 'Eagle Claw', MC-130E(Y) 64-0565 struck the ground during the ensuing mêlée at 'Desert One' (with a startled 'Delta Force' leader Col 'Charlie' A. Beckwith on board!) yet flew safely all the way to Germany. In South-East Asia, the three machines lost either flew into the ground as a result of pilot error or were hit in their revetments by the frequent Viet Cong mortar attacks. In addition to copious quantities of titanium armour plating bolted around crew compartments, the rear cargo door is modified to permit drops at speeds of up to 250kts—100kts faster than the basic C-130. A slingshot may volley pallets weighing up to 2,200lb out of the rear hatch at altitudes as low as 600ft, with staggering accuracy.[2] The older 'Echo' marks can snatch too. The aircraft drops a 'kit' which, once assembled, links the intended 'prize' to a 525ft tether attached to a 24ft × 6ft helium-filled balloon. The nasal proboscises of the 'Combat Talon'

clutch and eventually winch in the 'victim' through the rear hatch (by then dragging behind the machine). The system can handle up to two men or a 500lb load. A successful 'catch' demands that the 'Herky Bird' be aligned along its velocity vector very precisely, using plenty of rudder, to ensure that the haul rides the rear ventral fuselage guides, while Teflon-coated wires strung between the wing tips and nose act as a safeguard against the balloon tether snagging the propellers. Although STARS is generally considered obsolescent, forays into troubled Central America have sometimes demanded the use of these scissor prongs.

Last but not least, the MC-130E/Hs also serve as mobile headquarters. For operations from austere locations the type can accommodate fuel bladders, or a 'command and control' or reconnaissance 'module'. The cloak-and-dagger occupants of the cabin invariably lead a separate existence from the puzzled cockpit crew. Theoretically, the tent-based interpretation and support team is capable of operating 'in the field' without back-up for up to a month at a stretch. The machine's rough-field, STOL (short take-off and landing) performance permits stop-offs on a stretch of autobahn or a firm piece of turf, where it can bring in food or medical supplies and evacuate the wounded. Superlatives aside, at the height of

[2]In its latest guise it is designated the High-Speed Low-Level Aerial Delivery System, or HSLLADS. More recently, MC-130s have been performing trials with Pioneer Aerospace-developed 'smart' pallets that can steer payloads from drop heights of 12,000–14,000ft on to 'precise' landing co-ordinates. The 3,600ft High Glide Recovery System (HGRS) parafoil can cope with loads of up to ten tons.

Above: The 41st and 43rd Electronic Combat Squadrons operate the 'Ghost Gray' EC-130H 'Compass Call' comint and C3/CM comjam Hercules bulging with avionics and cooling scoops and fitted with a huge tail-end 'soccer net' of communications antennae. (Author)

SPECIAL OPERATIONS UNITS

Squadron		Equipment	Code	Location
Primary, Active SOF				
8	SOS	MC-130E/H		
9	SOS	HC-130P/N		
16	SOS	AC-130H/U	–	1st SOW, Hurlburt AFB, Florida; HQ AFSOF
20	SOS	MH-53J		
55	SOS	MH-60G		
7	SOS	MC-130H		39th SOW, RAF Alconbury, England; European Command
21	SOS	MH-53J		
67	SOS	HC-130P/N		
1	SOS	MC-130E		353rd SOW, Kadena AB, Okinawa; Pacific Command
17	SOS	HC-130P/N		
31	SOS	MH-53J		
1551	FTS	MH/TH-53J	–	Kirtland AFB, New Mexico RTU
Air Force Reserve and Air National Guard				
193	SOG	EC-130E	PA	Olmsted Field, Pennsylvania
815	WOF	WC-130E	–	Keesler AFB, Mississippi
919	SOG	AC-130A	–	Duke Field, Florida
Active support, Air Combat Command				
7	ACCS	EC-130E	KS	Keesler AFB, Mississippi
41	ECS	EC-130H	DM	Davis-Monthan AFB, Arizona
43	ECS	EC-130H	SB	Sembach AB, West Germany

East-West tension the 'Combat Talon' was tasked with several less altruistic jobs. Within NATO, its task was to sneak well beyond the FEBA (Forward Edge of the Battle Area) and deposit teams of SOF troops equipped with portable devices for partisan 'guerrilla atomic and chemical attacks'. Special Atomic Demolition Munitions ('SADM mines') were stockpiled in readiness for such nuclear combat, the goal being for the stealthy 'Talons' to deposit twelve-man squads who would 'assist US-sponsored indigenous leaders in establishing control over Soviet Bloc political and social structures', aerial manoeuvres that were until very recently rehearsed during 'Flintlock' exercises flown from RAF Sculthorpe and Wethersfield in England. Similar sorties were also generated for US Navy SEALs based at Machrihanish on the Mull of Kintyre and in support of tough South Korean 'grunts' on 'Team Spirit' exercises in the Pacific theatre. These forms of warfare are still possible, but attention has now shifted towards the support of US forces engaged in deep reconnaissance and sabotage.[3]

FLYING HOWITZERS

Of all Hurlburt's SOW forces, the gun-bristling AC-130s must rank as the best known. Deployed to South-East Asia from September 1967 under Maj Ronald W. Terry's 'Super Spook' Task Force to smash the never-ending convoys of North Vietnamese trucks

[3]Being dropped off, or parachuting, from one of these aircraft is infinitely preferable to the rumoured (and, if true, outrageous) technique of 'toss' bombing a rubber-clad trooper from the rotary weapons bay of the Buccaneer!

winding their way down the Ho Chi Minh Trail through Laos and Cambodia, the 16th SOS nowadays flies ten ghost-grey AC-130H 'Pave Spectre' marks which liaise with ten War-veteran 'A' models operated by the 711 SOS, Air Force Reserve (AFRes), up the road at Duke Field (Eglin Auxiliary Field No 3). 'We operate only in areas where we enjoy total air superiority' was the frank remark made by an AFRes crewman from AC-130A 53-3129, which made a courtesy visit to RAF Greenham Common in July 1981 (and which, incidentally, had been converted from the first production Hercules and was appropriately nicknamed 'The First Lady'). Nevertheless, the 'Spectres' enjoy a brisk trade which has seen them deployed to the Panama Canal Zone for clandestine recce missions over troubled El Salvador and Nicaragua under the code name 'Bield Kirk' and, more recently, to the Gulf. The AC-130's battery of 20mm 'Gatling' guns, 40mm Bofors 'pom-poms' and 105mm howitzers are 'directed' by a ballistics computer married to three cargo hold Fire Control Officer (FCO) consoles which display the imagery generated by the gunship's EW, AN/AAD-7 FLIR and AN/ASQ-145 Low Light-Level TV (LLLTV) sensors. AN/ASD-5 'Black Crow' traffic-sniffing electronic apparatus and a Korad AN/AVQ-19 laser ranging/designating gun were thrown in for good measure. Data gleaned from these devices can be taped for subsequent analysis, making the 'Spectre' an extraordinarily effective reconnaissance platform for counter-insurgency (COIN) operations. 'Black Crow', for example, can pinpoint radio transmitters, while LLLTV and FLIR can highlight the whereabouts of enemy forces hiding under a cloak of rain forest.

The days of the 'Spectre' are far from numbered. Twelve new AC-130U models equipped with Mil Std 1553B avionics-integrating databuses, modern generation MFDs and the F-15E Eagle's AN/APQ-70 synthetic aperture radar (capable of ground-mapping and beacon-plotting) are being developed by Rockwell International and will shortly oust the tired AC-130As from the AFRes inventory. At $48 million a copy, there must be plenty of faith left in the old beast yet. In common with the 'Combat Talon', the 'Spectre' features a 'female' AAR capability to extend its range or time on station and work hand in hand with special-duties F-117As as part of the broader manoeuvres performed by the US Central and Special Operations Commands. All three types navigate by infra-red and INS and have been spotted comparing notes in formation over the Mojave Desert!

Additional specialist marks of Hercules exist for tactical support and other clandestine work. Air Combat Command boasts a force of fifteen EC-130H 'Compass Call' C3/CM 'comjam' (communications-jammers) split between the 43rd ECS (Electronic Combat Squadron) at Sembach AB, Germany, and the 41st ECS at Davis-Monthan AFB, Arizona, designed to listen in on and simultaneously disrupt the enemy chain of command. These are accompanied by seven EC-130E Airborne Command & Control Centers (ABCCC), the survivors of ten developed to co-ordinate air strikes during the Vietnam War, which are currently headquartered at Keesler

AFB, Mississippi, under the 7th ACCS (Airborne Command & Control Squadron). The aircraft are equipped with a roll-in, roll-out ABCCC II AN/ASC-15 command battle staff module in their cargo bays with accommodation for up to sixteen personnel, and the crew utilize FM, VHF and UHF secure radio equipment, teletypewriters, maps and grease pencils to pick up and relay target co-ordinates and other such information from FAC (forward air controllers), tac-recce and EW support aircraft to friendly strike jets. Two new Unisys ABCCC IIIs were delivered on 5 January 1991 as part of a modernization initiative, featuring new digital systems, including satcom (satellite communications) relay links, Collins JTIDS (Joint Tactical Information Distribution System, a two-way system which feeds target co-ordinates and data relating to enemy anti-aircraft defences direct to the cockpit displays of friendly fighter-bombers) and revamped radio systems, designed around twelve automated computer 'battle' consoles managed by an AN/UYK-502 computer. This automatically sequences the appropriate radio systems—three satcom, eight UHF, eight VHF and four HF radios—built into the 47ft long module. The system may even relay colour and infra-red target photographs derived from 'Argus' or ATARS direct to attacking aircraft or ground stations, within minutes of their collection.[4] The two new ABCCC III modules became operational a matter of days prior to the outbreak of hostilities in the Gulf, and were thrown into the mêlée to help co-ordinate Coalition strikes, where they generated a total of 400 hours during the course of forty long-endurance combat sorties while operating from Riyadh in Saudi Arabia. Optical discs fed into the ABCCC IIIs contained the plans for each day's ATO (Air Tasking Order), and an operator was able to call up that fragmentary part ('frag') pertaining to the fighter or bomber he or she was talking to. It provided smooth co-ordination of what might otherwise have been total air chaos.

Perhaps the most unusual of all are the four 'psyops' EC-130E 'River Riders' of the Pennsylvania Air National Guard's 193rd SOG, which feature huge axe-head antennae under their wings, plus a dorsal fin extension and facilities to trail cable. They are code-named 'Volant Solo' and their job is to interrupt and overpower enemy civilian and military transmissions working on AM and FM radio, VHF and UHF television and military HF and VHF communications bands and broadcast specially prepared TV and radio propaganda, intermingled with live transmissions in

Above: 'Pave Spectre' 'Plain Jane' shows off her 'Black Crow' sensor. This tracks the ignition and sparking systems of trucks and other vehicles. (Author)

Below: The AC-130A 'Spectre' uses this array of AN/AJQ-24 stabilized tracking set, AN/ASQ-145 LLLTV and AN/AVQ-19 laser target designator/rangefinder to acquire and provide firing solutions for its battery of 'Gatling' guns and howitzers. (Frank B. Mormillo)

[4]ATARS and 'Argus' are discussed at the close of Chapter 1 in the context of Teledyne Ryan Aeronautical UAVs. The ability of 'Argus' to relate target images in 'near real-time' via ABCCC aerial battle command posts was first demonstrated during an autumn 1992 'Green Flag' electronic warfare exercise at Nellis AFB, Nevada.

Above: The Pennsylvania ANG operates eight Lockheed transporters, four dedicated to the 'Volant Solo' psychological warfare role and the remainder outfitted for 'Comfy Levi' comint duties.

Spanish, Farsi or whatever is required, using 'disc jockey' linguists seconded from the US Army and friendly nations. The goal is to demoralize the enemy ground forces, grab the attention of the civilian populace and do whatever else is required in the psychological warfare arena in support of US and allied interests. They have seen plenty of action. During the recent Gulf War, for example, three of the aircraft flew from Riyadh in Saudi Arabia and Abu Dhabi International Airport to transmit reassuring messages to the citizens of Kuwait City, and the same aircraft were instrumental in convincing droves of Iraqi tank crews to abandon their vehicles and surrender. In the process, they also established a record USAF 21-hour-long sortie. The air crews have flown this mission in their modified 'Fat Alberts' since 1978. Building on its recent success, the unit is modernizing its machines in a Lockheed-Ontario-led programme which is replacing the dorsal fin extension with four 'bullet' VHF transmitters, along with provisions to boost power output by an order of magnitude of 10kW. This will enable them to transmit colour TV in any format used around the world. Co-located with the 'Penny Guard' 'Volant Solos' are an additional four EC-130E 'Comfy Levi' Hercules, which fly with various palletized cargo modules rigged for the 'Senior Scout' sigint mission. Very little

is known about their assignment, but it has been reported that two of these aircraft may be reconfigured as 'Volant Solos' by 1997.[5]

Not part of the SOF, and engaged on special mission and reconnaissance duties of an altogether different nature, are the unarmed WC-130E 'Storm Trackers' of the 815th Weather Observation Flight, which share logistics support with the armada of ACC's ABCCC Hercules at Keesler AFB. Until very recently these formed part of much larger force of aircraft based in Mississippi and Guam which blithely flew into the heart of thunderstorms, the eyes of tornadoes and the walls of hurricanes to gauge their ferocity and direction (and thus the potential havoc they might wreak), to assist with the timely evacuation of villages, towns and even cities and to help with weather briefings for long-range strike crews. The bulk of the fleet reverted to pure cargo-hauling during 1991 following the stand-down of US nuclear forces, though the 815th, an AFRes unit, has been given a temporary reprieve and continues to fly this vital but bizarre form of reconnaissance. Mis-

[5] The nature of sigint is aired in the next chapter and a description of the DC-130 UAV mothership programme, another sub-mark of special-duties Hercules, can be found in Chapter 1. Additional 'stock' cargo C-130Es have from time to time been covertly equipped with sigint receivers and flown on classified missions along the former 'Iron Curtain' by the 7405th Operations Squadron out of Rhein-Main AB, Germany. These formed part of the great fleet of sigint craft described in the next chapter which generated data in support of the US Army and USAF Electronic Security Command. The overall record for refuelled time aloft is believed to be held by the RAF. During the Falklands War in 1982 Flt Lt Terry Locke and his C-130K crew spent a staggering 28 hours 3 minutes in the air.

Above: Wearing glossy FS 16473 'Aircraft Gray' are the WC-130E 'Storm Trackers' of the 815th Weather Observation Flight, stationed at Keesler AFB, Mississippi. Their most recent task was to fly into the heart of Hurricane 'Andrew', which devastated Florida on 24 August 1992. (M-Slides)

sions of note include the recent monitoring of Hurricane 'Andrew', which devastated Florida on 24 August 1992. Capt Robert Pickrell flew his crew into the thick of 'Andrew' to monitor winds and pressure and later reported that the instrument panel vibrated so violently that he was unable to read the 'neeeddlles-aand-ddiialls' for 5–10 seconds as the aircraft buffeted in $+2g$ to $-1g$! The machine was also thrashed by pea-sized hail for a quarter of an hour, which stripped paint off the wings' leading edges and crumpled some of the sheet metal. Who says that only strike crews know the meaning of danger?! In all, the unit penetrated the eye of the storm more than 40 times during seventeen separate sorties, providing vital meteorological data.[6]

SUPER JOLLY

Complementing the circus of Hercules are the heavy-lift rotary-wings, composed chiefly of Sikorsky/United Technologies Model S-65s, delivered to the USAF from 1968 as the HH-53B/C and nicknamed 'Super Jolly Green Giant' in deference to its predecessor the HH-3E. Initially issued to squadrons in South-East Asia, where the type performed sterling service extracting downed airmen from under the noses of the North Vietnamese and Laotians, a grand total of 64 'Super Jollies' were eventually ordered, including

twenty CH-53C 'Pave Knife' models built exclusively for special operations and field radar support work, many of which gained fame in the Son Tay rescue effort, the hectic evacuation of Saigon (Operation 'Frequent Wind') and the bloody *Mayaguez* incident in May 1975. Fifteen years on, the 41 survivors have undergone an extensive update called Project 'Pave Low III Enhanced' and reassignment *en bloc* to the SOF as 'new' MH-53J marks.[7] 'Pave Low III' dates back to 1977 when an initial nine machines were converted to the all-weather standard and assigned to Hurlburt and to the Kirtland AFB, New Mexico-based 1550 Aircrew Training & Test Wing (now known as the 1550th Combat Crew Training Wing) where all 'Super Jolly' training is centred. There then followed a considerable period of gestation before the full-scale programme got under way, eventually funded after it became apparent that the IFR limitations of the very similar Navy/Marine RH-53D Sea

[6]A solitary RAF Hercules W.2 (XV208), its nose fitted with a 'barber-shop' sensing proboscis and its spine sporting the relocated mapping radar, serves as a meteorological research tool, stationed at the Royal Aircraft Establishment at Farnborough and on detachment as required. It first flew in this guise on 31 March 1973, and it continues to fly today in its distinctive glossy livery.

[7]Thirty-three aircraft were converted up to 1990 to join eight survivors of the earlier HH-53H model (including two attrition replacement HH-53Hs converted in the mid-1980s). The eight 'Hotels' have since been updated to full 'Juliet' 'Pave Low III Enhanced' standard to bring the inventory up to the 41 machines mentioned, though these aircraft retain their distinguishing cantilever drop-tank braces. The refit was undertaken at the Naval Air Station at Pensacola in Florida, which is responsible for the maintenance and overhaul of all H-53s on the US inventory.

Above: The capacious Sikorsky S-65 series formed the basis for 41 MH-53J conversions. This 67th ARRS HH-53C was photographed whizzing over its old base of RAF Woodbridge, Suffolk, shortly before it underwent full conversion to the 'Pave Low IIIE' configuration. (Author)

Below: The 'Pave Low III Enhanced' modifications to the 'Super Jolly' included this collection of nasal blisters associated with the TI AN/AAQ-10 FLIR, AN/APQ-158 TF/TA radar and self-protection receivers/countermeasures. Aerodynamics were not enhanced, but night-time and under-the-weather capability certainly was. (Author)

Stallion had contributed to the failure of Operation 'Eagle Claw': of the eight ochre-coloured machines that lifted off from the deck of the *USS Nimitz* on the fateful night of 24 April 1980, only one (an early 'air abort') returned to the carrier. Crews had to fly through sandstorms using only altimeter and attitude director instruments while relying on 'dead reckoning' navigation techniques. They rapidly became exhausted, resulting in problems with vertigo (attitude disorientation); it is not a rare

occurrence when pilots are obliged to negotiate sandstorms over deserts or blizzards over ice caps or are forced to stay in the clouds too long. 'Pave Low III Enhanced' was designed specifically to overcome these limitations, and it proved its worth during Operation 'Desert Storm'. It comprises off-the-shelf INS and Doppler coupled to a projected map, plus Texas Instruments AN/AAQ-10 FLIR and multimode AN/APQ-158 terrain-following/terrain-avoidance (TF/ TA) radar to permit NOTE operations at speeds of up to 170kts in quarter-mile visibility with ceilings as low as 150ft! It also features a much enlarged fuel capacity, totalling 12,500 US gallons (including new 450 US gallon drop tanks), which doubles its radius of action to some 400 miles, along with Loral AN/ALQ-157 IRCM to decoy heat-seeking missiles. At night, the crews follow their dangerous profession by means of the dashboard read-outs and Aviation Night Vision Imaging System 6 goggles (NVG), which 'give a dreamy picture of objects out of the windshield'. With the crew keeping an eye on proceedings, the TF/TA may be coupled to the autopilot to permit closely supervised automatic terrain-following flight—a feature shared by the big 'Combat Talon'.

The MH-53J may carry 38 combat troops or 22 litters in addition to its routine crew of pilot, co-pilot, flight engineer, at least one maroon-beret pararescue jumper (PJ—a marksman, survival specialist and medic wrapped up in one) and an aerial gunner who enjoys access to three GE GAU-2A/B 7.62mm calibre miniguns (each capable of spraying up to 4,000 rounds a minute) or .50in Brownings, installed to provide covering fire during 'hot' drops and retrievals in 'Injun' country'.

Ever since the first 'Pave Low IIIE' was rolled out on 17 July 1987, freshly reconfigured aircraft have been gradually equipping the RTU at Kirtland AFB and three Special Operations Squadrons in Florida, England and the Pacific. The New Mexico-based 'Super Jolly School' also operates four ex-USMC TH-53A Sea Stallions for initial Model S-65 familiarization, while the operational units enjoy the support of HC-130N/P 'Kingships', which serve as command and control posts, and HC-130H 'Combat Shadows', which furnish hose-and-drogue AAR support or act as forward-located fuel stations. The 'Kingships' can be distinguished by their unique dorsal hump housing AN/ARD-17 'Cook Tracker' receivers, originally devised to plot re-entering capsules from spacecraft but actually of far greater use in picking up faint distress signals from below. The combined units are renowned for their daring rescue exploits. While stationed at RAF Woodbridge, the 21st SOS *Dust Devils* and 67th SOS *Night Owls* ran a hectic schedule. On 14 January 1989 a pair of their 'Super Jollies', commanded by Capt Dennis M. London and

Capt David W. Freeman, with aerial 'gas trucks' in tow, flew 1,700nm through Force 8 Atlantic gales to pick up 32 sailors from the 42,000-ton bulk carrier *Yarrawonga*, holed below the waterline 400nm west of Ireland. No other machine was capable of performing this task under such austere conditions, and for good reason too: the units' overriding objective is to ensure that there is always a CSAR presence within 30 minutes' flying time of Air Force One, the President's air taxi. Because of the tiring pre-positioning flights involved, invariably followed by extensive periods of inactive standby, the crews long ago nicknamed the mission 'duck-butt support'! The two units were moved from RAF Woodbridge to Alconbury on 20 May 1992 and are to be joined by the MC-130H-equipped 7th SOS, which is moving in from Rhein-Main in Germany; together they will comprise the 39th SOW. A similar reconsolidation is taking place under the 353rd SOW at Kadena in Okinawa. These are the two biggest concentrations of SOF aircraft to be found outside of the mainland United States.

FROM GRENADA TO THE GULF

For more than a decade now the SOF has been priming itself for limited 'crisis contingency operations'. It was given a taste of these in October 1983, shortly after it became apparent to the CIA that Cuban workers, being trained by a select group of Soviet *Spetsialnoye Natznacheyne* (Spetsnaz), were preparing to launch a *coup* on the former British colony Grenada. The lives of 1,400 American citizens were deemed to be at risk.

At around midnight on Monday the 24th, an airborne troop of eight SOS MC-130Es converged on the island to deposit SEALs, an element of the Delta Force and 75th Rangers, most of whom dropped to earth using daring HALO (high-altitude, low-opening) procedures. Sent in to destroy gun positions which endangered the subsequent Marine Corps and 82nd Airborne reinforcements, they were backed by 'Spectres' flying racetrack patterns over the landing zones for up to sixteen hours at a stretch, which successfully knocked out several People's Revolutionary Army heavy emplacements and armoured vehicles which threatened to inflict significant damage. Loitering 'feet-wet' off the coastline, Pennsylvania ANG 'psyops' EC-130Es broadcast pre-recorded tapes to pacify the bewildered locals, including evacuation instructions. Resistance was stiffer than anticipated but the island was secured within eight days and the students were repatriated before Havana could intervene with heavy forces. The success of Operation 'Urgent Fury' rejuvenated flagging American morale and served as a springboard for further international policing actions. It also provided the SOF with the biggest boost in funding enjoyed since the Vietnam War. However, nineteen US servicemen were listed as killed or missing in action and a further 116 as wounded. Had better reconnaissance and heavier

clandestine firepower been used to soften up the defences prior to the main assault, the casualties may have been much lighter.

When CIA attention next focused upon Panama, reconnaissance products were used to much greater effect. Drug trafficking, the ill-treatment of US servicemen and other excesses on the part of Panamanian dictator Gen Manuel Noriega proved too much for the Americans, who had regretfully helped to install the puppet to power in bygone years. President Bush would stand no more and okayed the JCS's plan, appropriately titled Operation 'Just Cause', to invade the troubled Central American country, reinstate democracy and secure the vital canal linking the Atlantic and Pacific. The effort 'fragged' a vast amount of air power, including 111 heavy-lift ferry missions. Joining four AC-130Hs already on station at Howard AFB on the night of 20 December 1989 were a force of five 'Spectres' (three Active and two Air Force Reserve machines) which flew in formation all the way from Florida to spearhead the assault. They arrived on station at Rio Hato and Tocumen airfields at 0045 local time, a quarter of an hour earlier than the originally scheduled 'H-hour' to offset an alerted Panamanian Defence Force (PDF). Six F-117As flew direct from Tonopah, receiving two AAR top-ups *en route*, to arrive as planned at 0100: two were 'air spares', two were tasked to support attempts by SOF troops to capture Noriega in the vicinity of his headquarters the Commandancia and to ensure that

his personal Learjet 35A would be unable to whisk him away from Paitilla airport and the final duo were committed to Rio Hato, where each deposited a time-delayed 2,000-pounder, designed to stun two élite PDF infantry companies while they remained asleep in their barracks. Although the enemy troops were out of their bunks and armed by this time as a result of the alert, the 'Nighthawks' delivered the desired blow: Army Lt-Gen Carl W. Stiner, who commanded the Panama Joint Task Force, later commented that the enemy 'began to throw down their weapons and run', many kitted with steel hats and guns but wearing only their underwear! The shockwave from a Mk 84 'hammer' is lethal to anyone within 400ft of the explosion and is capable of 'blowing out ear-drums' at ranges of up to half a mile. Stiner specifically chose the 'Bat Planes' for the task as these were the only aircraft that could guarantee the necessary accuracy and 'wallop'. The bombs did not hit their intended aimpoints, but they had the desired effect all the same—adequate reconnaissance saw to that. Their task accomplished, the crews flew the exhausting 3,000-mile trip back to Nevada, arriving home just in time for breakfast.

Below, left and right: Lockheed's paddle-bladed YO-3A was powered by a 'quiet' 210hp air-cooled Continental 10-360 piston engine, which incorporated a muffled exhaust silencer designed for acoustic stealth. Fourteen were built for the US Army and were introduced to combat in Vietnam in 1970. Their job was to creep over the jungle and spot Viet Cong positions. (Lockheed)

Above: Smoke rises from Panama, following pin-point blasts from the AC-130A/H 'Spectres' of Col George Gray's 1st SOW and of the AFRes 919th SOG. (US DoD)

Col George Gray, 1st SOW commander and Air Force SOF co ordinator in Panama, still had his work cut out for him. 'Spectres' orbiting at 7,000ft laid down suppressive fire in support of Army 82 Aviation Brigade and Task Force 160, knocking out nine V300 armoured personnel carriers and ZPU-4 AAA sites which were proving to be a thorn in the flanks of regular 'trash-hauling' C-130Hs and clusters of multi-service helicopters entering the landing zones at Rio Hato, Torrijos and Puma. In all, eleven Hercules took minor hits. With tankers on call to top up their fuel reserves, the 'Spectres' flew armed-recce sorties of up to 18.2 hours' duration. Joining the ensemble were four MC-130Es and HC-130s, which acted as bladder-and-drogue refuellers in support of the short-winded 'helos', together with five 'Pave Low' MH-53Js and four MH-60G 'Pave Hawk' rotary-wings which assisted with Ranger movements and the timely evacuation of endangered diplomats. Altogether the units logged a grand total of 1,200 hours during the operation, adding to the 1,980 hours accumulated by Army Apaches, Blackhawks and Chinooks. Noriega was eventually apprehended at the Vatican Ambassador's residence on 3 January and flown out by MC-130E to Florida to be arraigned on a drug indictment; limited resistance from the

'Dignity' battalions petered out altogether shortly after the announcement of his capture, and by 22 January Panama had been deemed 'secured'. Skilful planning and on-the-spot reconnaissance had brought about another much prized American victory.

Operations during the Gulf War sucked in virtually the entire AFSOF. Leading the assault on the night of 17 January were two pairs of 20th SOS MH-53Js, which acted as pathfinders for US Army AH-64A Apache gunships from the 101st Aviation Brigade, sent in to knock out Iraqi radars and AAA installations at two key sites to open up a 'radar-black' corridor into enemy airspace. This could then be prised apart further by fixed-wing forces. Only the 'Pave Low IIIEs' offered the kind of precision navigation required, and the operation was a complete success. Further MH-53Js penetrated enemy territory to deposit teams of US and British special forces, who would conduct hit-and-run sabotage and reconnoitre suspected targets in support of Coalition air and rocket strikes. One special forces team ferried into Iraq two days before the cessation of hostilities stumbled upon 29 'Scud' missiles which were being readied for a strike against Israel. Altogether the 'Pave Lows' alone accounted for sixty such missions, including the timely extraction of downed airmen such as TARPS Tomcat driver Lt Devon Jones. The forte of the 'Combat Talons' was 'bull**** bombing', and to prove the point processions of the beasts operating out of Riyadh and King Abdul Aziz Air Bases dropped a staggering 17 million propaganda leaflets promising safety if the enemy surrendered (and making a few other choice remarks relating to their well-being if they decided to stay their ground) during forty sorties into enemy territory. They also employed live ammunition in the form of giant 15,000lb BLU-82/B high-capacity light-case explosives, eleven of which were rolled out of the back of the cargo holds on to the hapless enemy below, annihilating everything at ground level within a three-mile radius. Drops were effected from FL170 and above, yet CEPs (circular error probables) were in the order of 50ft! (The 8th SOS was subsequently unofficially re-labelled the '8th Bomb Squadron' in recognition of its feats.) Backstage at altitude, stately squads of EC-130E/Hs assisted with their ABCCC, sigint, 'psyops' and comjam roles, while AC-130 'Spectres' became embroiled in battle area observation and the destruction of armour. Unfortunately, one of their number was brought down—the only AFSOF loss of the entire war. In the early morning light of 31 January AC-130H 69-6567 was hit by a SAM missile and all fourteen crew members perished when the aircraft subsequently crashed into the sea. It should have returned to Riyadh or King Abdul Aziz

Air Base at the first hint of sunrise, but the crew elected to stay on station in support of US Marines who were under threat from a 'Frog-7' surface-to-surface missile site in the thick of the battle to recapture the Saudi town of Khafji. In all, AFSOF operations in the Gulf proved to be an outstanding success, ridding the organization once and for all of the stigma attached to the expensive and embarrassing failure at 'Desert One' in Iran twelve years earlier.

WATCHFUL WARTHOGS

Providing covering fire for the SOF is ACC's growing force of O-for-observation OA-10A 'Warthogs', equipped with the devastating 30mm GAU-8/A Avenger gun, AGM-65 Maverick missile and a wide variety of 'iron' and cluster bombs. The machine is renowned throughout the fighter community for its odd looks and impressive armament; acknowledging this, the crews of the 'Warthogs' refer to their steeds as 'ugly but well hung'! Designed and fabricated by the now defunct Fairchild-Republic company at Farmingdale, New York, which produced no fewer than 713 of the basic A-10A mark (including a solitary night/adverse weather twin-seater) between 1975 and 1984 for tank-busting duties in the notional European 'battlefront', the aircraft is gradually being reallocated from active, ANG and AFRes fighter squadrons to TASS (Tactical Air Support Squadron) units, with three new assignments: 'keeping enemy heads down' during CSAR extractions, a mission known as ResCAP (rescue combat air patrol); additional SOF support in the controversial field of counter-insurgency (COIN) operations; and forward air control (FAC) observation—spotting and marking targets on the FEBA.

The decision to trade roles from 'tank-buster' to armed observation originated in 1987 with Gen Robert D. Russ, the chief of what was then USAF Tactical Air Command. The FAC force at that time consisted of 77 Rockwell International OV-10 Broncos and 34 Cessna OA-37 Dragonflys (excluding a limited quantity of OT-37s), which lacked the range, endurance and speed necessary for the hazardous ResCAP mission.[8] A total of 220 aircraft have since been earmarked for adaptation to the 'all-up' OA-10A configuration, which combines the existing 'Pave Penny' passive laser tracker, LN39 INS and Avenger gun with a new FLIR (three of which are currently under evaluation) linked to a GEC wide-angle head-up display and the Rockwell-Collins CP-1516/ASQ automatic target hand-off system (ATHS) which relays target co-ordinates over secure radio links to friendly strike aircraft. The first unit to form with the provisional (retitled as opposed to fully reconfigured) OA-10A FAC model was the 23rd TASS, 602nd

Tactical Air Control Wing, based at Davis-Monthan AFB, Arizona, which deployed sixteen aircraft to King Fahd Airport in Saudi Arabia on 24 November 1990 as part of the vanguard of the 'Desert Shield' build-up of forces in the theatre.[9] Operating as 'Fast FACs' with traditional Vietnam War-era 'Nail' call-signs, the 23rd threw itself into action the following January at the outbreak of hostilities. 'Nail' mission symbols which accumulated on the flanks of the machines' fuselages totalled 190, one of these aircraft (76-547/NF) accounting for the destruction of fourteen trucks, twelve armoured vehicles, 23 anti-aircraft guns and four missile launchers. Fellow 'Warthog' drivers stationed at King Fahd for ResCAP duties similarly proved the machine's prowess in that role. The first such successful mission provided covering fire during the extraction of downed TARPS Tomcat pilot Lt Devon Jones (see above), who was plucked from enemy-held territory on 21 January. The entire force of 194 A-10As and OA-10As generated over 8,500 sorties, during which the aircraft accounted for the destruction of more than 1,000 tanks, 1,200 artillery pieces and 2,000 other vehicles. They also 'bagged' a pair of enemy helicopters. On the debit side, the OA-10's batteries of underwing Tracor AN/ALE-40 chaff/flare dispensers were unable to provide complete protection against the occasional meandering heat-seeking missile shoulder-launched by Iraqi troops. OA-10A 76-543 (call-sign 'Nail 53') was brought down in this manner on 19 February 1991. Lt-Col Jeffrey D. Fox ejected, but he was unable to evade capture. One of his junior colleagues, Lt Patrick B. Olsen, was even less fortunate. On 27 February he took some hits in OA-10A 77-197 ('Nail 51') and elected to bring the aircraft back. Tragically,

[8]The Bronco is also used by the US Marine Corps and several client nations—including Morocco, Indonesia, Thailand and Venezuela—for FAC and COIN duties. Of special note are the USMC's dozen OV-10D-NOS (Night Observation, Surveillance) Broncos, which serve with VMO-1 at New River MCAS, North Carolina, and VMO-2 at Camp Pendleton, California, equipped with an AN/AAS-37 laser target designator and FLIR turret and an auto-video tracker (plus a 20mm gun and provisions for 2.75in rockets). Thirteen OV-10A/D aircraft from VMO-1 and VMO-2 provided battle-area FAC during the Gulf War from Al Jubail Air Base as part of Marine Air Group 13. Two of the daytime-only OV-10A variants were lost to enemy shoulder-launched SAM missiles—BuNo 155435 on 18 January 1991 (crewed by Lt-Col Clifford M. Acree and his observer CWO Guy L. Hunter) and BuNo 155424 on 25 February (crewed by pilot Maj Joseph J. Small and observer Capt David M. Spellacy). Capt Spellacy was killed and the other three crewmen were captured. Their proximity to enemy forces precluded rescue.

[9]An additional TASS has formed in South Korea while additional OA-10As are scheduled to be assigned to the following two reserve 'Warthog' units: the 47th FS, AFRes, at Barksdale, Louisiana, destined to receive a dozen aircraft in early 1993; and the 104th FS, ANG, at Baltimore, Maryland, which is receiving six aircraft during 1992. In turn, the 23rd TASS is scheduled to be deactivated and the aircraft will be transferred to the 21st TASS at Shaw AFB, South Carolina. Further squads of OA-10As are scheduled to form at McChord AFB, Washington, and Pope AFB, North Carolina.

Above: The 47th FS, AFRes, located at Barksdale, Louisiana, is home for a dozen OA-10As. The first unit to form was the 23rd TASS, which flew in the thick of the action during the Gulf War with traditional 'Nail' call-signs. LASTE (Low Altitude Safety Enhancements) and the ATHS (Automatic Target Handoff System) will maintain the aircraft in the Fast-FAC role for years to come. (M-Slides)

Below: A dozen OV-10D-NOS (Night Observation, Surveillance) Broncos serve with the US Marine Corps' VMO-1 at New River MCAS, North Carolina, and VMO-2 at Camp Pendleton, California, each equipped with an AN/AAS-37 laser target designator and FLIR. Daytime-only OV-10A variants are also operated by the units, and export versions of these still serve with the air arms of Morocco, Indonesia, Thailand and Venezuela. (M-Slides)

the 'Hog' flipped over and crashed on its return. The wreckage was later buried *in situ*. However, several badly scarred airframes returned safely with uninjured pilots strapped in their armoured titanium cockpit 'tubs'. The ability to absorb plenty of battle damage by means of redundant flight systems and control surfaces was designed into the aircraft from the beginning, and this quality proved its worth over the battlefields of Kuwait.

Further modifications to the OA-10A's electro-optical countermeasures to keep it abreast of anti-aircraft threats are in progress. Safety is also receiving a great deal of attention. The USAF loses an average of two aircraft annually in low-level crashes, and the demands of single-seat observation may exacerbate this unfortunate statistic. Chief amongst the safety improvements is LASTE (Low Altitude Safety and Targeting Enhancement), which is being added as aircraft undergo depot-level maintenance at McClellan AFB, California. LASTE comprises a ground proximity warning system, a new radar altimeter, a bombing computer, a speed brake warning system and refinements to the flight control system to provide an automatic 'up vector' when the gun is fired. The latter counteracts the aircraft's tendency to dip its nose when the Avenger is spun into action, while the new CCIP (Continuously Computed Impact Point) aiming facility provided by the bombing computer permits pilots to hit targets accurately with the Avenger's depleted uranium armour-piercing 'slugs' at slant ranges of two miles. Future updates under study include IDIMS, which works much like the ATHS but combines it with GPS/Navstar for added accuracy. Such facilities will weave it further into the 'netted' SOF system, to act as the 'forward eyes' of rearguard command and control posts. Given a reprieve by the Gulf War, where its outstanding performance saved it from a dusty fate in the desert boneyards of the south-western United States, the type has found a new niche. Its lack of aerodynamic aesthetics—apparently a prerequisite for any piece of SOF hardware—will merely serve to ease its transition from 'fighter' to armed observation jet. Its 330kt cruise speed (and 2hr 'bombed-up' loiter capability when operating up to 250 miles from its FOL) represents a leap ahead of the Bronco and Dragonfly. With 1,174 rounds of 30mm ammunition to play with, the watchful, sharp-shooting 'Warthog' has the potential to be substantially more mischievous too.

Below: The Cessna OA-37 Dragonfly, alias the 'Tweety Bird' was designed for COIN and FAC duties but, in common with the aged O-2 Skymaster and 'vanilla' OV-10 Bronco, is gradually giving way to the battle-hardened OA-10A 'Warthog'. (M-Slides)

5. SENTINELS

WHEELING ALONG their circuitous paths at a distance from the FLOT and sensitive borders are the world's great armadas of discreet surveillance aircraft, dispatched to act as the electronic 'ears' of the military command, control, communications and intelligence (C3I) network. Their job is essential to the smooth operation of today's fast-moving military forces, as overseers and co-ordinators amidst a morass of swirling aircraft and fleeting ground targets and as gatherers of sensitive information pertaining to the enemy's C3I and radar, fighter, missile and rocket forces. Sensor suites range from passive comint and elint intelligence-gathering receivers designed to catalogue an opponent's electronic order of battle (EOB) and day-to-day movements, tasks bearing the generic mission title of sigint, to active-mapping using multimode radars, which can plot both friendly and enemy air, ground and naval forces to provide an *overall* perspective of events in 'real time'. When properly managed, the various data gleaned from these 'platforms' form a composite patchwork from which can be extrapolated a perspective of the enemy's intentions and his movements—and his weaknesses too—which can be exploited by the timely disposition of friendly ground and airborne forces for maximum effect (a feature known for some time as the 'force multiplier').

ELECTRONIC EAVESDROPPING
Keeping an ear turned to the enemy is the task assigned to some of the world's most bizarre-looking machines, each bristling with radomes and other antennae which lend them a definite air of the sinister. The 'Dragon Lady' is counted amongst the best.[1] Indeed, several of these aircraft are crewed by sigint and EW specialists known as 'Crows' and themselves carry names associated with the occult, such as Raven. Individually, the machines are tuned in to a specific branch of the radio frequency spectrum, ranging from HF, VHF and UHF communications and early warning and height-finding devices which work in those lower bands up to 1,000MHz; through acquisition, tracking and illuminating radars operating at much higher frequencies, up to 20gc (20,000MHz); to precision

telemetry and guidance systems up to 40gc and beyond, into the millimetre-wave 'top end'. Each listening package covers only a portion of this broad range, requiring the data to be gleaned from a number of sources and 'fused' by an army of ground specialists who 'tweak' the signals, listen to tapes and conjure up a fuller picture of the opposition's defensive and offensive networks. Several intelligence squadrons which fly no aircraft but merely liaise with the airborne elements are dotted around the world. Processed, the various data may be 'pulled' from the constantly updated libraries for a number of uses: comint to ascertain a foreign nation's or opposing army's intentions; elint to counter his anti-aircraft forces with carefully prescribed countermeasures; and telint to monitor his progress in the fields of rocketry and weapons development. During peacetime, great banks of information are tediously catalogued by such organizations as the United States' Joint Electronic Warfare Center at San Antonio, Texas, which holds the information in a 'threat library' for use in contingency operations; and by military development units affiliated with EW and such programmes as the SDI (Strategic Defense Initiative), alias 'Star Wars'. In wartime, or in times of tension, where 'near real-time' information is amalgamated with catalogued intelligence, the data are made available to theatre commanders for such diverse uses as plotting the whereabouts of a specific enemy artillery radar and furnishing an entire EOB on an air base operations room computer, to help air crews map out flight-plans which bypass the thickest concentrations of enemy anti-aircraft activity.

At the top of the league and pushed aloft by a quartet of P&WA TF33 turbofans are the majestic Boeing RC-135 'Rivet Joints', USAF's giant elint-gatherers painted in a glossy Aircraft Gray and white livery and wearing the insignia of the 343rd RS and its parent Wing the 55th, headquartered at Offutt AFB, Nebraska. Overseas FOLs include Mildenhall in England, Hellenikon in Greece (latterly Soudha Bay in Crete), Riyadh in Saudi Arabia and Kadena, Okinawa, providing a global listening capability. As

---

[1] Refer to Chapter 1, where the U-2R sigint-related 'Senior' projects are aired in further detail.

one of the current Mildenhall 'Crew Dog' patches exclaims: 'In God We Trust—Everyone Else We Monitor'!

Modelled from the hugely successful Boeing KC-135 Stratotanker, of which no fewer than 732 were built at the company's Seattle, Washington plant, the RC-135 began life as Project 'Golden Fleece', the goal of which was to produce an automated, super-sensitive, direction-finding receiver able to monitor all 'traffic' in the 30MHz to 40,000MHz frequency range, covering everything from early warning emitters to telemetry signals. Using bulky computers and 'man in the loop' monitoring in the cabin, the system was designed to be capable of picking up elint, telint and urint (unintentionally radiated intelligence, such as that generated by radar side- and back-lobes) and of noting every nuance in the signals—frequency, pulse width and repetition rate, relative bearing (known as DOA, or direction of arrival)—while being able to differentiate complex sources (such as especially frequency-agile emitters, or multi-beam systems) as *individual* threats. In all, the package had to cope with up to ten million pulses a second! The only way to achieve this was to combine

Below: Fourteen of the giant 'thimble-nosed' RC-135V/W 'Rivet Joint' sigint spyplanes serve with the USAF's 55th Wing at Offutt AFB, Nebraska, and overseas at several detachments under the motto 'In God We Trust—Everyone Else We Monitor'! (Frank B. Mormillo)

200 square feet of flat, spiral, direction-finding interferometers with signals deciphering super-heterodynes (which mix incoming waves with those from lower frequencies to create a recognizable 'beat'), pack them into large 'Chipmunk' cheeks bolted on to the flanks of the Boeing and process the electronic medley by means of what then amounted to an onboard 'super computer'. 'Sorting the wheat from the chaff' was a task accomplished by two sets of receivers, one a wide-open crystal video set able to pick up main beam transmissions and the other a group of ten narrow-band receivers which swept across their assigned frequency range three times a minute to pick up urint side- and back-lobes which did not directly 'paint' the aircraft; in this manner, the system first collated the time and DOA of the signals, which were then passed on to the computer and 'tagged'. The package then examined the various 'tags' it had accumulated in order to differentiate the various radar types, before proceeding to analyze them in terms of their operating frequencies, pulse repetition rates and so on, overseen by four operators' positions. Styled the AN/ASD-1 (the whole package, including ground 'finder' support and analysis, was termed the UAS-7), the gear began flight-test work in 1961, clearing the way for an initial production run of ten RC-135Bs which joined the ranks of SAC's 55th SRW—an elint-only reconnaissance Wing from 1964—six years later, after having

RC-135 'RIVET JOINTS'

RC-135V (8)	RC-135W (6)	RC-135U (2)
55th Wing, Offutt AFB, Nebraska		
63-9792	62-4131 and -4132	64-14847
64-14841 to -14846	-4134 and -4135	-14849
-14848	-4138 and -4139	

Four RC-135As were flown by the 1370th Photo Mapping Wing during the 1960s before reverting to the cargo role and subsequent reconfiguration as KC-135D tankers during 1980. The follow-on RC-135B and additional conversions formed the basis of the fleet listed above. The 55th also possesses one TC-135W trainer (62-4129).

been reworked into the operational RC-135C 'Big Team' configuration. Known initially as 'Ferret' because of the radar-sniffing role, the type later received the code-name 'Rivet Joint'. Continuous updates to the AN/ASD-1 over the past quarter of a century, including major reworks and additions to the fleet from basic stock during the 1970s, have kicked the surviving models along the alphabet to form a collection of sixteen machines flying in three configurations: eight RC-135Vs and six RC-135Ws equipped with elegant 'thimble' radomes housing extra sideways-looking antennae, and two of the RC-135U mark which feature gawping noses and tail boom extensions in addition to wing-tip housings optimized for 360-degree elint coverage.

Today's heirs of the force, Gen John Loh's Air Combat Command, continues to fly sigint missions out of Offutt AFB in Nebraska and the domestic and overseas FOLs, with global reach. In the early days the bulk of air time was spent probing North Vietnamese, Chinese and Soviet air defences in support of tac-air and SAC's sizeable bomber establishment—and not without hazard. Several were stricken from the inventory over the years owing to 'operational causes'. Others received 'lucky near misses', includ-

Left: Two 'snub-nose' RC-135U 'Rivet Joints' operate alongside the more slender models, gathering elint and calibrating new EW systems. (Author)

Below: 'Chipmunk Cheeks' are a distinctive feature of the USAF's 'Rivet Joint' series. These pack the 200 sq ft of flat, spiral direction-finding interferometers associated with the AN/ASD-1 elint system. (Author)

ing an RC-135U which was shot at on 16 September 1980 while monitoring Libyan defences. During the Gulf conflict, three flew from Riyadh on refuelled missions of up to 24 hours' duration, pinpointing enemy C3I and radar installations for subsequent attack by F-117A Stealth bombers and 'Wild Weasel' strike aircraft, and collected further elint. Plans to retire the older RC-135Vs as part of the post-Cold War draw-down were subsequently shelved!

Additional weird and wonderful telint sub-variants bearing fanciful 'Cobra' code-names are attached to the untamed icy vastness of Alaska, assigned to the 24th Reconnaissance Squadron of the 6th Reconnaissance Wing at Eielson AFB. Their primary tasking is to fly out of Shemya AFB—known as Detachment 1, or more simply as 'The Rock'—at the tip of the Aleutian archipelago in the Bering Strait on 24-hour call and loiter near the Sea of Okhotz, to provide an airborne extension to the Shemya-based 'Cobra Dane' radar tracker and seaborne 'Cobra Judy' radar operated aboard USNS *Observation Island*. Their equipment is twofold, comprising telint receivers tuned to Russian rocket telemetry signals and advanced upward-looking optical BFCS (Ballistic Framing Camera Systems) and MRCS (Medium Reso-

Above: A 'slick' RC-135V awaits its crew at RAF Mildenhall, one of its many overseas operating locations which also include Soudha Bay in Crete, Riyadh in Saudi Arabia and Kadena, Okinawa. Like its 'Rivet Joint' stablemates, the aircraft has a gross take-off weight of 299,000lb. (Author)

lution Camera System) trackers built into the starboard side of the aircraft, designed to monitor reentering Russian dummy warheads. The BFCS images all objects of interest while the MRCS photograpghs individual re-entry vehicles, permitting size and yield to be postulated. The work is conducted in support of nuclear arms verification, and more recently in connection with the US 'Star Wars' effort. It is a largely unsung job which demands superlative aviators. Aircraft commanders alone must possess a minimum of 2,500 hours' flying time before they are even considered—hardly surprising when they might well have to face night landings in dense fog, in crosswinds of up to 25kts! Crews—which also include two navigators and a gaggle of specialists in the main cabin—stick together in teams for each twoweek-long rotational alert duty and only upgrade to the AC's or 'Nav 1' seat after accumulating 200 hours of operations as a 'Number Two'. The unique force of specially adapted aircraft includes two RC-135S

RC-135 COBRAS

Serial	Model	Code-name	Notes
6th Wing, Eielson AFB, Alaska			
55-3121	RC-135T		Redelivered Dec 1979; crashed 5 February 1985
59-1491	RC-135S	Rivet Ball[1]	Redelivered Jan 1967; crashed 13 Jan 1969
61-2662	RC-135S	Cobra Ball III	Redelivered Nov 1983
61-2663	RC-135S	Cobra Ball I	Redelivered Oct 1969
61-2664	RC-135S	Cobra Ball II	Redelivered Jan 1970; crashed 15 March 1981
62-4128	RC-135X	Cobra Eye	Redelivered July 1989
62-4133	TC-135S		Redelivered July 1985 as replacement for 55-3121
62-4137	RC-135E	Rivet Amber[2]	Redelivered Jan 1967; crashed 5 June 1969

[1]Originally a JKC-135A nicknamed 'Nancy Rae' 1961–63, then reconfigured as RC-135S 'Wanda Belle' 1963–67.
[2]Originally RC-135E 'Lisa Ann' Mar–Dec 1966.

'Cobra Balls' and an RC-135X 'Cobra Eye', plus a solitary TC-135S trainer and liaison machine. Their duties have proved much more hazardous than those undertaken by the 55th Recon Wing. Four have been lost since 1967, all ostensibly to technical problems or pilot error and not hostile fire. However, related losses of Korean KAL airliners—including a polar-routed Boeing 707 brought down by Soviet fighters while straying from its flightplan over Murmansk on 23 April 1978, and the loss of a Jumbo jet (the ill-famed Flight KE007, with 269 passengers and crew members on board) to a Su-15 'Flagon' interceptor near Sakhalin Island on the 1 September 1983, while en route from Alaska to Seoul—demonstrated just how eager the Soviets were to down the marauding Americans. At a distance, even in bright moonlight, night-flying RC-135Ss equipped with their distinctive optical tracking 'windows' bear an uncanny resemblence to their civil Boeing counterparts.[2]

Possessing a greater reach than even the farthest satellite outposts of Government Communications Headquarters, Cheltenham, are the Royal Air Force's secret but modest trio of R Mk 1P Nimrods, assigned to sigint duties in support of imported and indigenous countermeasures development, much like the American 'Rivet Joints'. These fall within the jurisdiction of No 51 Squadron at RAF Wyton—the bastion of Britain's 'spy plane' force of Canberras and Nimrods. The first in the series, XW664, was launched on its operational career on 31 October 1973 when Flt Lt Lambert captained the premier training sortie. Sigint tasks continued to be performed by the squadron's aged collection of Comet 2Rs until the two extra R.1s (XW665 and XW666) arrived and the Squadron was formally declared operational on the type on 10 May 1974, complete with 'Red Goose' insignia on the fins. The cream and white livery had given way the toned-down 'Hemp' camouflage by 1980 (described by the crews as 'various shades of turd'), at which juncture additional ESM self-defence gear in the form of Loral 1017A 'Yellowgate' wing-tip pods began to make its appearance. Monitoring assignments could task the machines on a global basis, though most operations focused initially on missions out of Akrotiri in Cyprus, Kinloss in Morayshire and the home-drome Wyton. All that changed while Wg Cdr B. N. J. Speed

Above: The wing-tip and tail elint receivers are exclusive to the RC-135U model. It employs the regular AIL/Melpar AN/ASD-1 and also the Raytheon AN/ALD-5 direction-finding set, the Hallicrafters/Systems Research Lab AN/ALA-6 pulse analyzer and the Loral Magnavox AN/APR-17 missile launch warning set, plus various QRC experimental systems. (Author)

was in charge. In April 1982 the Argentine invasion of the Falkland Islands shifted attention to the South Atlantic and, as part of RAF-wide retrofit to several 'heavies', the Nimrods were outfitted with an aerial refuelling proboscis to extend their range. Newly redesignated R.1P, the aircraft were deployed to Ascension Island and thence, by means of 'pyramid' flights of Victor K.2 tankers, on sigint monitoring tasks adjacent to both the Islands and the Argentine mainland. Covert operations from Chile were also probably carried out. Precisely what part No 51's aircraft or personnel played during Operation 'Corporate' is unknown; however, that the unit was subsequently awarded the battle honour 'South Atlantic 1982' indicates extensive operations in the region. Later becoming part of No 18 Group, No 51 Squadron got into action once more in support of

Below: The cockpit of the RC-135 'Ferret' is barely distinguishable from the standard Stratotanker series; the heart of the sigint system rests in the top-secret main cabin. (Bruce de Lis via USAF)

[2]A large number of other 'sky spies' have been based on the C-135 and commercial 707 series, including the EC-135 'Looking Glass' airborne command and control posts which at one time kept up a constant chain of airborne aircraft as part of the United States' NEACP (National Emergency Airborne Command Post) system and the US Navy's more recent E-6A TACAMO (Take Charge And Move Out) acquisitions, which employ very-low frequency (VLF) communications relay systems. Both are concerned with the command and control of American nuclear forces—NEACP with bombers and TACAMO with the submarine portion of the triad.

Above: EC-135N ARIA space-tracking Stratotankers have been in use since the Apollo programme of the late 1960s. Their giant nasal radars are the largest of of their kind in the world. Recently supplemented by the slightly larger EC-18B ARIA variant, the aircraft serve with the 4950th Test Wing at Wright-Patterson AFB, Ohio. (M-Slides)

Operation 'Granby', using Seeb in Oman as a spring-board for monitoring missions over the Persian Gulf. Again, the equipment fit and accomplishments remain among the Ministry of Defence's best-kept secrets, but it has been reported by historian Andrew Thomas that at least one member of the unit was subsequently decorated for gallantry. Currently commanded by Wg Cdr P. M. Blee, No 51 will continue with its specialized duties for the foresee-able future, leaving Comet contrails over the world's troublespots, while its MR.2P companions assigned to maritime patrol from Scotland skim over the Atlantic and North Sea to keep an eye on oil rigs, fishing rights, illegal shipping and naval movements on and below the waterline.

SIGNAL TARGETING

Battle area sigint aircraft have a different objective: rather than glean volumes on enemy practices for future reference, their job is to acquire as much as possible within prescribed wavebands as quickly as possible and to relay this crucial information— optimized to help defeat the opponent's caravanserai of AAA and SAM radar and weapons trailers—to the 'end user' in a matter of minutes. Most of these emitters are shifted about from one pre-surveyed site to another as a matter of routine, or have total mobility as an integral part of an armoured forma-tion. As such, they represent a protean threat, and the elint needed to counter them—especially for the much-coveted strike crews' EOB, used in mission-planning—must be updated on almost an hourly basis.

At the height of the Cold War it was the West, and notably the United States, which fielded the most capable elint machines tasked in support of threat evasion and suppression: the US was the only nation which could afford to spend megabucks in pursuit of gigaHertz. Inevitably, also, it was the ubiquitous Phantom which put one leg forward to volunteer for the duty. Litton-Amecom supplied the AN/ALQ-125 hardware and this was eventually fielded in 23 machines (replacing the SLAR fit in the Phantom's flank compartments) and distributed between three units, the 67th TRW at Bergstrom AFB, Texas, the 38th TRS at Zweibrücken in Germany and the 15th TRS at Osan, South Korea, which achieved IOC with the system during 1982.

TEREC 'tactical ferreting' provides complete 360-degree coverage, though, in common with many elint systems, left- or right-look is selected depending on the aircraft's position relative to the enemy while flying in 'racetrack'. TEREC is pre-programmed prior to take-off to 'sniff out' ten types of enemy radar, any five of which can be assigned 'high priority' status during the course of the mission. When the AN/ALQ-125 picks up one of the priority threats it tracks them long enough to enable it to obtain a series of DOAs, or bearings relative to the Phantom. By matching these with relative aircraft position (based on current position furnished by the aircraft's on-board AN/ARN-101(V) digital navigation system), the system is capable of triangulating the position of the threats. During this 'auto search', the back-seater or 'Wizzo'

Above: RAF Wyton plays host to the RAF's 'spyplane' force, which includes five Canberra PR.9s and a trio of Nimrod R.1Ps. The R.1Ps can be distinguished from regular maritime patrol variants by the dorsal sigint antennae sprouting from the fuselage and No 51 Squadron 'Red Goose' insignia on the fin. XW665 was captured on film while staging through NAS Keflavik, Iceland, in August 1989. (Scott Van Aken)

uses two displays to monitor the proceedings: a control panel relating to the five priority emitters, which light up when TEREC is listening to a relevant radar; and a 'location' panel, which displays all the pertinent information—bearing, estimated range and lat/long co-ordinates—in easy-to-read digits when one of the lit-up buttons on the control panel is pushed. This information can then be relayed over secure radio to friendly C3I, electronic support and strike aircraft. More importantly, at the push of the 'DL' button TEREC automatically passes on all available information relating to the five priority emitter types near-instantaneously to ground-based T-PEPS (TEREC Portable Exploitation Processors) and TRTs (TEREC Remote Terminals). Further elint can be gleaned from the aircraft's nine-track tape recorder following aircraft recovery. Processed in a T-PEP, this is capable of providing a complete EOB based on the AN/ALQ-125's 'full spectrum search' mode. TEREC represented a leap forward in tactical elint, made possible by developments in electronics in the late 1970s. However, it was a decade ahead of today's 'netted' JTIDS (Joint Tactical Information Distribution System) and other strike-orientated 'near real-time' C3I distribution systems, to which it was ideally suited. Instead, the bulk of the information it gleaned merely tended to collect dust in the 'hard rooms' of fighter operations bunkers in Europe and the Pacific. It was a classic case of 'all dressed up with nowhere to go': the data obtained during peacetime operations was of little relevance in the Gulf, the one occasion when it could have been put to combat use, and resources were not made available to fly-in the 26th TRW's entourage of TRTs and T-PEPS to Turkey. Those few TEREC machines re-assigned from Zweibrücken to Incirlik for Operation 'Proven Force' were very quickly press-ganged into much-needed optical reconnaissance duties, to which they were equally well-suited.[3]

An alternative system which might have been used with great effect in the Gulf but for the fact that it was permanently grounded five years earlier was the PLSS/SLATS (Precision Location Strike System, also known as the Signal Locating and Targeting System). The object of PLSS, also born out of Project 'Pave Onyx' in 1970, was to do precisely what TEREC had the potential to do: plot enemy radars *and* convey the co-ordinates of the target to friendly strike aircraft, even to 'smart' bombs being lobbed at the enemy, in virtual 'real time', by means of the modern 'netted' threat distribution introduced by JTIDS. Vast sums were lavished on the PLSS/SLATS effort over the course of fifteen years; it utilized extremely complex technology that had to be developed in a secret, 'black world' environment. Its key advantage over TEREC was that it used a combination of three TR-1As flying racetrack, each rigged with Harris Corp Distance Measuring Equipment (DME) interrogators and an elongated 'pinched' nose containing twin passive phased-array receivers provided by E-Systems, to furnish DOA and wavelength. Atomic clocks at pre-

---

[3]See Chapter 3 for a fuller account of the RF-4 and its combat history.

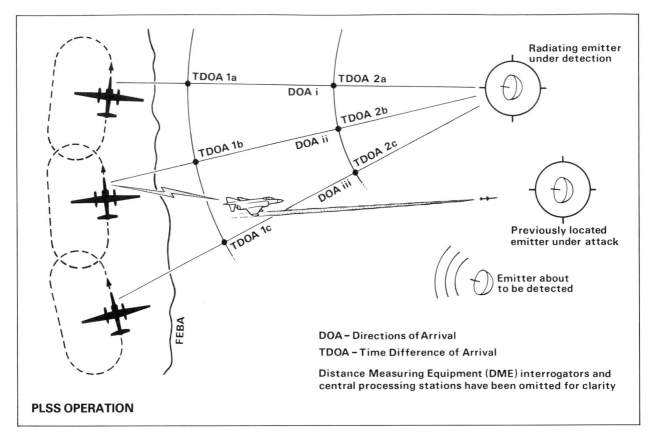

Radiating emitter
under detection

TDOA 1a

TDOA 2a

DOA i

TDOA 2b

TDOA 1b

DOA ii

TDOA 2c

DOA iii

TDOA 1c

Previously located
emitter under attack

Emitter about
to be detected

FEBA

DOA – Directions of Arrival

TDOA – Time Difference of Arrival

Distance Measuring Equipment (**DME**) interrogators and
central processing stations have been omitted for clarity

PLSS OPERATION

surveyed sites behind the FEBA provided the necessary ingredient to help determine the time difference of arrival (TDOA) of the multiplex signals being picked up by the triad. Between them, and with not a small amount of computer cogitation back on the ground, a complete picture of the enemy EOB could be generated in 'near real-time' at ranges of up to 300

Below: The only photograph to have been made available showing the PLSS-configured U-2R (in the centre).

miles. Trials of its ancestor the Advanced Location Strike System (ALSS) were held in Europe during 1975 with Col Stratton in charge, flown aboard five Ghost Gray-camouflaged U-2Cs (one of which, 56-6700, was abandoned by Capt Robert Rendleman owing to autopilot control problems and pancaked into a forest near Winterberg). Twelve years later the newly developed PLSS was thrown into action against the simulated threat-spotted desert wastes of northern Nevada during a 'Green Flag' EW exercise. There, under strict supervision, the system proved its ability to plot emitters to within a few feet and direct strike traffic on to the target. However, continued teething problems effectively axed the project the following year, when nobody could come up with the $50 million needed for a European demonstration effort: the whole package was simply burdened by complexity. Instead, the USAF is working on a simpler, more autonomous version to be carried aboard 'soloing' 'Dragon Ladies' for dissemination through current 'netted' channels. All that is in the public domain so far is its code-name, 'Senior Smart'.

BATTLEFIELD OBSERVATION

At the other end of the performance envelope are the petite propeller-driven machines designed to keep a watch on opponents by trudging around the periphery of a battle zone with eyes and ears to the ground. The US Army operates the most prodigious range. In addition to its OH-58D observation Kiowas, gunship helicopters and plethora of small ground-launched, short-range observation UAVs equipped with video cameras, the mainstay of the force comprises the Ghost Gray Beechcraft Guardrail and Grumman Mohawk families, outfitted to perform the more sophisticated tasks of radar-reconnaissance and sigint.

The twin-turboprop Beechcraft series, which can operate from unimproved airstrips, is the most prolific. Several hundred of the 'vanilla' light transport variants have been acquired from the Wichita-based manufacturer since 1964 for liaison duties by all three US services, with a select number specially adapted by the US Army for sigint- and urint-gathering assignments, in two key marks, the RU-21 King Air (based on the civil A90/A100 series) and the heftier RC-12 Huron (derived from the Super King Air B200C series), the latter equipped with eavesdropping sensors code-named 'Guardrail' and 'Left Foot'. The composite force of RU-21A–D/H and RC-12D models is distributed between Active units and elements of the National Guard, the leading edge of the force being forward-deployed to Germany at Wiesbaden and Stuttgart, under the 1st and 2nd Military Intelligence Battalions respectively (with additional forces serving with Aerial Surveillance Companies at Coleman Barracks and Ramstein). The latest in the series is the RC-12K, equipped with the Guardrail Common Sensor System (G/CSS). This can acquire both comint and elint, effectively combining the functions of the RV-1D Mohawk (described below) with those of the older 'Guardrail V' RU-21H and RC-12D models which it is gradually replacing, and is designed to support the service's ATACMS (Army Tactical Missile System) units in addition to collecting pure sigint. Self-protection equipment includes an AN/ALQ-162 'Compass Sail' continuous-wave jammer to defeat the SA-6 SAM and AN/ALQ-136 to fox ZSU-23/4-class triple-A systems, permitting flights over hostile territory. The RC-12K is in production with orders (plus options) amounting to 31 aircraft. A new Model RC350 Guardian, with a 3ft-expanded wing span for greater cruise economy and 27 per cent more cabin space, was developed by Beechcraft immediately following the cessation of hostilities in the Gulf and is currently being offered on the international market for overland and maritime surveillance, with optional sigint fits. The

Below: Grumman OV-1D Mohawks provided extensive battle-area reconnaissance of the jungles of Vietnam and, more recently, the deserts of Kuwait and Iraq. This particular machine, its AN/APS-94F SLAR clearly in view, carries the mission symbols to prove it. (Author)

prototype Guardian features a derivative of Raytheon Electromagnetic Systems Division's AN/ALQ-142 ESM set, whose Rotman direction-finding 'lenses' are tucked away in wing-tip pods, designed to pick up emitters in the 0.2–18GHz range.[4] The fuselage has been turned over to HF/VHF and UHF equipment. A multi-element direction-finding array located beneath a large black ventral radome feeds the twenty narrow-band comint receivers that can be installed. All audio data can be relayed directly to a customized pair of ground vans that would work with a typical airborne squad of half a dozen Guardians, three of which would be airborne at any one time. Loiter time is up to six hours at an altitude of 35,000ft, making it an impressive surveillance package.

First flown in prototype form on 14 April 1959, the OV-1 Mohawk is a multi-mission twin-seat surveillance aircraft honed to battle area observation using cameras, radar and infra-red devices. The elint function is a more recent development. Its trident-tailed arrangement (designed for maximum stability to counteract the yaw-inducing asymmetric sensor appendages and bulbous side-by side cockpit) is uniquely Grumman in origin, as is the use of ejection seats, also unorthodox for an Army machine. However, the gently whining Avco-Lycoming T53 turbo-props powering its unusual bulk render it difficult to detect at all but short distances. The machine was originally manufactured in four key photo- and radar-recce variants, all optimized for the surveillance of small fortifications such as hamlets or bunkers which are of special importance to field officers: the OV-1A, sixty-four of which entered the inventory equipped with KA-30 and -60 cameras (featuring optional LS-59A photo-flash pods for night-time work); 101 of the OV-1B, which introduced an all-weather AN/APS-94A SLAR (fitted in an off-axis 'canoe' to ensure adequate ground clearance); 133 OV-1Cs, which were equipped with with the airborne portion of first-generation UAS-4 infra-red detection equipment to supplement the OV-1A's basic camera fit; and 37 of the OV-1D mark, capable of switching between infra-red and SLAR with only about an hour's worth of ground preparation. Blooded in South-East Asia, where 23 aircraft were lost to hostile fire over the steamy jungles of South Vietnam and Laos while flying surveillance sorties in pursuit of the elusive Viet Cong, the type proved to be both a source of fear and and an object of curiosity to its enemies, who must have been astonished at the comings and goings of its armament. It was sporadically equipped with machine guns and 2.75in high-explosive rockets for 'self defence', and frequent Air Force objections to the Army's encroaching on its territory with armed fixed-wing types occasionally led to ridiculous directives which obliged the latter

service to dispatch defenceless Mohawks for prolonged periods of action.[5]

Today's still substantial fleet, which flies mostly stand-off missions, is completely unarmed, preferring instead to use the aircraft's wing stations principally for additional fuel during ferry flights or for Sanders AN/ALQ-147(V)2 'Hot Brick' infra-red countermeasures pods, designed to defeat man-portable heat-seeking missiles, which pose a far more serious threat than small-arms fire. All current assets carry the 'Delta' suffix: a further 108 OV-1Ds were converted from old stock through the 1980s during an extensive structural and systems upgrade, and at least two of these were supplied to Israel in 1976.[6] Standard equipment for the OV-1D includes an updated AN/APS-94F SLAR or AN/AAS-24 infra-red line-scanner (plus back-up KA-60C and KA-76 cameras), and no fewer than 110 of these aircraft have received Block 1 upgrades—comprising improved T53-L-704 engines and added communications equipment—to keep them in service through to the end of the century. More significant to the dicussion here are the thirty-six specially adapted RV-1D models designated 'Quick Look II'. Working in co-operation with the radar surveillance types, these are fitted with AN/ALQ-133 ESM receivers optimized for stand-off elint. In common with the Beechcraft 'snoopers', the bulk of the surviving force remains forward-deployed to Germany, serving with the mixed aviation companies 'barracked' with the 1st and 2nd MIBtns at Wiesbaden and Stuttgart, each of which operates a dozen OV-1Ds and six RV-1Ds. Further examples continue to ply their clandestine trade from South Korea, keeping a check on the hostile border country.

Making up in capability for what they lack in terms of glamour, the Mohawks and Guardrails provided round-the-clock surveillance in the Gulf, operating primarily from Al Qaysumah in Saudi Arabia. The

---

[4]The AN/ALQ-142 is carried by US Navy's SH-60 LAMPS (Light Airborne Multi-Purpose System) Mk 3 helicopters for maritime sigint. Six older ex-US Army RC-12D aircraft have been procured by the Israeli Defence Forces, which are expressing an interest in the new models.

[5]This type of petty squabbling and rivalry is precisely the sort of nonsense which Senate Armed Service Committee Chairman Senator Sam Nunn is currently trying to rid the US military of, as part of his call for a 'no holds barred' review of service roles and missions. The military were due to report with proposals which contain a 'strong commitment to change' in November 1992. Among the most likely major changes are the shifting of USAF A/OA-10s to the US Army and the establishment of a combined—*de jure* as well as *de facto*—SOF aerial recce-strike, CSAR and COIN force. Refer to Chapter 4.

[6]An additional four were authorized for shipment to Pakistan at the height of the Afghanistan War to help keep an eye on the mountainous border region, but their eventual disposition is unknown.

Above: A dozen of the RV-1D 'Quick Look II' elint models of the Mohawk continue to serve in Europe alongside 24 OV-1Ds of the US Army's 1st and 2nd Military Intelligence Battalions barracked at Wiesbaden and Stuttgart, though these aircraft are shortly to be ousted by the RC-12K 'Guardrail' (Scott Van Aken)

Below: The older Beechcraft RU-21 King Air comint aircraft are gradually being replaced by much more advanced RC-12K G/CSS (Guardrail Common Sensor System) aircraft from the same manufacturer. Thirty-one of the newer version are on the order books. (M-Slides)

intelligence they garnered proved particularly crucial in support of the US 18th Airborne Corps' daring heliborne flanking operation fifty miles deep into Iraq which spearheaded the Coalition land force's offensive on 24 February 1991. Twenty-eight machines of the 15th MIBtn from Fort Hood, Texas (including attachments from the King Air-equipped 224th MIBtn and the Huron-outfitted 1st MIBtn), flew more than 475 combat missions, logging 3,900 flight hours. These mission levels were unprecedented. Despite the comparative vulnerability of the aircraft, only one was lost (RC-12D 80-23375, from the 1st MIBtn), to what were described as 'operational causes'. Total assets committed to the theatre included 32 OV/RV-1Ds (which accounted for 700 sorties), eleven RC-12Ds and fifteen of the RU-21 series which bore such racy names as 'Great Balls of Fire', 'Catch 22', and 'From Riches to Rags'.

MARITIME SNOOPERS

Sigint tasks extend to naval air arms, with the goal of providing a 'fingerprint' of enemy ships. Trudging through the clouds on endless patrols are the US Navy's secretive squads of Lockheed EP-3E Orions, code-named 'Aries'. A dozen machines are assigned to this duty, each with a crew comprising an EW Aircraft Commander (EWAC) and a Mission Commander (MC) plus fifteen sigint and radar-recce personnel, including at least two fully rated NFOs who bear the trade-names EVAL (EW Tactical Evaluator) and EWAN (EW Navigator). The crew members operate a mass of specialized gear, embracing dual AN/APS-115 ASW (anti-submarine warfare) radar, an

AN/ALD-8 direction-finding receiver, AN/ALQ-78 automated ESM, an Argo AN/ALR-52 radar receiver, a United Technologies Laboratory AN/ALQ-110 elint analyser and a GTE-Sylvania AN/ALR-60 comint receiver, plus IFF and radar countermeasures designed primarily to foil enemy fighters that may be deployed to curtail the aircraft's sneaky monitoring operations.[7] While its efficient quartet of Allison T56-A-15 turboprops provides excellent range and endurance (on two engines the machine can trundle along at 1,500ft for 14½ hours), the EP-3E is confined to two bases—fleet air reconnaissance countermeasures squadrons VQ-1 at NAS Agana, Guam, and VQ-2 at NAS Rota, Spain—which somewhat limits the scope of operations. To fill that void, previously occupied by Douglas ERA-3 'Whales', Lockheed are adapting sixteen carrier-borne S-3A Viking ASW jets to the ES-3A sigint and BGPHES (Battle Group Passive Horizon Extension System) roles at their Palmdale facility. The aerodynamic testbed, BuNo 157993, first took to the skies in this revised form in September 1989, and the initial production example, BuNo 159404, followed on 15

---

[7]Two EP-3B aircraft (ex-P-3B BuNos 149669 and 149678) were converted for the task during 1969, later modified to EP-3E standard and joined by an additional ten EP-3E models (ex-P-3A BuNos 148887, 148888, 149668, 150494, 150497, 150498, 150501-150503 and 150505) between 1971 and 1975. Owing to fatigue problems, these are about to be supplanted by twelve new conversions, to be performed by Lockheed Aeromod Center Inc at Greenville, South Carolina. Japan's Kawasaki Heavy Industries is building five licence-manufactured EP-3s for the Japanese Maritime Force, the first of which was delivered in March 1991. An additional three or four may be procured after 1995.

Above left: Some of the EP-3E's sigint antennae are visible from this underside view—especially the 'farms' under the tail and wing tips. (Author)

Above: The aerodynamic test-bed for the ES-3A sigint Viking was BuNo 157993, which first took to the skies in September 1989. Carrying almost identical listening apparel to the EP-3E 'Aries', sixteen examples are being converted at NAS Cecil Field, Florida (depot centre for the similar S-3A/B Viking ASW fleet), and will form with VQ-5 and VQ-6 for land-based and sea-going deployments. (Lockheed)

Below: An ICAP EA-6B Prowler from VAQ-130 *Zappers* shows off its typical ALQ-99D fit of 'listening football', two drop tanks and three jamming pods. The maximum crew is four, comprising a pilot and three NFO/ECMOs. (Via Peter E. Davies)

May 1991. The remaining operationally configured aircraft, which feature equipment almost identical to the sigint avionics carried by the 'Aries', will be converted at NAS Cecil Field, Florida, to form two new squadrons, VQ-5 at NAS Agana and VQ-6 at NAS Cecil Field, which will deploy aboard the 'flat-tops' as two-plane detachments. New Link 11 UHF/HF communications equipment forms part of the revised kit, which is manifested as three new radomes and 35 blade antennae, operated by a four-man crew. The aircraft have plenty of life left in them. Although the last example of the podgy Viking left Lockheed in

Above: Crouching on one of the USS *John F. Kennedy*'s catapults in March 1978 is an EXCAP EA-6B of VAQ-133 *Wizards*. The Prowler series performs sigint in addition to pure jamming and is also fitted with one of three comint/comjam packages—the AN/ALQ-92, the AN/ASQ-191 or the latest AN/ALQ-149. (US Navy/Norman Polmar)

Below: The black-tailed EA-6B Prowlers with the Hefner symbol of fecundity indicate their membership of the US Marines' VMAQ-2 *Playboys*. The USMC operates twelve aircraft in three four-ship detachments. (Via Ben Knowles)

1978, the machine was designed for an impressive 13,000-hour fatigue life (since amended upwards by 30 per cent) and so has sufficient unexpired airframe life to see it in service well into the twenty-first century.

Also undergoing a major Advanced Capability (ADVCAP) modernization programme is the US Navy's sizeable EA-6B establishment, which operates from ship and shore on two related ESM assign-

ments: active radar- and communications-jamming in support of US and allied air strikes; and passive sigint, which is used to provide a constantly updated EOB 'threat library' in support of Carrier Group operations. Alluding to its Grumman feline origins and the lurking nature of its mission, the Prowler ranks as the world's most sophisticated self-contained ESM platform. The kingpin of this capability is its Eaton-AIL AN/ALQ-99(V) tactical jamming system (TJS). Whereas its predecessors the 'Whale', EA-6A Intruder and EB-66C Destroyer used barrage noise-jamming between brief 'listening' sessions spanning 10–15 seconds, the Prowler's TJS introduced the radical concept of 'look-through', whereby the system could tune in on enemy radars, analyze and record them *and* then respond with simultaneous spot-noise jamming, carefully tailored to the threat. Moreover, only the receivers were built into the airframe, housed in a fin-top 'football' fairing; the accompanying jammers were contained in up to five 950lb underwing pods, permitting the latter suite to be modified on a mission-to-mission basis.

First test-flown on 28 May 1968 with Grumman test pilot Don King at the controls and built up around a massively strong titanium keel, the EA-6B airframe was designed with a minimum 4,000hr fatigue life intended to include 950 exacting steam-

EA-6B PRODUCTION

Bureau Numbers	Nos built (remaining)	
Basic		
156478 to 156482	5	(2)
158029 to 158040	12	(9)
158540 to 158561	11	(6)
EXCAP		
158779 to 158817	19	(10)
159582 to 158587	6	(5)
ICAP I		
159907 to 159912	6	(5)
160432 to 160437	6	(6)
160609	1	(1)
160704 to 160709	6	(3)
160786 to 160791	6	(5)
161115 to 161120	6	(5)
161242 to 161247	6	(5)
161347 to 161352	6	(5)
161774 to 161775	29	(2)
ICAP II		
161776 to 161779	4	(2)
161880 to 161885	6	(6)
162223 to 162230	8	(6)
162934 to 162939	6	(6)
163030 to 163035	6	(6)
163044 to 163048	5	(4)
ICAP II Block 86		
163049	1	(1)
163395 to 163406	12	(12)
163520 to 163351	12	(12)
163884 to 163892	9	(9)
164401 to 164403	3	(3)

As of January 1990, 103 aircraft were on the inventory, comprising seventy-five ICAP II and twenty-eight Block 86 machines. Further examples were undergoing conversion or had not yet been delivered.

EA-6B UNITS

Unit	Nickname	Remarks
VAQ-129	*New Vikings*	Fleet Replacement (Training)
VAQ-130	*Zappers*	
VAQ-131	*Lancers*	
VAQ-132	*Scorpions*	
VAQ-133	*Wizards*	
VAQ-134	*Garudas*	
VAQ-135	*Black Ravens*	
VAQ-136	*Gauntlets*	Customarily forward-deployed to Atsugi, Japan
VAQ-137	*Rooks*	
VAQ-138	*Yellow Jackets*	
VAQ-139	*Cougars*	
VAQ-140	*Patriots*	
VAQ-141	*Shadow Hawks*	
VAQ-142	*Grim Watchdogs*	Disbanded 1991
VMAQ-1	*Screaming Banshees*	MCAS Cherry Point, NC; formerly VMAQ-2 Detachments X, Y and Z
VMAQ-2	*Playboys*	
VMAQ-3	*Moondogs*	
VMAQ-4	*Seahawks*	

All aircraft are headquartered at NAS Whidbey Island, Washington.

catapulted launches and arrested recoveries ('cats' and 'traps', extended to 1,500 in 1985). Entering service on 29 January 1971 with Fleet Replacement Squadron VAQ-129 *New Vikings* at NAS Whidbey Island, Washington, by 18 November 1988 the force had reached full strength with the commissioning of VAQ-142 *Grim Watchdogs*, the thirteenth carrier-deployable Tactical Electronic Warfare Squadron (TACELRON) to form. First in the queue were VAQ-132 *Scorpions* and VAQ-131 *Lancers*, which achieved IOC in July and October 1971 respectively, just in time for combat evaluation in troubled South-East Asia on board the carriers USS *America* and USS *Enterprise*. Known as 'standard' or 'basic' models, the eight aircraft, twelve pilots and thirty ECMOs (Electronic Countermeasures Officers) not only provided round-the-clock jamming support in a stand-off 'feet-wet' mode off the coast of North Vietnam but also generated a torrent of intelligence derived from the AN/ALQ-99 'football' receiver, on-board AN/APR-27 defensive receiver and Sanders Associates AN/ALQ-92 communications-jamming (comjam) device. EOB maps could thus be constantly updated for use by the carriers' Intruders, Corsairs and Phantoms for 'Alpha' and 'Delta' strikes deep into enemy airspace, while the opposition's Sino-Soviet-supplied radar and communications installations also came under close scrutiny in support of the

Naval Air Systems Command. These sigint missions included 'Wild Bill' elint flights against 'Height Finder', 'Bar Lock', 'Fire Can', 'Whiff' and 'Flat Face' emitters, conducted in concert with RA-5C Vigilantes, and 'Comfy Coat' comint, using the listening portion of the aircraft's AN/ALQ-92 comjam. The intensity of operations can be gauged from the activities of Cdr Lucio Diloreto's *Lancers*, which amassed 456 'traps' on deck, 166 of them at night! In all, the units flew 720 combat sorties.

In the post-Vietnam years, production continued apace with newer, more sophisticated models featuring deception-jamming, increased band coverage, much improved computer analysis and data storage capabilities and more finely tuned elint and comint/comjam apparatus. These programmes comprised the AN/ALQ-99A Expanded Capability Prowler (EXCAP, beginning with BuNo 158799 in January 1973); the -99D Improved-Capability Phase One (ICAP-1, starting with BuNo 159907 in March 1976); the -99F ICAP-2 (staring with BuNo 161776 in January 1984); and today's ADVCAP (commencing with test-bed BuNo 156482, re-delivered for test trials in October 1989), which is joining the Fleet as this is being written. Under an continuing CILOP (conversion in lieu of procurement) programme, older surviving airframes have been progressively updated to bring them into line with the latest production models, which continued to trickle out of the Grumman 'Ironworks' until the last of the electronic stalkers (BuNo 164403) was delivered in August 1990. ADVCAP, which is being applied to 95 airframes, includes exotic command and control systems such as JTIDS, a GPS/Navstar receiver, extended ALQ-99 frequency coverage through to

Below: ICAP II Prowler 'AE/605' was assigned to VAQ-132 *Scorpions* aboard the *USS Forrestal* during 1986. The unit introduced the 'standard' Prowler to combat in 1972 and has been flying progressively updated marks ever since. The grey tactical paint scheme used today weathers rapidly and is frequently touched up by the Plane Captains as a corrosion control measure, further adding to the patchy finish. (Grumman)

band 10, AN/ALQ-165 ASPJ (Advanced Self-Programming Jammer) and a brand new Lockheed-Sanders AN/ALQ-149 comjam system, along with new P&WA J52-P-P409 turbojet engines and aerodynamic improvements to reduce the aircraft's critical approach speed.[8] Shipboard programming is provided by TEAMS (Tactical EA-6B Mission-Planning System). This not only assists the crews with the taxing process of working out 'master radiate' timing but can actually 'talk' to the AYK-14 computers of the 'Electronic Tadpole' to 'download' and process sigint to catalogue EOBs in any given theatre. In this manner, the aircraft and its crew of three or four (varying with mission requirements) provide an all-in-one EW system unrivalled by any other air arm.

The closest competition comes from the USAF/ Grumman EF-111A Raven, 42 of which were converted from standard 'Ace' model fighter-bombers to the jamming configuration and re-delivered between 4 November 1981 and 23 December 1985, stuffed with the highly automated AN/ALQ-99E version of Eaton-AIL's Jamming Subsystem and linked to an ALR-62(V) radar-warning receiver to create its own all-up TJS. Two dozen of the forty remaining jets are now being realigned under the 429th ECS at Cannon AFB, New Mexico. Their mission is fundamentally similar to that of the Prowler, except in two crucial respects: the two-man crew hone their talents

Above: ICAP II EA-6Bs of VAQ-130 *Zappers* from the USS *John F. Kennedy* take on 'gas' from an Air Force Boeing. The *Zappers* provided ESM support for both land- and sea-based strike packages and claimed the first combat shoots of the AGM-88 HARM anti-radar missile. (US DoD)

towards automated jamming as opposed to the broader role of ESM, with only minor man-in-the-loop intervention; and their mission assignments include 'close-in' and 'penetration escort' jamming as opposed to just stand-off work. Moreover, the more specialized tasks of comint and comjam are outside its domain. Instead, these jobs are undertaken by four-engine turboprops operating with the code-names 'Comfy Levi' and 'Compass Call'.[9]

Matured in the post-Vietnam years, the AN/ALQ-99 has proved crucial in several Middle East operations.

---

[8] The Prowler's underwing pods each cover one of the following: bands 1/2 (VHF and band A), band 3 (band B), band 4 (band C), band 5/6 (bands D/E), band 7 (bands E/F), band 8 (bands G/H), band 9 (band I) and band 10 (band J). Typical configurations on the four underwing and belly pylons include a symmetric load of two fuel tanks and three jammers, e.g. band 7/tank/bands 1 or 2/tank/band 9. Two (or more) aircraft will fly in 'loose-deuce' formation with complementary AN/ALQ-99 pods and software for the 'footballs' and may work together using the TACAN antennae to provide a co-ordinated initiation of jamming.

[9] 'Comfy Levi' and 'Compass Call' are described in the context of AFSOF in Chapter 4.

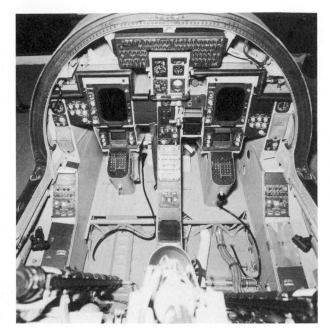 

Above, left and right: The ICAP I EA-6B's forward and aft cockpits are shown to advantage here. The pilot and front-seat NFO have since been given an INS and updated instruments to assist with captaining the aircraft and the comint/comjam role; the rear ECMO's displays have always been 'cosmic' and comprise computer-driven control pedestals and large Detail Display Indicators to flash up the radar threats. (Grumman)

This involvement began in 1981 during the US Navy's initial confrontation with Col Qadaffi's infamous 'Line of Death' and came to head five years later. On 24-25 March 1986 EA-6Bs from VAQ-137 *Rooks* and VMAQ-2 Detachment Y provided sigint and covering support for A-6E Intruder strikes against Libyan patrol boats during Operation 'Prairie Fire'. The boats had been harassing the Sixth Fleet, and they were quickly dispatched. On 15 April things hotted up again during Operation 'El Dorado Canyon', the punitive strike against Tripoli, Benina airfield and the Al Jumahiriya barracks, with EF-111As from the 42nd ECS *NATO Ravens* and EA-6Bs from VAQ-135 *Black Ravens* entering the fray. VAQ-135 flew from USS *Coral Sea* and nearby Sigonella on special-duty comint/comjam missions. The next round of action focused its attention further east, in the Persian Gulf. Prowlers first became involved in the region following an unprovoked (and unsuccessful) Iranian 'Silkworm' missile attack on the frigate USS *Jack Wilson* on 18 April 1988. During a series of counter-attacks by A-6Es and AH-1T SeaCobra helicopter gunships, which destroyed two Iranian oil platforms along with the frigate *Sahand* and fast patrol boat *Joshan*, EA-6Bs from Cdr Jeff Harris's *Black Ravens* provided fifteen hours of non-stop radar-disrupting cover. The machines also introduced the off-the-shelf

Collins AN/ASQ-191 comjam equipment into service, and it was at this juncture that the US Navy publicly admitted that for some time the Prowler community had been flying with enlisted Farsi langauge experts on board, who would monitor communications in support of the aircraft's vital sigint tasking. It has been reported that censored portions of the resultant comint and EOB data pertaining to the Iranian military was conveyed to Iraq, to maintain the status quo between the two warring nations, at the time engaged in a nine-year-long war of attrition. The United States was eager not to see either emerge as victor and was quite happy to watch the bloody proceedings continue unabated. Following the cease-fire and Saddam Hussein's incursion into Kuwait, the Prowlers redirected their powerful jamming and sigint apparatus against Iraq. Eventually, Operation 'Desert Storm' tasked eight Prowler TACELRONs to carriers operating from the the Gulf and the Red Sea, which provided cover for nearly every Coalition air operation undertaken throughout the six week-long air war. A USMC detachment at Sheikh Isa, Bahrain, brought theatre forces up to 46 aircraft, supported by squads of the similarly outfitted EF-111A Ravens which flew with the 7440th Combat Wing from Incirlik, Turkey, and with the 48th TFW(P) from Taif in Saudi Arabia. The USAF's supersonic AN/ALQ-99E 'platforms' alone accounted for 400 combat sorties/ 2,150 hours, providing a fair chunk of the in-force capability. Now that the dust from the whirlwind action has settled, the US Navy is looking forward to integrating the ADVCAP EA-6B into its ranks, while tentative Congressional plans exist to turn the USAF Ravens over to the sea-going fraternity. The issue has

not yet been resolved, but it forms part of the latest review of service roles in an effort to reduce expensive duplication—particularly with regard to costly 'concurrency' in future upgrades. Certainly the USAF would be very upset indeed to lose its Ravens, and the 'Spark Vark' possesses no carrier capability whatsoever—a point settled twenty-six years ago when the Navy's own fighter version was consigned to the scrap

Above: EF-111A Raven 67-052 spent the first eight years of its career with the 42nd ECS at RAF Upper Heyford. In April 1986 it was a participant in Operation 'El Dorado Canyon' and the following year carried the artwork 'Cherry Bomb'. The aircraft now serves with the 430th ECS at Cannon AFB, New Mexico. (USAFE)

Below: A pair of EF-111A Ravens on the ramp at RAF Upper Heyford, Oxfordshire, display their svelte, supersonic-capable airframes and variable-geometry 'swing' wings. The aircraft feature the Eaton-AIL AN/ALQ-99E JSS. Upper Heyford's Raven force flew 400 combat sorties during Operation 'Desert Storm'. (Author)

Above: The Raven's cockpit is jammed full of flight instruments and nav and attack gear. To the right is the EWO's AN/ALQ-99E Detail Display Indicator, a much more automated affair than that installed in the Prowler, which has two ECMOs and two sets of controls and displays with which to monitor proceedings. (Grumman)

EF-111A CONVERSIONS

USAF serial numbers	Nos converted (remaining)	Remarks
66-013 to -016	4 (4)	
-018 to -021	4 (4)	
-023	1 (0)	W/o 14 Feb 1991
-027 and -028	2 (2)	
-030 and -031	2 (2)	
-033	1 (1)	
-035 to -039	5 (5)	
-041	1 (1)	
-044	1 (1)	
-046 to -049	4 (4)	
-050 and -051	2 (2)	
-055 to -057	3 (2)	66-056 w/o 2 Apr 1992
67-032 to -035	5 (5)	
-037 to -039	3 (3)	
-041 and -042	2 (2)	
-044	1 (1)	
-048	1 (1)	
-052	1 (1)	

USAF EF-111A squadrons equipped with the internally mounted AN/ALQ-99E included the pioneering 388th ECS Griffins (subsequently redesignated the 390th ECS *Deny, Deceive, Defeat*) at Mountain Home AFB, Idaho, and the 42nd ECS *NATO Ravens* at RAF Upper Heyford, Oxfordshire, England. In the summer of 1992 the EF-111As were consolidated into one squadron under the 430th ECS *Tigers*, 27th FW, at Cannon AFB, New Mexico.

Left: The 42nd ECS' Saudi detachment (assigned to the 4404th Composite Wing) returned to RAF Upper Heyford from Dhahran for the last time on 26 June 1992, the three aircraft concerned bearing 'Volt' call-signs. About to climb out of the cockpit of 67-048 is Capt Jeff Coombes, who had ejected from EF-111A 66-056 (nicknamed 'Babyjam') twelve weeks earlier on 2 April. The unit disbanded on 10 July and all USAF Ravens were consolidated under the 430th ECS *Tigers* at Cannon AFB, near Clovis, New Mexico. (Author)

Above: Aircraft from the 390th ECS(P) *Tronfighters* fly in formation over Saudi Arabia. Assigned to Taif, the unit denied the Iraqis crucial radar data, forcing them to resort to inaccurate 'blind' barrage firing. One aircraft was lost on St Valentine's Day 1991: 66-023 tumbled into the ground during a threat-reaction 'jinking' manoeuvre, killing its crew, Capts D. L. Bradt and P. R. Eichenlob Jr. (US DoD)

heap—but its ability to fly at low level, at transonic speeds, even by night, deep into hostile airspace as a matter of routine, is a task which Prowler crews do not relish.

HARD-KILL

In addition to providing carrier crews with active jamming support and a constantly updated EOB, the EA-6B Prowler has the potential to destroy enemy emitters using Texas Instruments AGM-88 HARM (High-speed Anti-Radiation Missiles). This 'hard kill' capability was incorporated into the fleet beginning in 1987.[10] After all, with the threats plotted, the opportunity to wipe them out proves irresistible,

particularly if you have the potential to respond with home-on-jam missiles! This move is one of several inexorable trends that will see dedicated 'soft' and 'hard' EW assets merge; however, it will necessitate developing a 'do-it-all' machine fresh on the drawing board.

As an adjunct to the land-based elint mission, but customarily thrown into the deep end of combat at the first hint of trouble, are the dedicated radar-destroyers. The mission—known to US crews as SEAD, or the suppression of enemy air defences—was developed in the aftermath of the 1962 Cuban Missile Crisis following attacks on US reconnaissance aircraft by radar-directed SAM and flak batteries. The mission was perfected during the war in Vietnam, where the American aviators confronted, head-to-head, the North's sinister Soviet-supplied anti-aircraft network under the trade-name 'Iron Hand'. Between February 1972 and January 1973

[10]The first EA-6B to fire HARMs was BuNo 158805, which loosed them off over China Lake, California, in May 1986. HARM 'OpEvals' were completed the following summer and all ICAP-2 machines had received provision for the anti-radar missiles by March 1988. As a matter of interest, the level of operations undertaken by the TACELRONs can be gauged from the staggering 56,454.8 hours accumulated by the EA-6Bs that year (taking their total aggregate hours to 383,729.3, 'cats' to 80,396 and 'traps' to 81,792!). HARMs were first fired in combat by the appropriately nicknamed VAQ-130 *Zappers* while operating from the USS *John F. Kennedy* during Operation 'Desert Storm'.

Above: 'Wild Weasel' air crews from the 81st TFS *Panthers* pose for the camera in front of one of their radar-killing F-4G Phantoms at Sheikh Isa, Bahrain. (Via Lt-Col Jim Uken)

Right: The EWO's position in the back seat 'pit' of the F-4G 'Wild Weasel' Phantom features back-up flight instruments and, below them, the digital panoramic and homing indicators, used to garner elint and to 'feed' targets into the machine's lethal armoury of AGM-88 HARM missiles. (McAir via John J. Harty)

Below: An F-4G crew prepare to start up and launch from Sheikh Isa, their mount carrying two AGM-88B HARM missiles interfaced with the jet's sensitive AN/APR-47 elint receiver. Sixty 'Weasels' and their crews were assigned to the base for 'Desert Storm', under the command of Col Ron Karp. (Lt-Col Jim Uken)

Opposite page: Wearing wall-to-wall AGM-88 HARM missiles and an experimental one-piece windshield, an F-4G lunges menacingly towards the camera. (USAF)

alone, 83 US aircraft fell prey to SAMs, yet studies indicate that these losses would have been at least five times greater but for the judicious use of SEAD and constantly re-tuned jammers, the continuing QRA development of which depended heavily on a steady and reliable stream of sigint.

In the post-Vietnam years the US military continued to update its fleet of 'Iron Hand' aircraft, while Europe lagged woefully behind.[11] In the main, the US Navy opted to concentrate on advanced ARM missile technology—notably updated models of the Texas Instruments AGM-45 Shrike and General Dynamics Pomona AGM-78 Standard ARM, and the brand new Navy-designed AGM-88 HARM—which could be 'strapped on' to a broad range of sea-going strike and EW aircraft.[12] The USAF, on the other hand, elected to field a further specialized variant of the combat-proven Phantom, stuffed to the brim with elint

apparatus interfaced with the Navy missiles for locate-and-destroy work. No fewer than 134 F-4G 'Advanced Wild Weasel Vs' were converted from Fiscal Year 1969 F-4E Phantom fighter stocks in two batches, some forty of which remain in service today.[13] Although now somewhat long in the tooth, the 'Weasels' continue to provide the 'big bite' for the USAF's SEAD forces, now headquartered under the 81st FS at Spangdahlem, Germany (the sole remaining active unit, at present disbanding), and the 124th FG at Boise, Idaho (a combat-capable training element of the Air National Guard). Despite its mid-1970s origins, the technology remains impressive and the size of the force belies its ferocity: just like their namesakes, once the Weasels' canines are engaged, they will retain a tight grip until their prey are in coma. Still with the anthropomorphic analogy, keen smell and cunning originally derived from the

IBM AN/APR-38A HAWC (homing and warning computer), which used interferometers and superheterodynes as part of 56 antennae added to the aircraft to pick up and analyze emitters at ranges of up to twenty miles (with elint reception at least three times

---

[11] European developments were confined to the Anglo-French Martel anti-radar missile which could be fitted to Buccaneers and Mirages and to the Soviet MiG-25 'Foxbat-E', discussed in Chapter 2.

[12] The ARMs themselves, when tied into the user aircraft's RWR or more specialized SEAD avionics, are capable of providing on-the-spot elint preparatory to a missile or bomb attack. This subject has been described more fully in the author's *Airborne Weapons of the West*, published by Arms & Armour Press in 1992.

[13] Modified during depot maintenance overhauls at Ogden Logistics Center at Hill AFB, Utah, including 116 between 1977 and 1981 and a follow-on batch of eighteen attrition replacements which were converted between 1987 and 1989. These ousted the Vietnam-era survivors of sixty F-105G 'Weasel Thuds' and thirty-six F-4C 'Wild Weasel IV' Phantoms.

as great). These would then be plotted on the Phantom back-seater's panoramic and homing indicator displays, ranked in order of priority according to the HAWC's threat programme software. The EWO in the 'pit' would then 'hand them off' to the ARMs, which could be fired at the enemy emitters at a relatively safe stand-off distance, off-axis from the target, while the pilot at the front was furnished with a threat bearing to assist with missile attack or a follow-up 'dive-toss' bomb run with cluster munitions. The AN/APR-38A was unique in that it was capable of providing threat type, bearing and range in 'real time' in the cockpit and, in a secondary role, the HAWC established itself as a highly effective elint tool, with the facility to collate the threats on Conrac magnetic tape recorders for post-mission analysis.

The entire system was 'revisited' from 1987 under Phase One of the Performance Update Program (PUP), the heart of which was a new Unisys WASP (Weasel Attack Signal Processor) which increased computer memory by a factor of eight and speeded radar interpretation sevenfold. LSI AN/ARN-101(V) digital navigation equipment also replaced the vintage analogue nav-and-attack systems. Redesignated the AN/APR-47, the system established its worth during the Gulf War. Sixty F-4Gs from the 81st FS *Panthers* and the 561st *Black Knights* were forward-deployed to Sheik Isa in Bahrain between August and December 1990 under the command of Lt-Col Ron Karp (with additional assets stationed at Incirlik in Turkey, to cover the northern sector), to provide SEAD for Coalition strike aircraft, including 'packages' of US Navy, Marine Corps and Saudi Arabian jets. Their reputation preceded them. After obliterating the Iraqi radar defences with the missile-launching war cries 'Shotgun', 'Rifle' and 'Magnum', the 'Weasels' (which always flew using distinctive beer brand call-signs such as 'Budweiser', 'Michelob', etc) by their mere presence proved sufficient to coerce the remaining enemy radar operators to 'shut up shop'—to switch off their emitters to avoid being 'bitten' by the Weasels' substantial armoury of ARMs and bombs.[14] However, in its elint mode the AN/APR-47 was capable of picking up the threats after only a few seconds' exposure to the enemy emitters, which were duly noted on the Conrac mission recorders. With aerial refuelling support, these 'Weasel Police' patrol tactics would last for up to three hours, to provide a constant umbrella for Coalition aircraft. On the 'hard kill' board, several crews chalked up impressive scores: the 81st FS's top-scoring crew was EWO Maj Ken Spaar and his pilot Capt Vinnie Quinn, with a dozen confirmed radars knocked out. There were some impressive aircraft too. Top of the league was F-4G 69-7207 from the 561st AMU (Aircraft Maintenance Unit), nicknamed 'Laura L' after the

wife of its Dedicated Crew Chief TSgt James R. Clark. This beast clocked up 223.7 flight-hours during 62 combat missions flown between 17 January and 3 March 1991. Evidence of just how busy the aircraft had become was also highlighted by a sister-ship (69-7263), assigned to DCC TSgt Alan Martin and appropriately nicknamed 'Number One SAM-Slammer', which fired 37 HARMs, two Mavericks and one Shrike.

Returning home that April, the force was shortly afterwards drawn down into its present organization, a knock-on effect of the post-Cold War cutbacks in defence expenditure. Despite their outstanding successes in the Gulf, the O&M costs—reputedly three times that of the F-16—prompted a scaling-down in line with the wholesale withdrawal of the Phantom from the US inventory. This has also put a firm lid on the prospective Phase Two of the PUP update, which would have added a new Directional Receiver Group. In their stead are the gaggles of easy-to-maintain F-16 'Electric Jets', which must rely on the built-in Loral radar warning receiver (RWR) kit to assist with missile attack. The latest AN/ALR-56M model of the RWR is theoretically capable of providing the relative azimuth of emitters to within about one degree; however, it features no critical rangefinding capability nor back-up elint functions, and it has no EWO to use the equipment to maximum effect. Longer-term measures are being taken to provide a podded 'strap-on' (known as 'Weasel in a Can'!). Meanwhile the prime contractors for the F-4G, McAir, are continuing to explore the possibilities of stripping the Phantoms of their specialized equipment and refitting it inside a number of F-15E Strike Eagles, which are already destined to receive added provisions for a modest elint package (yet to be settled) by 1997. In the interim, the old Vietnam War-era 'Weasel' watchword 'Cave Putorium!' has become a European trademark.

Unlike the Royal Air Force, which opted for pure imaging-systems for its recce-strike GR.1A Tornados, Germany's *Luftwaffe* and Italy's *Aeronautica Militare* have gone the whole hog are and fielding a specialized Electronic Combat-Reconnaissance (ECR) version of the Panavia 'swinger', known to the programme leaders in Germany as the EKA (*Elektronische Kampfführung und Aufklärung*). As with

<hr>

[14]The announcements 'Shotgun', 'Rifle' and 'Magnum' signified the launch of Shrike, Maverick and HARM missiles respectively and were made as a warning to friendly aviators to avoid possible confusion with enemy SAMs. By night only the faint plumes from the missiles' rocket motors are visible, and the daring tactics of the 'Weasels' make their presence, but not their precise whereabouts, known, which might otherwise cause confusion. The force is being wound down as part of the F-4 phase-out, but fortunately some of the 'institutional knowledge' is being preserved by means of liaison with the RAF's and the *Luftwaffe's* Tornado squadrons.

Above: The second *Staffel* of *Marinefleigergeschwader* 2 (2/MFG 2) was the first Tornado unit to specialize in the HARM anti-radar missile. The mission is passing over to the *Luftwaffe's* Tornado Electronic Combat-Reconnaissance, one of which is shown here; thirty-five aircraft are being adapted to the task for JBG 32 at Lechfeld and JBG 38 at Jever. Italy is also buying the Tornado ECR, and the first of sixteen (serial MM7079) flew from Turin/Casselle in late July 1992. (Author)

the American 'Wild Weasel' kit, the mission equipment is a fully integral part of the Tornado's avionics. It comprises a Honeywell-Sondertechnik infra-red imaging system (IIS), a nose-mounted FLIR and a TI/Deutschland GmbH Emitter Location System (ELS) interfaced with the TI AGM-88 HARM. Litton-Litef ODIN (operational data interface) data-link equipment provides a microwave relay of critical threat information to suitably equipped friendly C3 and fighter-bomber aircraft. The German prototype (serial number 9803) first took to the air on 18 August 1988 and has been followed by 35 operational models produced under Batch 7 (the last, following six batches totalling 324 jets manufactured for the *Luftwaffe* and the *Marineflieger*) for distribution between *Jagdbombergeschwader* 32 at Lechfeld and JBG 38 at Jever, delivered between May 1990 and January 1992, which are currently in the

process of training on their new mounts. These are not yet fully mission-capable and will be refitted with the IIS and ELS after qualification tests are satisfactorily completed, beginning in December 1992. Like the AN/APR-47, the ELS is a high-sensitivity, broad-frequency system optimized to locate the 'terminal threats' which guide triple-A, SAMs and air-to-air missiles to their targets, and it backs that capability up with a modern channelized receiver. This avoids the shortcomings found in both wide- and narrow-band receivers (the former suffering from poor selectivity owing to their broad 'sniffing' facility and the latter from limited coverage owing to their inherent selectiveness) to ensure a high probability of interception of all pertinent signals and the rapid display of the threats on the cockpit CEDAM (combined electronic display and map), all of which can be recorded for elint purposes. The IIS is also state-of-the-art, capable of providing horizon-to-horizon coverage in 'real time' and of 'fusing' this with additional information from the FLIR and ELS. Italy's sixteen Tornado ECRs, due to enter service during 1995, will use an almost identical kit except for the IIS, which is to be substituted with an E-O video-camera which offers both 'real time' viewing in the cockpit and up to 30 minutes' worth of taped, high-

resolution imagery which can be digitally enhanced following aircraft recovery. Interest has been expressed by the US Navy, which is considering repackaging the ELS portion of the hardware into pods for carriage as an optional extra by the F/A-18D(CR). France is treading a similar path. Thomson-CSF has developed ASTAC, an elint pod which can glean its data either autonomously or with manual pilot intervention. Secretly tested on a Mirage F1CR from the French MOD Flight Test Centre at Bretigny near Paris during the 'brassboard' stage of development, it demonstrated the ability to plot radars at ranges of up to 250nm from an altitude of 35,000ft. Working in the C to J bands in which most radars operate (with the facility to be further expanded into the K band at the upper end), ASTAC is said to be able to handle 200 emitters simultaneously and, by means of interferometric techniques, to plot the azimuth of these threats to within half a degree! Self-contained in a 13ft-long pod weighing a mere 400kg (882lb), it exemplifies the great strides forward being made by Western European firms in what was an American stronghold. The beauty of these packages is their small size: as a USAF officer associated with the 'Golden Fleece' programme noted, modern micro-electronics are permitting systems the size of the AN/ASD-1, 'which took up the bulk of an RC-135, to be tucked away into a pod small enough to be carried by fighter-category aircraft.' Further advances in automation will soon provide a capability commensurate with that of the giants.

GOD'S-EYE-VIEW

There is no substitute for bulk when several tons of active radar-mapping gear needs to be hauled aloft. The larger the radar aperture, the greater the image quality, even when using SAR techniques. It is a

Above: The Grumman E-2C Hawkeye is far more than just a cheaper alternative to the big Boeing AWACS. Its AN/APS-125 (or newer -145) rotodome is able to track up to 250 'bogeys' simultaneously, using three radar operators and ARPS (Advanced Radar Processing System). A gross of this latest type have been manufactured since its first flight on 20 January 1971, mostly for the US Navy and Coast Guard but also for several overseas clients, including five aircraft for Egypt, four for Israel, four for Singapore and eighteen for Japan (one of whose machines is pictured here). (Grumman)

Right: NATO's eighteen E-3A AWACS fly from Geilenkirchen in Germany, split into three squadrons which are crewed by personnel from eleven of NATO's sixteen member nations. This example was caught in the moody evening twilight while taking on fuel over cloudy England. (USAF/SSgt David Nolan)

simple equation that microelectronics cannot as yet redress. By virtue of their one- or two-man crew, small fighters also lack the ingredient of teamwork ('people-in-the-loop') essential to airborne C3I. In this field the US continues to reign supreme, although Russia's Ilyushin Il-76 'Mainstay' has made minor inroads. The fiasco of the British Nimrod AEW.3 venture, which foundered after billions of pounds had been spent on the fabulous beast, remains a source of considerable embarrassment to the Ministry of Defence, frustration to the beleaguered contractors and annoyance to the British taxpayer. The RAF's 'Magic Roundabout' squad of aged Shackletons was eventually replaced by seven of Boeing's E-3D Sentry Airborne Warning & Control Systems (AWACS), giant airborne C3 radar outposts, based on the 707-320C airliner, which cruise at altitude with distinctive 'whirly-top' Westinghouse rotodomes capable of monitoring twelve thousand cubic miles of airspace during each ten second, 360-degree scan.

The 100-ton 'flying radar' was evolved from a pair of EC-137D test-beds, the first of which flew on 5 February 1972. USAF orders followed for two dozen

of the so-called 'core' E-3A mark, which went on to equip the 552nd Airborne Control Wing (ACW) at Tinker AFB, Oklahoma, beginning on 24 March 1977. Equipped with AN/APY-1 ODR (Overland Downlock Radar) and IBM CC-1 computer processing, the Sentry plots, interrogates (via IFF) and maps all aircraft within its scan and projects the synthesized data on to nine SDCs (situation display consoles) and ADUs (auxiliary display units) tucked into the long cylindrical cabin. The crew then vector friendly fighter aircraft on to hostile targets, keeping tabs on the proceedings right through to missile launch, if necessary, via TADIL-C data-link and jam-resistant 'Have Quick' radio. The AN/APY-1 works in several modes, including passive detection, full-power beyond-the-horizon scan and shorter-range pulse-Doppler non-elevation or elevation scan. Improvements followed on the production line with a second batch of ten 'standard' E-3As which introduced a full maritime tracking facility by means of new AN/APY-2 ODRs and a combined pulse-repetition frequency-scanning mode for the simulataneous tracking of ships and aircraft. These machines have since been upgraded to the E-3C mark with the installation of five additional SDCs and jam-resistant communications, including the 'netted' JTIDS, while the original two dozen have been progressively re-fitted with CC-2 computers and most of the other features of the E-3C to bring them up to an intermediate E-3B configuration. Thirty-four USAF machines continue to equip the 552nd at Tinker AFB, with permanent detachments further afield at NAS Keflavik, Iceland, Kadena AB, Okinawa, and Elmendorf AFB, Alaska, flown by a standard crew of

Above: The RAF received the first of seven CFM56-powered E-3D Sentrys on 4 July 1990. The force operates with No 8 Squadron and the first example is seen here during an acceptance flight near Mount Rainier in Washington. (RAF)

Below: AWACS in action during 'Desert Storm'. Crewmen plot aerial and maritime targets being tracked and interrogated in 'real time' by the giant Westinghouse AN/APY-1 or -2 rotodome and supply suitable vectors and intelligence over secure 'Have Quick' radios and JTIDS, or file the intelligence data in the computer. (USAF/SrA Kathy Bradley)

seventeen personnel apiece. Mainland European members of NATO opted for a co-purchase of eighteen machines as a means of sharing the high acquisition costs. Headquartered at Geilenkirchen, Germany, they operate with multi-national crews and are officially registered in Luxembourg (serials LX-N90442 to '459) and sport the coat of arms of the Grand Duchy on their tails. As related above, Britain went it alone with an order for seven E-3Ds (ZH101–107), which formed initially at RAF Waddington with the receipt of its first aircraft on 4 July 1990 before moving on to RAF Lossiemouth under No 8 Squadron on 30 June the following year, while France also voted for an independent fleet comprising a quartet of E-3Fs, the first of which arrived at Le Bourget, near Paris, in November 1990. To date, the only other sales have involved five KE-3As with an AAR drogue capability for Saudi Arabia. The aircraft are the in the

'big league' in terms of acquisition costs. Indeed, Japan expressed a strong interest in four of the E-3J model but dithered over the acquisition process during domestic budget wrangles; as the production line at Seattle has since closed down, future production would be based on newer Boeing 767 airliner stock.[15]

A limited ESM capability is also creeping on to the aircraft. RAF Sentrys already feature prominent wing-tip Loral 1017 'Yellowgate' pods, while NATO's force is beginning to sprout 'canoe' bulges on its flanks. The chief goal is to provide a passive detection capability which can act as go-between when the radar needs to be shut down temporarily, to avoid

Below: The Norden 'Pave Mover' radar was first tested on F-111A 66-053. The production AN/APY-3 system, later retitled Joint-STARS, is being installed on E-8C airframes. (Grumman)

[15]Boeing 707 production was phased out the with the last militarized basic model in 1987 and finally ended with the last British E-3D derivative in May 1991. In all, Boeing produced 1,011 airframes. A total of 422 commercial models remain in use, and some of these may provide the basis for future conversions. The manufacturers estimate that, with safety improvements, the airframes will be good until around the year 2140!

broadcasting the radiating Boeing's presence. However, there exist plenty of possibilities to garner elint. This supplementary feature is becoming increasingly important as the aircraft settle into their new role as pivots of the modern 'netted' C3I scheme of things. Even in its current format, AWACS' 'all-seeing eye' proved to be especially useful during Operation 'Desert Storm' in vectoring Coalition fighters on to their opponents, as exemplified by the 'interesting' engagement between *Al Quwwat al-Jawwiya Assa'udiya* (Royal Saudi Air Force) F-15 pilot Capt Al-Shamrani and his eventual prize of two Iraqi Mirage F1E-Qs—the second 'double kill' of the conflict—on 24 January 1991. He was extremely eager to down his quarry, but AWACS operators persuaded him to refrain from squeezing the trigger until they had placed him in the optimum position to launch his missiles. Had he not received this assistance, his 'kills' would in all likelihood never have taken place and the Mirages—believed to be carrying deadly Aérospatiale AM39 Exocet anti-shipping missiles—

Below: The E-8A J-STARS test-beds were modified by Grumman at its Melbourne Systems Division in Florida, which will remanufacture 22 used 707-300 airliners into the production E-8C configuration. The final delivery is due to be made in 2001. (Grumman)

might have broken through the cordon and caused untold carnage to Allied shipping. AWACS crews covered the entire theatre of operations, split into three zones: 'Cougar' (west), 'Buckeye' (central) and Boston (east). Four of 552nd ACW Wing boss Col Gary Voellger's twenty aircraft were airborne out of Riyadh at all times on 14–16hr patrols, controlling up to 7,000 air-to-air, tanking and strike 'events' each day. As one crew member put it before the cessation of hostilities, 'Saddam won't be able to sneeze without us knowing it!' That may have been going a bit too far, *mais sans doute*, as its more recent French operators would confide, AWACS did prove itself as the 'all-knowing one', which assisted the Coalition forces in reaching their initial objective of complete air supremacy.

Other star performers during 'Desert Storm' were the USAF's two E-8A Joint-STARS (86-0416 and -0417), also derived from the 707 series and still undergoing development when hostilities broke out. Their contribution led Gen Merrill McPeak, US Air Force Chief of Staff, to say 'we will not ever again want to fight without a Joint-STARS kind of system.' Army commanders reckoned that, by comparison, they had fought previous wars 'blindfolded'. The two test aircraft, flown by the 4411th Joint-STARS

squadron commanded by Col George K. Muellner, deployed from Florida on 11 January 1991 and flew their first mission only 72 hours later, on the express orders of Coalition C-in-C 'Stormin' Norman'. Stationed at the Saudi capital of Riyadh alongside the AWACS, they were able to track Iraqi armour and other ground-based weapons at a distance of up to 155 miles from the battlefield while cruising at FL350. During the Gulf War the aircraft flew all 49 scheduled missions, fulfilling their ATO by 100 per cent—an outstanding achievement for what was a duo of prototypes.

The heart of the J-STARS is its belly-mounted Norden AN/APY-3 phased-array mapping radar, housed in a fixed, 26ft-long ventral gondola, originally developed under Project 'Pave Mover' for use in Europe.[16] As used during the conflict, the Norden radar system works in two ways. In a wide-area MTI (moving target indicator) mode, sharpened by pulse-Doppler processing, clutter suppression interferometry and adaptive clutter cancellation, the package produces a 'real-time' ground map covering 50,000 square kilometres at a go. This is computer-processed into straightforward colour graphics which depict anything radar-significant that moves. In the SAR mode, high-resolution images are obtained of ground terrain, installations and fixed targets, to provide attack pilots and intel specialists with extremely accurate renditions of specific targets and

locales. How the two modes work together in 'near real-time' was best explained by Gulf veteran Capt James Dew, who reported that 'With MTI we would see very, very large numbers [of Iraqi ground forces] in convoys coming down a road. It was mind

Above: The two development E-8A Joint-STARS on the wing (86-0416/N770JS in the lead position, and 86-0417/N8411 nearest the camera). Powered by four JT3D-3B engines rated at 18,000lb thrust each, the machine uses Norden AN/APY-3 MTI/SAR radar to track moving and fixed ground targets at ranges of up to 155 miles. (Grumman)

Below: The Joint-STARS main cabin will feature seventeen operator consoles crewed by up to fifteen radar operators and two communications experts. During the Gulf War the two test Joint-STARS aircraft generated 49 dawn-to-dusk combat sorties each averaging 10.4 hours' duration, flying with a hybrid crew comprising Grumman and US service personnel. (Grumman)

[16]An initial European Operational Field Demonstration (OFD) was made in the autumn of 1990 but the results were overtaken by events in the Persian Gulf. The original Norden 'Pave Mover' 'brassboard' radar was fitted into an F-111E for early flight trials, in competition with the losing Hughes submission (also fitted to an F-111 test-bed). The recce-strike adaptations of the 'Vark' are aired in Chapter 3.

JOINT-STARS SUPPORT TO OPERATION 'DESERT STORM'

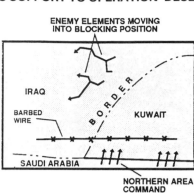

February 24: G-Day

- Lower centre: Northern Area Command Force in breaching operation
- Linear heavy return at lower portion is barbed wire moving in wind
- Upper right-hand portion shows Iraqi elements moving into blocking positions, which Coalition interdicted by air strikes

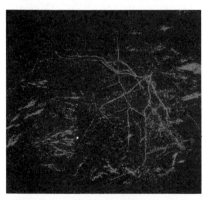

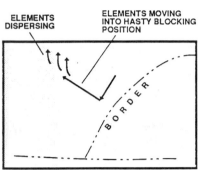

February 25: G + 1

- Enemy elements moving NW into blocking positions
- Engaged and destroyed while on the move
- Note: Three elements dispersing on north side of road

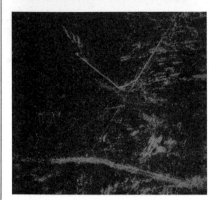

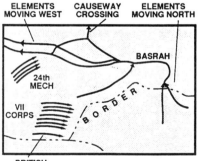

February 26: G + 2

- Lower left: VII Corps in attack on RGs; British 1st Armoured Division in south
- Traffic in KTO moving north out of Kuwait, towards Basrah
- Traffic from Basrah moving west on two parallel routes south of Euphrates
- 24th Mech moving to interdict routes
- Upper centre: Traffic moving north across causeway

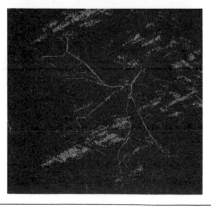

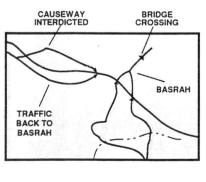

February 26: G + 2

- Larger scale of previous panel
- Causeway interdicted, traffic blocked
- Traffic flow is back to Basrah along the two parallel routes
- Small amount of traffic crossing Euphrates at Basrah

Above: The F-15E Strike Eagle uses SAR radar for ground attack. J-STARS can convey radar pictures of enemy positions deep behind the lines to ease the process of target acquisition. This particular aircraft belongs to the 492nd FS at RAF Lakenheath, England; it is undergoing preparations for a mid-day launch, 21 April 1992. (Author)

boggling. In fact, sometimes there were so many you couldn't even count them all. Then, all of the sudden, you don't see any more traffic. What does that tell you? It tells you they left the road or stopped. Then you would use your SAR, and shazaam! All the sudden, we've got the exact number of vehicles, where they are parked, and we would relay that information to fighters and the Army so that they were able to address the situation quickly.' J-STARS proved crucial. On 22 January one of the machines located a sixty-vehicle convoy at a range of 124 miles, moving towards Kuwait. Not long afterwards an air strike was called in, and this obliterated 58 tanks. On the opening day of the ground offensive, 24 February, J-STARS successfully identified Iraqi forces which were moving into a ground-blocking position, and again helped to direct suitable air strikes to keep the corridors open. Other targeting helped to track the elusive Iraqi 'Scuds' (a feat requiring field-tuning of the radar system, which evolved as the war progressed). The co-ordinates were treated as 'rich pickings' for use both by strike jets and B-52 bombers and by Coalition MLRS (Multiple Launch Rocket System) batteries, 'saving countless Allied lives' according to Maj-Gen Stephen Silvasy, US Army

Deputy Chief of Staff for Concepts, by ensuring that Coalition ground forces were never outmanoeuvred. Finally, J-STARS monitored the Iraqi retreat from Kuwait City, setting up a 'turkey shoot'. Gulf missions were flown by night and lasted for around twelve hours, crewed by Grumman and service personnel. In all, 54 sorties were flown, during which the aircraft logged more than 600 hours.

In J-STARS' fully operational format, any of the material generated by MTI and SAR may be called up on as many as fifteen of the seventeen colour screen operator consoles installed in the main cabin, for immediate sorting and relay to friendly strike aircraft. The radar data are also simultaneously transmitted via secure links to ground stations, including mobile five-ton lorries sporting 100ft telescopic aerials.[17] Occupying the giant machine are a 'standard crew' of 21 USAF and Army personnel—pilot, co-pilot, flight engineer, navigator/EWO and up to seventeen radar operators—who would typically expect to fly an 11-hour-long sortie; but the aircraft can accommodate double that number of people for extended air-refuelled missions lasting for up to twenty hours. Production by Grumman at its Melbourne Systems Division in Florida will eventually

[17]Two of the multifunction consoles—any two—would be used for communications work. The test aircraft committed to war featured only ten consoles, and all data were relayed via six US Army ground stations. This is the key difference between the E-8A test-beds and production model E-8Cs, which will also incorporate JTIDS for use in the modern 'netted' C3I system.

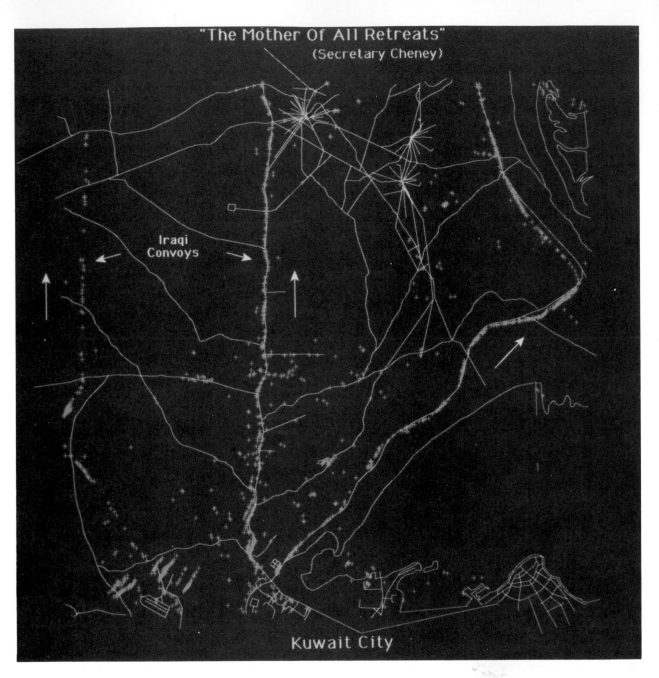

"The Mother Of All Retreats"
(Secretary Cheney)

Iraqi Convoys

Kuwait City

total 22 E-8C airframes (including the revamped test-beds), all based on used 707-300 airliners which are being gutted, stripped down to bare metal and refurbished at Lake Charles prior to receiving J-STARS avionics. The final airframe is due to be delivered in the year 2001.

J-STARS is just one of the latest systems to enter the world of integrated command, control, communications and intelligence. When fused with products generated by high-flying satellites, AWACS/SUWACS, short-range intelligence from UAVs, pictures gleaned by recce-strike jets and even close

Above: J-STARS MTI combat radar imagery in action, as viewed on one of the operator's consoles, showing thousands of Iraqi vehicles fleeing north from Kuwait City. Each small '+' symbol represents a vehicle or closely knit cluster of vehicles retreating north along several different road segments. The radar system effectively denied the enemy its night sanctuary. The SAR images created by the Norden radar also served as target reference shots for F-15E Strike Eagle crews, as the fighter's APG-70 radar would generate much the same kind of imagery at closer range. (Grumman)

intelligence from SAS, Spetsnatz or Delta Force troops hidden in dunes or hills overlooking the enemy, military commanders can now watch every move the opposition makes.

GLOSSARY

AAA — Anti-Aircraft Artillery. Also known as 'Triple-A'.

AAM — Air-to-air missile.

AAR — Air-to-Air Refuelling.

ACC — Air Combat Command. USAF. Formed on 1 June 1992 and amalgamating combat and reconnaissance assets previously flown by Tactical and Strategic Air Commands.

ADI — (Pilot's) Attitude Director Indicator. An artificial horizon instrument which can present pitch steering commands (the companion Horizontal Situation Display is used to present steering commands) based on inputs from the navigation computers or from external transmissions.

AEW — Airborne Early Warning.

AFSOF — Air Force Special Operations Forces. USAF.

AGL — Above ground level. Measured in feet.

AGM — Air-to-ground missile.

ALE — Airborne Countermeasures, Ejection. A chaff, flare and decoy dispenser.

ALQ — Airborne Countermeasures, Special Purpose. Pod or installation.

ALSS — See PLSS.

ARM — Anti-radiation missile.

ASARS — Advanced Synthetic Aperture Radar System. The Goodyear/Loral ASARS-1 equipped the SR-71A and the Hughes ASARS-2 the TR-1A/U-2R.

ASW — Anti-Submarine Warfare.

AVTR — Airborne Video Tape Recorder.

AWACS — Airborne Warning and Control System, usually associated with today's Boeing E-3 Sentry, but introduced to combat thirty years ago by Lockheed's EC-121 'Big Eye'.

BAe — British Aerospace.

Band — Waveband. See RF.

'Canned' — Used to denote strictly defined flight plans, including climb and descent procedures.

CAP — Combat Air Patrol. Also known as MiGCAP.

C3 — Command, Control & Communications. Includes overall co-ordination of the air and ground forces from airborne C3 posts as the EC-130E 'Comfy Levi', E-3 AWACS, etc. The term 'C3I' (C3 and Intelligence) is also used. 'C3/CM' refers to C3 Countermeasures, or the jamming of enemy C3 systems as a deliberate offensive ploy. See also Comjam.

CCD — Charged Coupled Device. Capable of turning camera pictures into digitalized signals for display in the cockpit, or for transmission and decoding into images back on the ground. CCDs are most often associated with 'real-time' cameras, whose imagery, like FLIR's, can be recorded on AVTR (q.v.) or transmitted for near-instant replay elsewhere.

COIN — Counter-insurgency.

Comint — Communications Intelligence. Part of Sigint.

Comjam — Communications-jamming countermeasures. Generally used in a purely defensive mode.

CSAR — Combat Search and Rescue of downed airmen, usually in territory dominated by enemy ground forces.

ECM — Electronic countermeasures. A device designed to disrupt enemy communications or radar systems. ECCM is a measure designed to reduce susceptibility to ECM.

Elint — Electronic Intelligence. Receiver working in the mid-to-high end of the RF spectrum, where radars operate.

E-O — Electro-optics. Includes TV and LLLTV (q.v.).

EOB — Electronic Order of Battle. 'Head count' of enemy electronic defences such as the whereabouts and types of anti-aircraft radars deployed.

ELS — Emitter Location System. An ESM device employed by the Tornado ECR variant.

ESM — Electronic support measures. Typically elint apparatus which listens passively to enemy radar signals but which implies subsequent ECM or other active measures. ESM is also used by the US Navy in lieu of elint.

EW — Electronic warfare (the science) or early warning (the radar emitter). Throughout this book the latter term has been written in full, to avoid confusion between the two terms.

EWO — Electronic Warfare Officer. A navigator (see WSO) who is skilled at electronic warfare techniques, having undergone additional specialized training in this field.

FAC — Forward air controller. Usually orbits in the vicinity of the FLOT (q.v.) to direct air and ground fire against enemy forces.

FLIR — Forward-looking infra-red. All bodies at temperatures above absolute zero radiate electromagnetic energy, ranging in wavelength from short cosmic rays, through gamma rays, X-rays, the ultraviolet, visible radiation, infra-red and so on. With FLIR, energy from the infra-red part of the spectrum is collected from a wide aperture 'window' and a thermal image is generated by rearranging the signal from the detector to form a spatial analogue of the original scene. The degree of infra-red emission from any body is subject to its properties as a 'heat' radiator, and thus the image is a 'false' one to the human eye. Darker objects tend to absorb heat more quickly by day and subsequently radiate heat more quickly by night. Heat generators such as people and engines show up well at all times. The resulting scene may be displayed in either the 'white hot' mode (which closely resembles a black and white photographic negative) or as a 'black hot' image (a positive image). In addition, most FLIRs are in fact slewable, just like an eye, and, depending on their location, may even be referred to instead as 'DLIRs' or 'SLIRs' (downward- or sideways-looking), for example those employed on the F-117A and Tornado GR.1A respectively. See also IRLS.

FLOT Forward Line of Troops. Also known as the FEBA (Forward Edge of the Battle Area).

FOV Field of view (of a sensor). Virtually all TV and FLIR devices have several fixed 'zoom' settings, or a variable FOV.

GC/GHz Gigacycle/GigaHertz. Used to measure radio wavelength, 1 GHz being one million cycles a second.

GPS/Nav Global Positioning System (based on Navstar satellites). A 'P decoder'-equipped aircraft can receive the signals and deduce its position to within 15 metres.

IDS Infra-red Detection Set. See FLIR.

IFR Instrument Flight Rules. The use of these is dictated by inclemental weather or darkness. This abbreviation is also sometimes confusingly used to refer to in-flight refuelling, which is more properly addressed by the term AAR.

IOC Initial Operating Capability. The first time a new aircraft or system becomes operational with a squadron-sized unit.

IRCM Infra-red countermeasures. A 'jammer' designed to foil heat-seeking missiles.

IRLS Infra-red line-scanner. Records still, optical images with a significantly enhanced resolution compared to that of a FLIR. This is effected by means of a string of infra-red spectrum detectors which in turn activate LEDs (light-emitting diodes). The LEDs' brightness is relative to the heat intensity of the radiating objects under scrutiny, and the resultant white-on-black, line-by-line scans are registered on standard film, also line-by-line, to create something akin to a monochrome negative. See also FLIR.

ISAR See *SAR*.

J-STARS Joint(-Service) Surveillance Target Attack Radar System. Otherwise the Grumman E-8A, which uses SAR and MTI radar to plot, respectively, fixed and mobile enemy ground forces.

JTIDS Joint Tactical Information Distribution System. A 'netted' secure radio system which relays target and threat data from command posts and other observers to strike and support aircraft equipped with Class 2 terminals. JTIDS is presented on the recipients' cockpit MFDs.

Laser Light Amplification by the Stimulated Emission of Radiation. A cascade of coherent photons. Its key advantage is its ability to travel considerable distances undiminished in intensity, thanks to its coherent, non-spreading beam. This makes the laser ideally suited for ranging and target marking, and considerably more accurate than radar. The Vietnam War witnessed the introduction of the first practical chemical lasers in combat.

Work is currently being undertaken to perfect a laser-mapping radar device; such a device was first tested nearly two decades ago as the AN/AVD-2, fitted to RF-4Cs.

LLLTV Low Light-Level TV (sensor). An airborne E-O version of a 'Starlight' scope.

LOC Lines of communication.

LORAN Long-Range Navigation (aid). Uses fixed ground transmitters (LORAN C) or mobile ones (LORAN D) to plot present position by comparing the TOA (time of arrival) of hyperbolic radio waves emanating from 'master' and subsequently triggered 'slave' transmitters at known locations.

LOROPS Long-range optical cameras. Typically of 66in focal length or more.

MAD Magnetic Anomaly Detector. Used to locate submarines which create a 'magnetic wake'.

MC/MHz Megacycles/MegaHertz. Used to measure radio wavelength, 1 MHz being one thousand cycles a second.

MFD (Cockpit) Multi-Function Displays. Can be either monochrome or part or full-colour.

MTI Moving Target Indicator.

NFO See *WSO*.

NOTE Nap-of-the-earth (flying).

OBC Optical bar camera. Used to take horizon-to-horizon swaths from altitude based on angled mirrors sitting in front of the lens, or prisms to combine two split images. See Panoramic devices.

Oblique Side-looking camera which typically 'shoots' a series of frames left or right; or the technique of using a vertical camera off-axis from the perpendicular, when the aircraft is banking, so as to point the sensor at the subject.

Panoramic A wide-open perspective; a vertical camera which scans laterally from horizon-to-horizon. Fore-to-aft coverage is catered for by multiple exposures 'bracketed' along the aircraft's flightpath, or by a strike camera. Panoramic cameras were first used during the Korean War.

Pave A prefix standing for Precision Avionics Vectoring Equipment, first used during the Vietnam War to denote any system developed (usually) by the Eglin Munitions Systems Division (known prior to 1990 as the Armament Development Test Center) with the object of enhancing navigation, reconnaissance or targeting accuracy.

PLSS Precision Location Strike System. An experimental elint package which was designed to convey precise target co-ordinates to SEAD aircraft and defence-suppression weaponry. Previously known as the Advanced Location Strike System (ALSS) and latterly as the Signal Location Targeting System (SLATS).

POL Petroleum, oil, lubricants (storage facilities).

RAAF Royal Australian Air Force.

RAP *Razvedchik Aviasionniy Polk*. Soviet/CIS Aviation Reconnaissance Regiment.

RAF Royal Air Force.

Real-time Reconnaissance images or other intelligence which is relayed to an airborne or ground station within 15 minutes of its collection (hence the term 'near real-time'). Also refers to the almost instantaneous display of sensor imagery in a reconnaissance aircraft's cockpit.

RF   Radio frequency. The part of the electro magnetic spectrum in which radios, radars and telemetry equipment operate. For military purposes NATO has divided this into a number of wavebands (or bands) beginning with HF, VHF and UHF (the latter further divided into bands A, B and C) and progressing through the alphabet through to the J band and beyond to the millimetre wavelength.

RPV   Remotely Piloted (i.e. unmanned) Vehicle. A Vietnam War-era term seldom used today.

RWR   Radar warning receiver. Commonly associated with self-defence and ECM but being put to increasing use for subsidiary elint duties in electronic combat aircraft such as the Prowler, Raven and Tornado ECR.

SAC   Strategic Air Command. Now absorbed into the new USAF Air Combat Command.

SAM   Surface-to-air missile.

SAR   Synthetic aperture radar. A SLAR (q.v.) which can produce photograph-like radar images by using line-by-line mapping techniques which create the same degree of detail as huge, high-powered conventional radars. ISAR, or inverted SAR, works in a similar manner but repeatedly tracks the same portion of ground or sea to build up a high-resolution image at extreme range. The acronym is also denotes Search and Rescue, nowadays commonly known as CSAR, or Combat SAR, to distinguish the two.

SEAD   Suppression of enemy air defences. The mission is also referred to by the USAF as 'Wild Weaseling'. During the Vietnam War it bore the generic title 'Iron Hand'.

Sigint   An all-embracing term which encapsulates various modes of passive electronic signal-gathering intelligence, including comint, elint, telint and urint (q.v.).

SLAR   Sideways-looking airborne radar. A ground-mapping device used for all-weather reconnaissance.

'Tech'   Technical Objective Camera. A panoramic or oblique framing camera used by high-flying USAF recce aircraft such as the SR-71A and U-2R.

Telint   Telemetry intelligence. This is customarily used for gathering information on foreign nations' rocketry and related flight-test work.

TEREC   Tactical Electromagnetic Reconnaissance (sensor). The AN/ALQ-125 elint system used by a special quantity of RF-4C Phantoms.

TFR   Terrain-following radar, designed to provide manual or automatic terrain-hugging flight when combined with cockpit displays and/or an automatic flight control system (AFCS, or autopilot).

TI   Texas Instruments.

TRA   Teledyne Ryan Aeronautical.

UAV   Unmanned Air Vehicle. The modern term for RPV. It is to be distinguished from the term 'drone', which refers either to a target vehicle or to a UAV which is pre-programmed to fly a 'canned' (q.v.) mission.

Urint   Unintentionally radiated intelligence, for example signals generated through day-to-day training with radars, including unwanted side- and back-lobes from emitters, which may be recorded surreptitiously and analyzed for various uses.

VFR   Visual Flight Rules. Clear weather; daytime.

WESTPAC   West Pacific (cruise) especially one made by a carrier and Air Group (CAG) to the Tonkin Gulf during the Vietnam War.

WSO   Weapons Systems Officer. A USAF term denoting a navigator trained as a weapons specialist in two-seat fighter-bombers (see also EWO). Most other air arms refer to him as a navigator. The US Navy uses the term 'Naval Flight Officer' (NFO), which embraces the Radar Intercept Officer (or RIO, e.g. the back-seater in the F-14 TARPS Tomcat) or as Bombardier/Navigators (or B/Ns, e.g. the EWOs who operate the mission equipment in the EA-6B Prowler). The concept evolved during the latter half of the 1960s, when fighters introduced complex navigation, electronic warfare and targeting systems.

INDEX